E-LEARNING

Strategies for Delivering
Knowledge in the Digital Age

MARC J. ROSENBERG

WITHDRAWN

McGraw-Hill

New York   San Francisco   Washington, D.C.   Auckland   Bogotá
Caracas   Lisbon   London   Madrid   Mexico City   Milan
Montreal   New Delhi   San Juan   Singapore
Sydney   Tokyo   Toronto

Library of Congress Cataloging-in-Publication Data
Rosenberg, Marc Jeffrey.
    E-learning . strategies for delivering knowledge in the digital age / Marc J. Rosenberg.
       p. cm.
    Includes index.
    ISBN 0-07-136268-1 (alk. paper)
    1. World Wide Web.   2. Internet in education.   3. Computer-assisted instruction.   I. Title: Strategies for delivering knowledge in the digital age.
 II. Title.

LB1044.87 .R68   2001
371.33′4—dc21   00-062209

McGraw-Hill

A Division of The McGraw·Hill Companies

5 6 7 8 9 0 DOC/DOC 0 9 8 7 6 5 4 3 2 1

ISBN 0-07-136268-1

This book was set in Janson Text by V&M Graphics.
Printed and bound by R. R. Donnelley & Sons Company.

How to Contact the Publisher
To order copies of this book in bulk, at a discount, call the McGraw-Hill Special Sales Department at 800-842-3075 or 212-904-5427.

To ask a question about the book, contact the author, or report a mistake in the text, please write to Richard Narramore, Senior Editor, at richard_narramore@mcgraw-hill.com

This book is printed on recycled, acid-free paper containing a minimum of 50% recycled, de-inked fiber.

To Harlene and Brian

Contents

PART II

New Approaches for E-Learning

PART III

Organizational Requirements for E-Learning

Web Address

The world of e-learning is constantly changing and evolving. To help keep this book on the cutting edge, I've created a Web site where you'll find:

- New and updated links to sites that are good examples of all forms of e-learning and sites that provide additional information on e-learning strategy
- Information on new e-learning resources (books, articles, newsletters, and conferences)
- E-Learning FAQs
- Selections from the book
- Tools to help you apply concepts from the book
- Opportunities to provide feedback to me

You can access this Web site at
www.books.mcgraw-hill.com/training/rosenberg

Foreword

"Busted," Sharon said, "they took my picture running a red light on Harbor Drive. Now I have to go to traffic school, plus pay $301 in fines. Fortunately for me, by taking a class on the Web, I can take care of this mess from home."

Alfonso, too, was confident: "We're going online to shift our global workforce to several new software packages. This is great because I was having trouble finding an instructor for the Ukraine and Belarus."

My mother was not to be left out: "I'm learning new knitting patterns for afghans on the computer."

New York Times columnist Thomas Friedman quoted Cisco's John Chambers: "The next big killer application for the Internet is going to be education. Education over the Internet is going to be so big it is going to make e-mail usage look like a rounding error in terms of the Internet capacity it will consume."

Sharon is a therapist. Alfonso is a training manager. My mother is an 80-year-old retired social worker. And John Chambers is CEO of one of the world's premier technology companies. What do they have in common? They and many, many others are drooling over e-learning.

There are good reasons for their unbridled enthusiasm. First, there is the promise of access that extends to my little old mother, 50-year-old pal, and a Ukrainian petrochemical engineer. The Web enables update, information, learning experiences, and collaboration wherever, whenever, and in the nick of time. Executives, often perceived as missing-in-action when it came to education and training, are now increasingly riveted by learning and knowledge online. The Web brings human capital front and center, where I think it belongs.

Marc Rosenberg thinks so, too. In this book he presents a rich discussion about e-learning, linked to strategic results, and capturing the concerns and priorities of individuals and executives.

Rosenberg understands the lone saleswoman who perceives the Web more as a library than a classroom, and turns to it because it's chock full of resources for selling. With just a few keystrokes she examines colleagues' presentations, fact sheets, product updates, and proposals, edits related documents, and repurposes them for her customers. Pressed for time, and selling in northern Canada in the dark of winter, she joins her company's global sales community for online chats, or reaches out beyond it to others who also want to get smarter about telecommunications products and services.

Rosenberg writes a book that executives, too, will want to read. There are rich examples from U S WEST, Merrill Lynch, and the Prudential, descriptions of what learning dotcoms are up to, and many anecdotes and experiences shared by fellow leaders. Lessons learned are often presented as meaty and manageable lists; for example, 13 reasons why the training department is dragging its heels on e-learning, and 6 questions to ponder when ratcheting up online learning to a meaningful and systemic architecture.

Here Rosenberg pushes beyond a classroom metaphor for e-learning and into knowledge management, and performance and decision support. This bigger tent definition for e-learning capitalizes on the technology and parallels what people really need.

But Rosenberg does not drool over e-learning. He admits to the gnarly issues and tackles them here. This book acknowledges the challenges of doing the technologically and strategically new. He does not gloss over the difficulties of working across conventional boundaries, effort that is typically a part of successful e-learning and knowledge management. Through balanced discussions about prior technology disappointments, juicy programs, dicey relationships, and guidelines for proposals and negotiations, Rosenberg provides both broad guidance and nitty-gritty tools.

For e-learning to realize its promise, much harder things than XML and screen design are involved. Success depends on strategy, sponsorship, and execution, all described here in tangible and authoritative ways. Calling for the "Four C's of Success: Culture, Champions, Communication, and Change," Rosenberg's is a sober voice regarding transforming Web promises to workplace performance through concerted organizational effort.

The hope that surrounds e-learning is with us today. Soon, while the Web will endure and evolve, the excitement about e-learning as the next great killer application is likely to fade. Now is the time to move forward to do the hard things that must be done to convert wondrous possibilities to dependable realities.

This is where Rosenberg's book comes in. While the book offers much that encourages enthusiasm for e-learning, it offers even more to the irreverent individual who smells the hype and vows to do better.

A young woman considering graduate school at San Diego State University recently said something like this: "Sure I know a little about the Web and online learning. But I won't be graduating until 2003 or even 2004. I mean, what's next after learning on the Web?" Must e-learning soon move from the In list to the Out? Is Wall Street's wobbly reaction to learning dotcoms a harbinger of the future?

Whether it is the Web or the next new, new thing, Rosenberg's message remains anticipation, connection, engagement, culture, collaboration, and systems. This message is In now, true today as it was for instructor-led training a while back. And it most certainly will be In tomorrow, as learning and knowledge attract fresh consideration through the engaging power of the Web.

Allison Rossett

Allison Rossett is a Professor of Educational Technology at San Diego State University and the year 2000 inductee into Training Magazine's HRD Hall of Fame. (http://edweb.sdsu.edu/people/ARossett/Arossett.html)

Preface

"The biggest growth in the Internet, and the area that will prove to be one of the biggest agents of change, will be in e-learning."

John Chambers,
CEO, Cisco Systems[1]

"In my lifetime, I've never seen hype and understatement walk hand in hand. But that's what we're seeing now. I'm convinced that our great-grandchildren will look back and wonder why we didn't get it."

Nicholas Negroponte,
Director, MIT Media Lab[2]

COMPUTERS ARE AN integral part of our lives. But how instrumental have computers been for learning? I often ask people how long they think that computer-based training (CBT) has been around. Five years? Ten? Fifteen years? Most people believe that CBT is a recent educational innovation. In fact, it's been around well over thirty years.

I remember my first professor of educational technology, Dr. Phillips. It was 1973 and I had just begun my master's program in the field and was fascinated with what Dr. Phillips was doing. Sitting at a Teletype terminal hooked to a mainframe, he was responding to multiple-choice questions generated by a computer program he'd written. Literally hundreds of keypunched cards stacked just right generated several simple questions, and even simpler responses. *Correct, Incorrect,* or *Try Again* was all the system could muster. As rudimentary as it seems now, back then it was a breakthrough, a significant new application of the pioneering "teaching machines" work that educators and psychologists were experimenting with in the fifties and sixties. Dr. Phillips would remind us over and over that it wouldn't be too long before everyone was learning from the computer.

Fast-forward to today. The technology is more sophisticated. Yet as late as 1998 most organizations reported only about 14 percent of their education programs were technology-based.[3] Why has such a promising innovation been so difficult to deploy? Why was Dr. Phillips's prediction so off the mark?

As innovations go, many people consider technology-based learning disappointing at best. A field of great promise has had such a relatively minimal impact. After thirty-plus years of experimentation and trials, isn't it reasonable to expect more progress? Are we destined to continue down a mediocre path, or are we on the verge of a real shift in how we view, build, and deliver superior, highly cost-effective learning and performance?

Why This Book ... and Why Now?

We are on the verge of a major sea change in learning. Internet technologies have fundamentally altered the technological and economic landscapes so radically that it is now possible to make quantum leaps in the use of technology for learning. Yet there is also a danger. If we focus too much on the technology itself and not enough on how well it is used, we will continue to fall short. But if we neglect the power of the Internet, we will never get off the ground. In the end, successful Internet-enabled learning, or "e-learning," depends on building a strategy that optimizes the technology within an organizational culture that is ready and willing to use it. But, as we will see, it isn't just a technical innovation that drives us to e-learning. Businesses need to get information—even information that's changing—to large numbers of people faster than ever. They need to lower the overall costs of creating a workforce that performs faster and better than the competition, and they need to do this 24 hours a day, seven days a week for people located around the world.

The question is no longer *whether* organizations will implement online learning, but whether they will do it *well*. Having the right technology and delivering good learning programs using that technology is essential but insufficient. An effective e-learning strategy must be more than the technology itself or the content it carries. It must also focus on critical success factors that include building a learning culture, marshaling true leadership support, deploying a nurturing business model, and sustaining the change throughout the organization. It must be pursued by people who are highly skilled and capable of executing effectively. And, it must move us to a view of learning that is much more than formal instruction or training—to one that sees learning in a much broader, organizational context—as in the growing of the intellectual capital of the firm, and the enabling of higher individual *and* organizational performance. Finally, it must be a strategy that can be developed, tested, and deployed at "Internet speed." For managers in the training business, this is a "do or die" issue. For managers running the business, it is do or die as well—as speedy, cost-effective performance improvement will be a key to winning in the marketplace.

Most organizations, including training organizations, don't have an effective, broad-based e-learning strategy. They have Web sites, courseware, and other artifacts of online learning. But without the strategic thread that holds it all together, based on "*why* do it," not just on "how to do it," most programs have been minimally impactful and/or short-lived at best. This book focuses on building such a strategy, and in doing so, provides a road map for growing and sustaining an e-learning culture. It is based on 20 years of observations, best practices (and worst practices), and conversations with numerous leaders in the fields of learning and learning technology.

There are six fundamental beliefs that I consider a foundation for the direction I'm taking. Keep these in mind as you move through the rest of this book:

1. *Internet technology is the key to a profound revolution in learning.* But technology—any technology—is a *tool*, not a strategy. Being proficient in the use of a word processor does not guarantee that you'll write the next best-seller. Likewise, the Internet cannot, in and of itself, improve the quality of the learning you put on it.

2. *There is an enduring and important role for traditional classroom instruction.* People who believe technology will totally replace great teachers in front of classrooms of highly motivated learners are as misguided as those who believe the Internet is a passing fad.

3. *Learning is a continuous, cultural process—not simply a series of events.* It values *and* transcends the classroom and the workplace. Access and opportunities to learn should be available to anyone, anywhere, and at any time. Organizational learning is as much about what happens *outside* formal learning programs as it is about the programs themselves.

4. *The broad field of learning encompasses more than education and training.* It is a genuine *discipline*, complete with a discernable body of knowledge, founded on systematic inquiry and empirical research that can be mastered through formal education and broad-based experience. Learning and e-learning professionals are not made overnight.

5. *You do not necessarily have to be in the education or training business to create opportunities for e-learning.* Further, it is important not to confuse learning (something we all do) with instruction (something that presumably supports learning). People learn all the time—you couldn't stop it if you wanted to. There are many public Web sites that are not instructional in nature yet provide information from which people can learn.

6. *Strategy development and implementation are never really finished.* You change it as your business changes. You adjust it as your people become more skilled. You redefine it as new

technological options become available. And, you constantly test it against the mission and vision of your business, making sure that you are always in alignment. To ignore the iterative nature of your strategy, including your e-learning strategy, would quickly result in stagnation—a death knell in the digital business world.

This book is for anyone—trainers, executives, consultants, and students who see the promise that Internet and related technologies will bring to the field of learning and performance and who want to be sure that when they implement their e-learning strategy, they'll do so in ways that will invite success. We are rapidly becoming very comfortable with computer and Internet technology and there is no question that in time a new generation of workers will *expect* to learn via this technology. But of course, waiting for a generational turnover is not an option.

The time is now to build an e-learning strategy that meets the needs of today's workers, some of whom are ready for this change, and others who will need help in the transition. And now is the time to build an even greater capability to deliver on this strategy for an increasingly computer-savvy workforce. At the very time businesses' need for learning and knowledge has outstripped what's possible using conventional training methods, e-learning will allow us to respond more effectively. E-Learning has never been so important, and our opportunities have never been greater.

A Strategic Focus

Too often we are so enamored with the opportunities that technology offers that we neglect the climate in which it will be implemented. And so the purpose of this book: to recognize that in order to leverage the potential of e-learning technology for sustained, beneficial change, a sound business and people-centered strategy is essential. The successful deployment of e-learning is absolutely dependent on understanding this important premise.

The focus of this book is about the Internet, for e-learning is a *Web-enabled* strategy. Certainly other technology delivery systems, such as CD-ROMs, have a role to play, but because they lack the inter-networkability that is fast becoming an *essential* element for e-learning, these non-Web technologies will play a subordinate role.

This is a book about strategy—e-learning strategy in particular. There can be no successful learning initiative without it. But strategy without a tactical framework and execution rings hollow. So we will also explore many of the key operational decisions that must be made for the strategy to be both successful and durable.

This is *not* a tactical "how to design Web-based training" book, although it does talk a lot about what quality Web-based learning is. It is not about authoring or programming, or which tools are better than others, and it does not go into the intricacies of user interface design or navigation. It does not provide deep insights into Java or HTML, nor does it deal with graphic packages, JPEG, MPEG, streaming video, or other production issues. There are many fine resources that deal with design, technology, and tools (see Appendix B). This book is also not about specific vendors and vendor products that are in the marketplace. The speed at which these products and their underlying technologies are changing would make this book obsolete before it is printed. While some vendors are mentioned, and URLs provided as examples or case studies,[4] recommendations of specific companies and products will be avoided; to do otherwise would again make the book obsolete almost immediately. It would also compromise an important cornerstone of this book—its product- and vendor-neutral nature.

This book is a *companion* to the many fine "how to" books out there, providing a balance between building great e-learning (design and technology issues) and implementing it (acceptance and support issues). Both are necessary for e-learning to succeed.

How This Book Is Organized

I've divided the book into three parts. Part One, "The Opportunity," sets the stage for understanding the business and technological drivers that are influencing radical changes in learning. Part Two, "New Approaches for E-Learning," explores these changes in more depth, providing a much broader perspective on e-learning options and approaches. Part Three, "Organizational Requirements for E-Learning," focuses on the key infrastructure, environmental, cultural, business, leadership, and organizational factors that can make or break an e-learning initiative. If you are wondering why your e-learning efforts aren't as successful as you'd like, look here.

The intent is to provide the insight and perspective to make the important strategy, quality, and operational decisions that are necessary for effective e-learning implementation. The critical success factors for e-learning will be explored, as will those actions that can kill even the most promising initiative. Within each chapter, examples will illustrate many key components of an effective e-learning framework. And at the end of the book, a summary of key learnings and questions are provided to help you formulate your e-learning strategy.

A lot of ground is covered, but no single book can go into as much depth on each topic as some people might like. In places, the level of detail provided is augmented by the resources listed in Appendix B.

Throughout this book you'll read *E-Learning Journeys*—stories of how corporate learning executives and other influential people in the field, in their own words, made their own personal transition to e-learning. These essays do more than just project the opinion of these leaders as they reflect on their career experiences; they also point out the challenges that everyone, at every level, will face as they move through this significant transformation.

This book assumes a basic to moderate level of reader familiarity with the foundation concepts of learning and technology. If you are responsible for the training efforts of your organization, or if you work in (or lead) your Corporate University, many of the issues you are currently facing will be addressed. Managers from the front line to the executive suite who are responsible for the learning and development of their people, or who want to bring the benefits of e-learning to their suppliers and customers, or simply consider such activities important enough to warrant their attention, should also find value in these pages. University faculty and students in learning, human resources, and business improvement fields will find that the strategic nature of this book offers a useful balance to the many processes and techniques that are part of their curricula.

Finally, since many of us have participated in some form of corporate training, perhaps even delved into some computer-based training, it's likely that some opinions will be challenged or reinforced, or both. The assumption is that you've had ample personal and business experience with the Web to be curious and want to explore the power of this new technology.

The book doesn't provide the "one way" for making e-learning work. In fact, there are many alternatives that can be pursued. Rather, we will address the fundamental reasons why the potential for e-learning has not been fully realized and how that trend can be reversed. When you're done reading, you'll still have work to do. There will be many decisions you'll have to make and many people you'll have to convince about the value of your vision before your efforts will bear fruit. My hope is that this book will be a valuable guide on your e-learning journey and give you a framework to be successful.

Acknowledgments

THERE ARE SO MANY PEOPLE who have supported me in this effort that I often think of it as a group project. I have learned a great deal from each of them and I thank them for the free exchange of ideas and best practices that I have tried to embed into this book.

I'd first like to thank my essayists, Barry Arnett, John Coné, Gloria Gery, Elliott Masie, John McMorrow, Maddy Weinstein, and Ray Vigil for their outstanding insight and perspective as they talked about their own e-learning journeys and their perspectives on the field. Their words of experience convey the great possibilities that lie before us as we transform learning.

There were also innumerable contributors of stories and suggestions that enhanced my words tremendously. My deepest thanks go to June Maul and Jonathan Jones for contributing the U S WEST story, and to Cathleen Fuchs, Brad Hall, Sue Pannacione, Jim Reed, Carol Rusin, Albert Siu, Daná Wilson, and Chris Wolff for their generosity in sharing AT&T's experiences. At Merrill Lynch, thanks to Sharon Gargano, Sandy Kurinsky, and the entire advanced FC training team for their terrific support. Thanks to Carline Dobson, Meg Hayden, Marie Murphy, and the people of Prudential's learning and leadership team for their story. To Suzanne Pink at nMinds, Darian Hartley at Dell

Computer, Dave Stevens at Lucent Technologies, Paul Pinkman and Liz McCraven at CRK Media, Ellen Wagner and Anne Derryberry at Informania, Marcia Conner at Learnativity.com, Betsy Alvarez and Alan Longman at Kepner-Tregoe, Brian Miller at Ninth House Network, Tom Kelly at Cisco Systems, Stan Malcolm at Performance Vision, and John Howe at General Physics Corp.—thank you all for your time and effort.

There would be no book without the support of colleagues at OmniTech Consulting Group and DiamondCluster International. Special thanks to Mathew Adlai-Gail, Ed Arnold, Nancy Bellis, Fred Belmont, Paul Carroll, John Faier, Woody Forthsyth, Michael Hoffman, Michael Krauss, Jim McGee, Chunka Mui, and everyone in the New Jersey office for their help and advice, especially Louise Adler and Phevie Mitchel. A special thank-you goes to Joel Krauss, Joan Lufrano and my colleagues "on the ground" in New York for their enthusiastic support and encouragement from day one.

This book is also a reflection of more than 60 years of combined experience and expertise reflected in my three reviewers— Rob Foshay of PLATO Learning, Pat Kelly of AT&T Wireless Services, and John Larson of Lucent Technologies. Actually, they were more like collaborators than readers. I thank them not only for the hundreds of great suggestions, but for their professional and personal friendship. I especially want to express my gratitude to my friend of more than twenty years, Allison Rossett, who has been a great sounding board and inspiration for me.

I would not have had the opportunity to write this book it it weren't for several people who took a chance and gave me my start in this profession: Diane Dormant, Richard Lincoln, Dean Spitzer, Harold Stolovitch, and Paul Tremper at ISPI, and Chuck Martinetz at AT&T—thank you all.

Finally, I'd like to thank my editor at McGraw-Hill, Richard Narramore, and his team, especially Jennifer Chong and Jane Palmieri, for their support throughout the process.

Oh yes, and my family—Harlene and Brian—thanks for your love and encouragement, and for putting up with me over the last eight months.

Marc Rosenberg
Hillsborough, New Jersey

About the Author

Marc Rosenberg, Ph.D., has been active in the field of learning and performance improvement for more than two decades. He has an international reputation as an expert on enhancing individual and organizational effectiveness. A highly regarded presenter, Marc has spoken at the White House and at over 200 professional and business conferences. He has authored more than 30 articles and is a frequently quoted expert in major business and trade publications, including *Context*, *Fast Company*, *Knowledge Management Magazine*, and *Training*. Marc is a past president of the International Society for Performance Improvement (ISPI) and holds a Ph.D. in instructional design, plus degrees in communications and marketing.

He is currently a principal with DiamondCluster International (www.diamondcluster.com), a premier business strategy and technology solutions firm. At DiamondCluster, Marc specializes in knowledge management, e-learning strategy and the reinvention of training.

Before moving into the consulting world, Marc worked for AT&T where he was instrumental in the development of the company's digital learning and performance management initiatives. He was one of the early pioneers in performance support, producing one of the first such tools in the late 1980s. Marc and his family reside in Hillsborough, New Jersey.

PART
I

The Opportunity

Learning Is a Lot More Than Training

"The illiterate of the 21st century will not be those who cannot read and write, but those who cannot learn, unlearn, and relearn."

Alvin Toffler

"It used to be that information supported the 'real' business; now it is the real business."

Thomas Stewart[1]

THE EXPONENTIAL GROWTH of information that characterizes modern business makes the need for learning more important than ever. But the sheer volume of what we have to learn and the speed at which we must learn it can be daunting. So much so that old models of learning acquisition are failing us. Meeting this challenge requires new thinking about how we acquire knowledge and skill, and how we deploy learning resources that can keep up with the knowledge economy.

Learning and training are often thought of as synonymous; they are not. Training is the way instruction is conveyed; it supports learning, which is our internal way of processing information into knowledge. But since there are many ways we can learn, an effective learning strategy must transcend training.

Some dictionaries equate learning with activities such as training or education. Others use broader cognitive viewpoints like "acquired wisdom, knowledge, or skill," or scientific-sounding behavioral definitions such as "a modification of behavior as a result of experience." While all of these definitions are useful, we can go further to define learning in a way that works in the context of organizations and businesses.

What Is Learning?

In business, learning is a means to an end. Generally speaking, that end is enhanced workforce performance, which in turn reflects its value—better products and services, lower costs, a more competitive posture in the marketplace, greater innovation, improved productivity, increased market share, etc.

In the context of business, learning is the process by which people acquire new skills or knowledge for the purpose of enhancing their performance. Companies want salespeople to learn new selling techniques so they can improve their sales results, which goes right to the business's bottom line. A hotel wants its desk clerks to learn more about customer service so they can be more helpful to guests, and, as a result, the hotel can increase occupancy rates and solidify brand loyalty. The independent plumber seeks to learn a new way to repair burst pipes so that s/he can do the job more quickly and thus handle more customers in the same amount of time. Investment houses want their stockbrokers to learn more about investment strategy so they can presumably provide a greater level of client service, while the firm can increase the amount of assets it has under management. In each case, learning enables an individual or groups of individuals to work faster, better, and smarter so that they and their organizations (or employers) reap business benefits.

The Role of Training

We have traditionally relied on training as the "default" approach to facilitating and improving performance, and instruction as the specific process that makes training work. Training/instruction is used when it is necessary to shape learning in a specific direction—to support learners in acquiring a new skill or to utilize new knowledge in a specific way or to a specific level of proficiency, and perhaps within a specific time frame. Airline pilots are trained to be sure that they can demonstrate all the skills and competencies necessary to operate an airplane safely and efficiently *before* anyone flies with them. Surgeons are trained because of the grave consequences that might result if they practiced their craft without certification of their skills—in advance. Police officers are trained not only because society needs to be sure they are skilled, but also to be sure that they employ their skills appropriately in situations where life and death decisions are made in split seconds. Customer care representatives are trained to respond appropriately with customers every time, and technical experts are trained to fix infrastructure or systems problems quickly so our businesses run smoothly.

Training can be delivered in many ways—in the classroom, over the phone, through a computer or via satellite, to name a few. And a variety of instructional approaches are used to get the job done, including lecture, case study, simulation, drill and practice, laboratories, and small group work. In the end, training has four main elements:

1. An *intent* to enhance performance in a specific way, typically derived via needs assessments and reflected in learning goals and instructional objectives.
2. A *design* reflecting the instructional strategy that is best suited to the learning requirement and the learner's attributes, as well as the measurement strategy that gauges the effectiveness of the training.
3. The *means and media* by which the instruction is conveyed, which may include the classroom, a variety of technologies, independent study, or a combination of approaches.
4. In high accountability situations, a more formalized *assessment* or certification capability.

A New Era

For 1999, *Training Magazine* estimated that $62.5 billion would be spent on corporate training, a 24 percent increase in five years. Of that amount, an estimated $4.5 would be spent on facilities and overhead, predominately classrooms, a five-year increase of just nine percent. Compare that figure to an estimated amount spent on outside services, $15 billion, representing a 66 percent increase over the last five years, most of it coming from increased purchases of hardware and education programs to be delivered over new technologies. In addition, expenditures in the training marketplace, money spent outside the organization for training products and services, has increased by 52 percent in the past five years. So while the demise of the classroom is clearly premature, it's also clear that companies are shifting their training investments to new strategies of technology and external services.[2]

Is this investment in corporate learning paying off? There is increasing evidence that these types of investments are related to corporate success, according to a 1997 study conducted by the American Society for Training and Development (ASTD). When a sample of publicly traded companies was split in half based on training expenditure per employee, the companies in the top half had higher average net sales per employee, and higher average annualized gross profit per employee than the companies in the bottom half. In addition, companies in the top half provided training to an average 84 percent of their workforces, whereas companies in the bottom half averaged just 35 percent of their employees receiving training.[3] But it's more than a question of whether learning pays off; it's about how we can improve the learning process so that the benefits can be *sustained*.

> **"In the 21st century, the education and skills of the workforce will be the dominant competitive weapon."**
>
> **Lester Thurow**

The Transformation Is Underway

The growing body of evidence that quality training can positively impact business performance is good news, but it is only part of the story. In the future, changes in society, business, and technology will limit the impact of traditional training. To continue moving forward, we must transform our perceptions of learning. Following are the five major areas of transformation.

From training to performance. The first transformation is about outcomes. Focusing on the act of training, including how much training activity takes place, is no longer adequate. Trainers must be more accountable; they must demonstrate a positive impact on worker performance in ways that benefit the company. In other words, training is accountable for the same primary measure as any other function: business value. Although powerful, training is just one way to improve performance. No performance improvement strategy is complete without leveraging a variety of powerful nonlearning interventions, such as having the right tools, creating a good work environment, providing adequate incentives and motivation, and giving appropriate feedback/coaching, to name a few. This broad-based view of performance improvement is often referred to as "human performance technology" (HPT).[4] Although beyond the general scope of this book, you should always take HPT into consideration as you formulate an overall learning and development strategy.

From the classroom to anytime . . . anywhere. The second transformation is about access. Widely distributed employees who are busier than ever are calling for delivery solutions that meet their needs and time frames. Learning must be available on a 24/7 clock, with delivery to the office, home, and hotel room. Time is emerging as a critical factor in learning. Employees want and need to learn according to their schedule, not the schedule of the training organization. They also want to learn as fast as possible. Managers want this, too, as it saves downtime due to training and increases overall organizational mobility. But others may want to learn more slowly, a little each week or whenever their schedule permits. While classroom training still has a critical role to play, the needs of employees who have different time requirements can be met most effectively by putting technology in the mix.[5]

From paper to online. Although no one still predicts we'll be working in a paperless world anytime soon, we have come to rely more and more on what's on our computer screens. The online revolution provides corporations with an extremely valuable capability—to update content immediately and continuously. Now, learners will not have to rely on so-called "student guides" given out in class that quickly become old and dated. Nor will businesses have to worry that people might act on last week's or last month's information, believing it is still accurate and valid. Online resources, including learning materials, can be kept fresh and relevant, making them much more valuable to employees over the long term.

From physical facilities to networked facilities. While there continues to be strong arguments for classroom learning, and for outstanding training facilities to support it, companies are now taking advantage of the digital age to link their facilities and their people through the Internet, and, more specifically, through intranets. In companies where these internal webs are built out, they've become the lifeblood of the business, carrying critical business information on sales, customers, products, and people. And learning is becoming a major user of these new corporate information highways. Some companies such as Aetna, AT&T, and SBC Communications have closed or drastically reduced their investment in large, centralized residential training centers, but other businesses continue to maintain these facilities. Those centers that remain have a changed role. They are becoming more specialized, moving to more advanced learning, team-based training, culture-building and problem-solving experiences. Courses that are introductory in nature or deal with specific processes or informational content are among the first to be moved to the Web. In many cases Web-based training is a prerequisite for attendance at a live course. This "clicks and mortar" approach is quickly being deployed at firms like AT&T, Andersen Consulting, Dell Computer, General Motors, IBM, Lucent Technologies, and Merrill Lynch.

From cycle time to real time. Speed is the defining characteristic of the digital world, and time is either a competitive asset or a competitive disadvantage. Twenty years ago I had a year to develop a two-week course. And that course was expected to have a life of several years before it needed major revisions. Sometimes, with stable or foundation content (for example, fundamentals of telecommunications, basic science, or communications skills), we can and should take the time to build the right learning programs that will remain relevant and interesting to people. In many other cases, however, we don't even have two weeks to develop the same course. In fact, an increasing number of training programs cannot be retaught even once without some maintenance. The days when training developers built a course, launched it, declared the project over and moved on are over. Today, cycle times, especially around knowledge, are so short that we are all but working in a real-time mode. That doesn't mean a rigorous training solution is inappropriate—it still might be the best solution. It's just that with such short time frames, using technology and more advanced instructional and informational design techniques are required if we are to keep up with the change all around us.

Learning itself can take time—more time than people or companies can afford to expend. The implications for organizing suppliers of information, including training, are huge. Updating becomes critical as training organizations struggle to stay current. And people are finding that the information they may have learned only weeks ago is now outdated. Going forward, learning will be a continuous process, not only because the content is changing, but because the needs of learners, as well as the needs of the organization, are also constantly changing. We have to find ways to improve learning efficiency, perhaps even to the point where less emphasis needs to be placed on direct learning acquisition for the same or even greater performance payoff. New tools, approaches, and organizational principles will be needed for this to happen.

> **"The only thing that gives an organization a competitive edge . . . is what it knows, how it uses what it knows, and how fast it can know something new."**
> **Laurence Prusak, IBM[6]**

Despite the power of training to contribute toward improving performance, we simply can't train everyone to do everything. If we did, we'd have employees in the classroom all the time—with little time left for work. We can't retrain people every time a new product is announced or every time the competitive landscape changes. We can no longer tell our sales force to leave their customers and come to the training center whenever we have something new to teach them, nor can we halt an assembly line to teach workers about every part change to a product being built. Changing people's perceptions about this will require a lot of effort, because it involves changing the culture they work in as well as influencing their beliefs about what training is.

Formal training may also be "overkill" when the content to be learned is more easily discerned from documentation or other information sources. Think of all that you do and all that you know. Some of what you know and what you can do required training, but much of your knowledge and capability did not. You learned by reading, watching someone else, trial and error, asking a question, or simply thinking through a problem on your own.

Organizations that have strong values regarding learning and performance improvement are usually the ones that have the support and resources necessary to carry learning to the workplace. They have instilled a broader learning culture, not a training culture, and have backed this up with leaders who see it as a significant competitive advantage. They have developed a compelling rationale for learning and have used it to help organizations navigate through difficult change. When these supports are in place, the journey from a focus on training as an activity to competence as an outcome, and the sustainability of that competence, is made much easier.

Unfortunately, in too many businesses learning isn't looked at this way. It's often viewed as an afterthought. Sure, most companies conduct training (some more systematically and comprehensively than others), but the question is whether they go beyond mere training to instill learning in the fabric of the organization.

Broadening Our Perspective: The Role of E-Learning

This expands learning's role in the organization. Despite more emphasis on technology, most training departments, corporate universities, and even organizations that have begun their transition from training to performance still function predominately with a training mindset. They have concentrated their resources, either by design or legacy, almost exclusively in the instructional arena.

E-Learning provides an opportunity for us to broaden this perspective. What we are beginning to note most about e-learning is its growing diversity, beyond courseware and instruction, to generating and disseminating information and directly supporting performance. Providing access to information that contains the collective wisdom of the company can be a powerful adjunct to training. So when we have a learning need that requires instruction, we can use training, and when there is a learning need that more appropriately requires information, we can use *knowledge management* (KM). In the chapters that follow, these two components of e-learning will be examined in detail. But to better understand their differences at a macro level, let's look at one example.

Today, communications companies serve two primary customer groups: businesses and consumers. (Some will argue that government represents another key customer group, but we'll put that aside for now.) One large communications firm set about to secure the data transfer business of a major global client. This client wanted to electronically move financial resources around the world instantly, and ensuring the accuracy and security of these transfers was essential. So the eventual contract was worth millions. Needless to say, the communications firm put its best people on the sales effort—several hundred sales executives, technical experts, and support personnel. These people did not need to be trained. They were already the best. But they needed to learn—quickly and securely. Every day, they needed to learn what was new about the customer, they needed to learn about each other's activities, they needed to learn about the competition. So how did they do it? They learned from each other, facilitated by a Web site designed exclusively for this purpose. Every day, new information—much of it supplied by the team members themselves—about the customer, competition, products, budget, the proposal, government regulations, and literally everything else that had to do with this sale was posted to this secure site. And every day, every member of the team not only interacted with it, they depended on it. Data, analysis, strategy, progress reports, e-mail, tools, discussion, and other features on the site created a community out of this far-flung team. And once the sale was made, the Web site was expanded and repurposed to support the broader sales force. Neither class-room nor computer-based training (CBT) would have worked here because of its structured nature, lack of flexibility, and long lead-time for development—this was simply not a training problem. In this instance, *knowledge management* was the best approach for enabling learning through the delivery of *information*. It worked so well that many on the team attributed the success of the sale in part to this new form of learning.

This same company serves millions of individual consumers, people who might spend five or $500 a month on their phone bill. These customers have needs that are normally met through a call center. The representatives they deal with, on the other end of the phone line, also have learning needs. But their life is more structured. In most cases, turnover is high and pay is moderate, at best. They are evaluated on how fast they handle calls and how many calls they can handle in addition to how well they treat the customer. They deal with an increasingly complex array of prod-ucts, services, promotions, and special situations that change daily. For these folks, time "off calls" is costly to the company, so learn-ing is more controlled. CBT, delivered directly to their workstation over the intranet, provides short, precisely tuned, and specifically scheduled instruction on specific skills and knowledge—customer relations, telephone sales skills, handling customer objections, product knowledge, marketing pitches, etc. Fifteen-minute CBT modules are scheduled when the call center's activity is slowest. Each week the representatives will learn something new. For these workers, knowledge management would be too unstructured, too unsuited for the rigors of the call center. However, *online computer-based training* worked extraordinarily well, because the nature of the learning need required *instruction*, not just information.

What did the global sales team and the customer service rep-resentatives have in common about the way they learned? Most of their skills and knowledge acquisition was facilitated through the same corporate intranet. Although each group had different require-ments (training versus knowledge management), a broad e-learning approach provided solutions in both cases.

In summary, while instruction and information both aid learning, they are different in many respects. Be careful not to confuse the two. If we mistakenly substitute one for the other, we can hinder rather than accelerate the learning process. These distinctions are shown in Table 1.1.

Table 1.1 Characteristics of Instruction and Information

Instruction	Information
• Focused on a specific learning outcome.	• Focused on a specific organization of content.
• Purpose defined by instructional designers, instructors, etc.	• Purpose defined primarily by users.
• Based on a strong diagnosis of user characteristics and needs, and targeted to meet those specific needs.	• Based on the characteristics of the particular knowledge discipline and targeted users.
• Sequenced for optimum memory retention.	• Sequenced for optimum reference.
• Contains presentation, practice, feedback, and assessment components.	• Primarily centered on effective presentation.

Be wary of claims that suggest instruction can be done away with in favor of information. The real challenge for learning, especially for e-learning, is the ability to distinguish the need for information (knowledge management) vs. the need for instruction (online training), and to understand how they work in tandem. This leads to the important determination of whether a particular skill or knowledge need is better met through training or through other approaches.

The Internet and Organizational Learning

Today, organizations are investing in corporate universities, elevating learning to the highest levels of the firm. They're appointing "chief learning officers" or "chief knowledge officers" with access to the top of the business. These new leaders seek not just to offer training courses, but rather to demonstrate a clear linkage between learning investments and business strategy, and to create and maintain a knowledge-creating and knowledge-sharing culture.

They seek, in the words of MIT's Peter Senge, to create organizations that are "continually expanding their capacity to create their future."[7] This is essentially the definition of a "learning organization." Given the massive changes in businesses and the increasing demands on employees, how can we effectively deliver on this learning promise?

One often-discussed approach is to build organizational learning into the business. That is, to create an environment and a culture that encourages knowledge generation and sharing, supports an atmosphere of learning from mistakes, and assures that what is learned is incorporated into the future activities, decisions, and initiatives of the firm. But with people so dispersed and so busy, with demands on our time so seemingly overwhelming, new tools are needed. The Internet is just such a tool. Certainly the Web is becoming essential in the work of business, but it is also becoming essential in the work of learning.

Learner Needs

Employee learning needs can be characterized in three key points: access, comprehensive approach to knowledge, and a balance between training and information.

1. Access is key. Without access to learning, nothing else matters. Employees need access to the information they require to perform their jobs, whenever and wherever they need it. Access has four dimensions: *technical*, as in having the infrastructure to connect to the information; *empowerment*, as in having (or taking) the authority or permission to retrieve and use the information; *flexibility*, as in accommodating the schedules of the learners and not the schedules of the trainers; and *time*, as in having the time to spend obtaining, reviewing, absorbing, and learning the information. In other words, if people can't get it, are not permitted to have it, have to reorder their lives in order to take advantage of it, or have no time for it, there is a fundamental management problem that must be addressed first.

2. Comprehensive approach. Once access is established, employees expect a comprehensive approach to information that's reliable, accurate, complete, organized, and labeled for easy retrieval and use. And they expect it all the time, not just for the few weeks they attend training classes. Knowledge that's inaccurate, dated, missing key points, hard to verify, or organized and labeled for a different use or users is pretty much worthless. This is the continuing struggle of any learning strategy—ensuring that the content is always the *right* content, in the *right* format, and continuously available.

3. Balance. A complementary balance between training and information is another key point. There are many types of information that do not have to be delivered in a course, and other skills or knowledge areas that must be delivered as training. One success factor is being able to differentiate on this point. When we require people to sit through training to learn something they could more easily look up, we waste their time and our resources. On the other hand, if we truly need to train people on a certain skill or competency, then simply referring them to a job aid or Web site would not be adequate. For example, product knowledge can often be delivered as information. But learning how to give CPR probably requires at least some formalized training and practice. One of the biggest errors practitioners make is confusing requirements for learning via training vs. requirements for learning by other means, such as accessing information or using tools to perform tasks for you so you don't necessarily have to learn them.

Business Needs

To meet employee learning needs, businesses also have three key requirements: the right information, an open culture, and an effective technology.

I. Information. Businesses need to deliver the right information to the right people at the right time, even though the content is constantly changing. If people are going to take time out to learn, this information better be well selected and organized for them to use. In an era of specialization, each individual needs a customized learning plan. The old "spray and pray" approach to training—i.e., "spray" it out to everyone and "pray" that it sticks— is an anathema to where organizations are headed. So the organization seeks to deliver precision learning—learning that is timely and geared to precise individual, organization, and business needs. As information requirements become more diverse, the traditional classroom system can no longer cost-effectively or speedily meet all of the demands.

2. Open culture. The organization requires a culture of open access to information and knowledge that encourages sharing knowledge rather than hoarding it. The free flow of information and knowledge is a requirement for a learning organization. When people protect what they know, fearful that sharing it with others somehow diminishes their security or power, the organization can't grow. Real learning organizations characteristically have incentives and systems in place that legitimize, encourage, and reward knowledge sharing, thus building the collective intelligence of the firm. Creating a learning culture is one of the first criteria for building an effective e-learning strategy.

3. Effective technology. Finally, the company requires a cost-effective technology that allows these needs to be met. Information that arrives too late to be used, is too difficult to access, or disrupts the normal work flow is of little value to individuals or to the firm. The increasing complexity of the workplace cries out for technology solutions that help people cope with the information explosion. With learning needed across geographic and organizational boundaries, across cultures and time zones, and across product lines and customer classifications, there is a need for a unifying technology that can, in a manner of speaking, create organizational learning in cyberspace. That unifying technology is the Internet/intranet. It will radically transform learning in the organization and lead everyone involved to reassess their role and purpose.

What Is Your Purpose in the New World of Learning?

Whether you are a chief knowledge officer, chief learning officer, training director, course developer, instructor, or other learning professional, you must determine the purpose of your part of the business. If you are a front-line manager, vice president, or CEO, you must ask yourself: What is the role of learning in the organization? How do I build a climate *and* an infrastructure to support learning? How do I justify learning and e-learning to the business? Asking questions like these is critical of the first steps in building a durable e-learning strategy.

Some people see training, and training organizations, as limited to the delivery of courses, primarily classroom courses. They see instruction as the only legitimate way to learn, and see training people primarily as teachers. They measure their success by how much instruction they deliver and how much people have learned when it's over. Their views of the Internet tend to center on its ability to expand the delivery of what they've always done by moving classroom instruction to online instruction, and that's all. Anything else is someone else's job.

Others have a much broader perspective. They look at improved business performance as the driver of what they do, and thus are more comfortable with new, noninstructional approaches to learning as legitimate growth areas for CKOs, CLOs, training departments, and training professionals. They tend to view the Internet as providing a unique opportunity to redefine themselves and their value in a knowledgecentric world.

The E-Learning Revolution

"Once a company gains a knowledge-based competitive edge, it becomes ever easier for it to maintain its lead and ever harder for its competitors to catch up."

Quinn, Anderson, and Finkelstein[1]

"The Web Changes Everything"

Business Week[2]

THROUGHOUT HISTORY, major technological advances have had the power to completely alter society. Often referred to as "restructuring" or "disruptive" technologies, they very quickly replace a previous technology, even if the previous technology had been a mainstay of life for a very long time. Johann Gutenberg created one of these restructuring technologies with the invention of a printing press for movable type in 1436, replacing 2000 years of handwritten, paper-based communication. This breakthrough allowed for mass duplication and distribution of information in the form of books, newspapers, etc. This eventually led to the advent of schooling, since people now needed to learn to read.

Since Gutenberg, the time frame between restructuring technologies has gotten shorter. Between the mid-1800s and the early 1900s, the telegraph, telephone, radio, and film rapidly altered the communications landscape once again, adding a dose of realism to communication that was never possible before. Just 40 years later, television dramatically disrupted our paradigm of communications further, leading to what Marshall McLuan popularized as the "global village." The sights, sounds, and experiences of people all over the world appear daily in our homes.

Today, the Web represents the latest restructuring technology, expanding the global village with instantaneous, two-way communication and a unique ability for anyone to participate and contribute. Access to the Web is fading as an issue. According to *Worth Magazine*,[3] more than 80 million Americans and 200 million people worldwide are on the Web, and these numbers are expected to double in two years. "In a nutshell: the future" is how *Worth* describes the Internet.[4] The Internet is also a significant part of the future of learning, but the journey has not been easy.

A Short (and Often Frustrating) History of Technology for Learning

The history of using technology for learning is replete with promise and disappointment. In 1922, Thomas Edison predicted that the motion picture would replace textbooks (and perhaps teachers) in the classroom. Clearly, Edison was better at inventing than he was at predicting. Yet film was the first true modern learning technology. As the United States prepared for World War II, military trainers realized there was no way they could reach the millions of service people around the world. While much training was left to field commanders, there was concern that the consistency and thoroughness of U.S.-based training, basic and advanced, would be lost overseas. The solution came as much from Hollywood as from the educational establishment—the army training film. Although many experiments were conducted earlier in the twentieth century, the Second World War provided a need for the massive deployment of these films, which covered everything from personal hygiene to weapons maintenance. So pleased was the military with the success of this approach that, after the war, they continued sophisticated research on the use of film, and later television, for learning. Based on this long tradition and interest, it's no wonder that the U.S. military is generally regarded as a pioneering and leading organization in e-learning.

The military didn't go it alone. They partnered with leading universities to bring the benefits of both behavioral and cognitive psychology to learning. There was lots of work done on many campuses in the United States and around the world. In the sixties, early "teaching machines" and "programmed texts" paved the way for embryonic computer-based training. Instructional films became more creative and covered more topics appropriate for children in schools. A flourishing commercial educational film business catered to both the public and private sectors with films on almost every topic imaginable. For those of us who are old enough, we remember film as a central part of our public school's curricula in the social and physical sciences in the fifties and sixties. Other technologies, such as the infamous filmstrip, also flourished.

But it was television that really got educators excited. TV could bring almost any form of learning to the classroom. Videotape could capture the very best instruction for continuous use. Live teachers were an endangered species, some would say—we'll all be learning off the tube. Airplanes would fly overhead all day, beaming programming to wide geographical areas. Cable would assure that even the most remote areas would get televised learning. Certainly we were not far from the vision depicted in one of the early sixties-era episodes of the original *Star Trek* TV series, where children sat for hours in front of a video screen in a teacherless class, happily absorbing all manner of knowledge.

But it hasn't turned out that way. In spite of a few extraordinary successes such as *Sesame Street*, educational television did not bring about a learning utopia. Why? First of all, the technology, while expensive, was easier to justify than the programming. Many colleges and universities spent millions of dollars wiring every corner of their campuses with cable only to find they had no money for programs or the staff to create them. Second, we really didn't know how to make instructional television. At a time when the nation was still amazed at the entertainment and informational capabilities of TV, most students found instructional "shows" too boring to watch. Although there's been some good use of instructional television in local schools and community colleges, most programs were devoid of any form of instructional design, and teachers didn't know how to integrate the learning into the classroom activities. Today, we have figured out how to use television for learning in specific situations. The PBS classroom television service and a wide range of adult/distance education done on TV are good examples, although they never reached the potential predicted for them in the 1950s. News programming can be eye-opening for history and social studies students. And videotapes can bring experts and once-in-a-lifetime events into corporate and school classrooms. But the main reason why television did not become everyone's teacher was because it lacked the very essential quality of teaching: the ability to interact with the learner, provide feedback, and alter the presentation to meet the learner's needs. TV was a one-way provider of information; it was really not instruction.

It was this necessity for interactivity that renewed efforts in the area of computer-based training (CBT). In the seventies and eighties a tremendous amount of effort was put into this field. It was hard work. Early mainframe efforts were marginal at best.[5] The advent of the personal computer was a turning point. As more PCs were deployed in offices and homes, CBT developers began to see an embedded base of hardware to run their programs. But this hopeful sign was short-lived, as differences in hardware, software, programming languages, and other technical barriers made universal availability more a wish than a reality. Programs had to be developed in different formats, an expensive proposition. And just when a program hit the marketplace, rapid changes in technology platforms made it obsolete. The conversion of 5¼ to 3½ floppy disks, the incompatibility of Apple, UNIX, and IBM-type computers, coupled with the complete lack of authoring and development standards, played havoc with the emerging CBT industry.

This went on as recently as the late eighties and early nineties, when a promising hardware technology known as "InfoWindows," developed by IBM and employing touch screens and interactive videodisks, couldn't survive as the technology changed, leaving it in the dust.

Another problem was that many of the programs were deadly dull. Limited by small hard drives, slow computer speeds, poor graphics, and a surprising disregard for what makes for good learning, most CBT programs never made it out of the box. Although developers did the best with what they had, most CBT programs at the time were text based and almost textbooklike. They primarily focused on an instructional strategy commonly known as "drill and practice." The learner would read a few screens, respond to a few badly written questions with minimal feedback, and then do it all over again. And, if you forgot something, it was practically impossible to search the program to find it again. Although some interesting efforts tried to break this mold, most programs were so bad that students quickly learned not to like *any* program. Guilt by association.

A third problem was caused by the rapidly changing knowledge base. CBT programs were hardly out the door when some of their content was rendered obsolete by a technological change, product update, organizational realignment, or a change in the competitive landscape. Content stability became a key criterion for determining if CBT should be built. But stability proved to be an elusive concept. What constitutes stability? A year? A month? Eventually, training planners grew more conservative, refusing to invest in CBT for fear of premature obsolescence and the high cost of updating. Add to this the large up-front investment needed to build a CBT solution and the questionable likelihood of achieving the large-scale use to justify that investment, and it was easy to see why people become so hesitant. Trainers only used CBT when there was either a lot of people to train over a very *short* period of time (justifying on short-term impact), or a large number of people to train over a long period of time and the content was *not* going to change (justifying on content stability). Even today, decisions about whether to build an instructional CD-ROM must take content stability into consideration.

While all this was going on, tremendous advances were being made in understanding how people learn. New principles of learning and motivation were incorporated into the emerging field of instructional design. Characterized by a systems approach, this so-called "soft" technology helped identify the critical success factors for learning and incorporated them into methodologies that began to be used to create more effective training. But the increasing awareness of what worked often ran into the limitations of the "hard" computer technologies of the time. In many cases this severely limited the instructional design strategies that could be employed. Today this problem can be mitigated if state-of-the-art approaches to instructional design, combined with new, more flexible technologies, are used.

So the computer-based training business, indeed the entire learning technology business, entered the nineties with four things going against it. First, technology changes made it almost impossible to serve all the platforms that were in use. Second, the limitations of both hardware and software rendered programs boring and unauthentic. Third, the growing instability of content, as well as development costs and time, made people gun-shy about spending the amount of money needed to build and deploy an effective system. And finally, the limitations and problems associated with computer technology, as well as a lack of awareness of current instructional design approaches, diminished the contribution of more advanced learning approaches.

John Hancock's Larry Israelite suggests that learning technologies have gone through repeated "cycles of failure."[6] A technology is developed and is then applied to solving educational problems. Expectations are raised that cannot be met. Many of the resulting learning programs are poorly designed and ineffective. The realization grows that the use of the technology has been inadequate and underproductive. Over a relatively short period of time, frustration and disappointment is manifested in the abandonment of the technology. People return to what they know—to traditional, tried-and-true instructional techniques. That is, until the next great technology comes along and the cycle is repeated. Like film, television, and other technologies, it seemed as though CBT was on a continuous cycle of failure and might never have a real impact on learning. Has the Internet changed all this? Will it break the cycle of failure? Israelite says it might, but only if we are careful about how we view and use the Web.

The Rise of a Web-Based Learning Industry

For the first time, Wall Street is taking notice of the e-learning industry. Bank of America, W.R. Hambrecht, and Merrill Lynch, among other financial institutions, now follow the e-learning industry for investors.

> **"The Internet has begun to radically change the teaching of adults in the U.S. who want to improve their skills or further their general education."**
> **Gary S. Becker, 1992 Nobel laureate, who coined the term "human capital"[7]**

The e-learning industry is very diverse. During the 1970s, Florida's Nova University (now Nova Southeastern University, www.nova.edu) stood almost alone as a pioneer in distance learning. Today Nova and almost all traditional higher education institutions are developing an Internet presence beyond simple promotional Web sites. Courses online, interaction with fellow students and instructors, and access to research libraries are just some of the capabilities that are emerging. Here are a few examples from the hundreds of colleges and universities offering online curricula:[8]

- Penn State University: www.worldcampus.psu.edu
- Florida State University: www.fsu.edu/~distance
- Kentucky Commonwealth Virtual University: www.kcvu.org
- State University of New York:
  sln.suny.edu/admin/sln/original.nsf
- University of Maryland: www.umuc.edu/distance/index.html
- Western Governors University: www.wgu.edu

Another growth area is in the for-profit university arena. The Apollo Group's University of Phoenix (www.phoenix.edu), Jones

International University (www.jonesinternational.edu), and Walden University (www.waldenu.edu) are examples among many of the for-profit "eUniversities" offering courses and degree programs following a traditional collegiate model.

The growth is not just courseware. Companies like Eduprise (www.eduprise.com) help build learning infrastructures and networks for higher education institutions as well as corporations. Tools from Blackboard (www.blackboard.com) and WebCT (www.webct.com) allow customers to create learning programs directly on the Web without investing in their own tools or infrastructure.

"Dotcom" online learning companies now proliferate on the Web. Some companies cater mostly to corporate clients (business-to-business), such as Knowledge Planet (www.knowledgeplanet.com), Vcampus.com (www.vcampus.com), and DigitalThink (www.digitalthink.com). Some cater to specific industry segments, such as the IT community (KnowledgeNet, www.knowledgenet.com, and NETg, www.netg.com), or the professional and business community (Skill Soft, www.skillsoft.com).[9]

Dozens of new "learning portals" have emerged on the Internet. These sites offer a one-location gateway to a variety of additional learning resources, some sponsored by universities, some by commercial training companies, and some by individuals. Want to learn something—English literature, computer programming, how to manage people or fix a faucet? Simply query the portal for a three-hour or a three-minute learning program. Some are free, some are supported by advertising, and others charge a course or subscription fee. Both consumer- and corporate-focused portals are represented in the following examples (visit these sites to explore the diversity of what's available on the Web):

www.about.com	www.learnitonline.com
www.click2learn.com	www.learn2.com
www.ehow.com	www.smartforce.com
www.headlight.com	www.smartplanet.com
www.hungryminds.com	www.thinq.com
www.learn.com	

Most of these portals offer prescreened learning programs to customers, many created by third parties. Many also offer books and other items for sale. There are also learning sites composed entirely of submissions by outsiders. Expert Central (www.expert central.com) lets people promote their own expertise on the web (experts for hire), and Fat Brain (www.fatbrain.com) lets individuals publish and sell their own intellectual property on the Web (books, courses, etc.)—for a share of the profits, of course. The number of commercial learning portals is too numerous to mention—some will disappear as quickly as they appeared, while others will grow or consolidate. Expect to see new and increasingly innovative variants of this concept in the future as companies move to have a presence in what analysts Trace Urdan and Cornelia Weggen call the three key e-learning market segments: content, technology, and services.[10] Over time, traditional and for-profit universities, online training companies, learning portals, and other forms of Internet-based e-learning businesses will likely form partnerships and other relationships to cover all these segments.

> **"There's an untapped frontier out there for building e-learning directly into e-business applications."**
>
> **Michael Hoffman, partner, DiamondCluster International**

Finally, many traditional and e-businesses are adding learning to their Web sites to provide more value for their customers and to create increased site loyalty. Examples include Kodak (www. kodak.com), and financial sites like Dow Jones (www.dju.com), ClearStation (www.clearstation.com), and TD Waterhouse (www. tdwaterhouse.com). "NDB University" on the National Discount Brokers Web site (www.ndb.com) offers lessons similar to other sites, but goes one step further, providing an online glossary as well as testing that includes feedback and links to review pages for missed questions. While some of these "lessons" may not be as instructionally advanced as some people might like, there is little question that learning is increasingly becoming a value-added feature on many e-business sites.

The Web is nothing short of the world's library. Easy to use, easy to update, and universal in its availability, it is the driver of the knowledge economy. And, because of this, it is a natural vehicle for learning.

E-Learning Defined

E-business . . . e-commerce . . . why not e-learning? There have been many terms to describe the use of technology for learning, but most are either antiquated or no longer appropriate for a digital world. We've used e-learning quite a lot already, so let's define it.

E-Learning refers to the use of Internet technologies to deliver a broad array of solutions that enhance knowledge and performance. It is based on three fundamental criteria:

1. E-Learning is networked, which makes it capable of instant updating, storage/retrieval, distribution and sharing of instruction or information. So important is this capability that it is fast becoming an *absolute requirement* of e-learning. As useful as CD-ROMs (and DVDs) are for instruction and information delivery, especially for rich media-based simulations, they lack the networkability that enables information and instruction to be distributed and updated instantly. So while CD-ROMs are indeed technology-based learning systems, they should not be classified as e-learning.

2. It is delivered to the end-user via a computer using standard Internet technology. This is a little tricky because the definition of just what is a computer is constantly changing. We see a merging of television and computers, in products like Web-TV, for example, as well as the delivery of the Web to cell phones, pagers, and personal digital assistants, such as the PalmPilot. The key characteristic is the use of standard Internet technologies, such as the TCP/IP protocol and Web browsers that create a universal delivery platform. While corporate business television (usually broadcast by satellite and often using a "student response system" to provide a level of interactivity) meets the first criterion—it can be updated and distributed instantaneously—it doesn't meet this requirement. However, new technology such as IP over satellite provides very fast connections and meets this requirement.

3. It focuses on the broadest view of learning—learning solutions that go beyond the traditional paradigms of training. E-learning is not limited to the delivery of instruction, characterized by computer-based training (CBT). As we will see throughout this book, e-learning goes beyond training to include the delivery of information and tools that improve performance. For the same reason, Web-based training (WBT) or Internet-based training (IBT) are simply more up-to-date descriptions of CBT and are also too limiting as a description of e-learning.

E-Learning spans distance, but distance learning's broad definition also includes correspondence courses, one-way television courses, or other approaches that don't fit any of the above criteria. So we can say that e-learning is a form of distance learning, but distance learning is *not necessarily* e-learning.

Finally, we do a disservice to the advancement of e-learning by referring it as "alternate learning" or "alternate delivery." Some people associate the word "alternate" with "second-rate" or "substitute," or to refer to a classroom equivalent. It can also be construed as describing a temporary or less optimal situation. The bottom line is that "alternate" is a poor choice of words if your goal is to reflect something that has lots of potential. It can become a self-fulfilling prophecy and set expectations that are not in line with your strategic direction. Furthermore, there's no particular reason that the goal of e-learning should be to simply emulate what could be done in the classroom.

Benefits of E-Learning

Why all the fuss? Table 2.1 identifies 11 major benefits of e-learning.

Mergers and acquisitions, global operations, short product life cycles, hypercompetition, instantaneous communications, the explosion of knowledge and "e-everything" are combining to fundamentally change the way we work and learn. Old models, including old models of instructional delivery, are no longer adequate. By combining the new technology of the Internet with new thinking of how people learn, durable e-learning strategies—strategies that actually work—are beginning to emerge.

Table 2.1 Benefits of E-Learning

1. *E-Learning lowers costs*	Despite outward appearances, e-learning is often the most cost-effective way to deliver instruction (training) or information. It cuts travel expenses, reduces the time it takes to train people, and eliminates or significantly reduces the need for a classroom/instructor infrastructure. When deployment is based on a sound business case, the significant startup investment can be quickly recovered through delivery savings.
2. *E-Learning enhances business responsiveness*	E-Learning can reach an unlimited number of people virtually simultaneously. This can be critical when business practices and capabilities have to change fast.
3. *Messages are consistent or customized, depending on need*	Everyone gets the same content, presented in the same way. Yet the programs can also be customized for different learning needs or different groups of people.
4. *Content is more timely and dependable*	Because it's Web-enabled, e-learning can be updated instantaneously, making the information more accurate and useful for a longer period of time. The ability to upgrade e-learning content easily and quickly, and then immediately distribute the new information to large numbers of distributed employees, partners, and customers, has been a godsend for companies trying to keep people current in the face of accelerating change.
5. *Learning is 24/7*	People can access e-learning anywhere and any time. It's "just in time—any time" approach makes an organization's learning operations truly global.
6. *No user "ramp-up" time*	With so many millions of people already on the Web and comfortable with browser technology, learning to access e-learning is quickly becoming a non-issue.

Table 2.1 *(Continued)*

7. *Universality*	E-Learning is Web-enabled and takes advantage of the universal Internet protocols and browsers. Concern over differences in platforms and operating systems is rapidly fading. Everyone on the Web can receive virtually the same material in virtually the same way.
8. *Builds community*	The Web enables people to build enduring communities of practice where they can come together to share knowledge and insight long after a training program ends. This can be a tremendous motivator for organizational learning.
9. *Scalability*	E-Learning solutions are highly scalable. Programs can move from 10 participants to 100 or even 100,000 participants with little effort or incremental cost (as long as the infrastructure is in place).
10. *Leverages the corporate investment in the Web*	Executives are increasingly looking for ways to leverage their huge investment in corporate intranets. E-Learning is emerging as one of those applications.
11. *Provides an increasingly valuable customer service*	Although not internally focused, a business e-commerce effort can be enhanced through the effective and engaging use of e-learning that helps customers derive increased benefit from the site.

Why Have an E-Learning Strategy?

With e-learning, we're not just introducing new technology for learning—we are introducing a new way to *think* about learning. Learning does not necessarily require training or instruction. People learn in many ways—through access to well-designed information, by using new performance-enhancing tools, through experience, and from each other. If we think about learning in this broad perspective, it will be easier to see new options for improving performance.

> **"Technology has revolutionized business; now it must revolutionize learning."**
> **Trace Urdan and Cornelia Weggen,**
> **W.R. Hambrecht & Co.**

Many efforts at using technology for learning have not been sustainable because few saw past the capabilities of new and promising technologies to understand the bigger picture. Many efforts often underestimated the complexities of the interactions between e-learning and the organization, and how truly difficult it is to change people's attitudes about what learning events are and what they can be. With so many stakeholders and business variables in the mix, a more strategic approach is necessary to ensure that e-learning has the best possible chance to succeed. A true e-learning strategy certainly addresses issues of technology and learning effectiveness, but it also addresses issues of culture, leadership, justification, organization, talent, and change. Finally, a comprehensive and well-defined e-learning strategy puts a line in the sand—it helps you focus your attention and lets your customers, clients, and employees know where you are headed. If you want to know if your e-learning initiatives have the potential for success, having a strategy to measure yourself against is a good place to start. Then, you have to execute.

A Strategic Foundation for E-Learning

E-Learning would be complex enough if all we wanted to do was to build and deliver high-quality training on the Web. Building an e-learning strategy, one that has a much greater likelihood of success, also requires us to address:

- *New approaches to e-learning*—including *online training* (the instructional strategy) that provides courseware and business simulations, and *knowledge management* (the informational strategy) that provides informational databases and performance support tools.

- *Learning architectures*—the coordination of e-learning with the rest of the organization's learning efforts. This includes building synergies with classroom training.
- *Infrastructure*—the use of the organization's technological capabilities to deliver and manage e-learning. From general Web access to so-called "learning management systems," the lack of a good infrastructure can stop e-learning in its tracks.
- *Learning culture, management ownership, and change management*—the creation of an organizational environment that encourages learning as a valuable activity of the business, supported by senior managers who are truly engaged in the process. Given a negative learning culture and a quality e-learning initiative, the culture almost always wins. And without an e-learning champion, the initiative may never get off the ground. The effective use of change management can help turn the tide.
- *Sound business case*—the development of a compelling business case that supports e-learning. The old measures of student days and tuition revenue just won't cut it anymore.
- *Reinventing the training organization*—the adoption of an organizational and business model that supports rather than limits the growth of e-learning. New approaches to learning will require new approaches to running, professionalizing, and measuring the training/learning function.

Together, these factors form a "strategic foundation for e-learning," which is depicted in Figure 2.1. The more pieces of the foundation that are supporting, rather than hindering, e-learning initiatives, the greater the likelihood that these initiatives can be sustained.

Think about how your company is approaching e-learning. Are your efforts unified or are they more like "everyone for themselves"? Are you arguing more about what authoring tool to use rather than what content to deliver? Are your instructors just a little worried about their jobs, believing that the Web will kill all classroom training? Are you stymied by an inconsistent or nonexistent infrastructure? Do you buy online courses by the bagful without really knowing what you're getting? Are e-learning funds always the first to be cut during a financial crisis? Do employees

Figure 2.1 The Strategic Foundation for E-Learning depicts all the critical components for successful e-learning initiatives.

feel they have to apologize for, or even hide, work time devoted to their own learning? These are pretty obvious symptoms of an ineffective strategy. This foundation can guide you through these and other challenges on your way to make it more effective and more durable.

A lot of what's missing in an e-learning strategy is often what's missing in a general learning strategy as well. This is a key point. Many companies have been less than successful in truly implementing organizational learning because these same factors were not taken seriously. If we're not thorough, we can easily be seduced by powerful software and computer technologies at the expense of issues of culture, leadership, access, change, and so on. We could also go awry by confusing the message (e.g., content) with the messenger (e.g., the Internet). Without a comprehensive strategic foundation, this situation is all too common and all too prone to failure.

Beginning with Chapter 3, we'll build this foundation, piece by piece. We'll address new forms of learning, but we'll go far beyond that as well, emphasizing the critical role these nonlearning factors play in a successful e-learning initiative. By the end of this book the framework will be complete, and will represent the best balance between e-learning and the organizational culture that can either support it or kill it.

An E-Learning Journey

by Elliott Masie, The Masie Center

Warp Speed for E-Learning?

I LOVE THE CONCEPT AND FUTURE of e-learning. I've been an advocate of the power of linking technology and training for years. Yet, I have this strange feeling that we are at a science fiction moment in the learning profession. Science fiction? Please explain.

As a science fiction fan, I tend to look at things from the cockpit of a large space vehicle. Many folks are describing this as a hyper-jump point in the learning industry. You know, that place where physics is suspended and the space rocket jumps to a whole other galaxy and even time in an instant. It saves a lot of pages in a science fiction book and a lot of minutes in a sci-fi flick to instantly leap. Is it true for the learning industry? Will e-learning *instantly* transform how organizations and human beings perform? Will we accomplish in a few years what dozens of years of CBT experimentation could never reach? It's certainly worth pursuing, and we will get there, but it is a longer road than we think.

The buzz predicting instant change in the world of learning is coming heavily from the e-commerce and e-business world. Fueled by the hope and hype of instant fortunes, new phrases drip off of business plans describing how technology will instantly change all aspects of learning. The biggest myth in this analysis is that adding technology to the learning process requires a whole new product and a totally different human experience. If I am talking about the impact of e-commerce on airline travel, it is easy to make the case that most of us will use technology to shop and purchase for travel choices. The same will be true for the process of shopping for and buying training.

Yet, imagine the difficulty of selling an online travel experience, where you took the vacation from the PC in your living room, rather than boarding an airplane. That is the size of the challenge for scalability of e-learning. It will not be an instant change for how we look for new skills. It will take years of success and failure as the art and science of e-learning evolves, as heroes emerge in this field and as the equivalent of a Steve Spielberg of e-learning design is born and grows up. The forecast is for a positive upward curve of adoption—we have come further in the past few years than in the previous twenty, but the journey will be measured in additional years or even a decade, not instant and massive change in the next 12 or 36 months.

There are two different "markets" that are impacting the world of e-learning—the stock market and the vendor marketplace. Each of them has a different rhetoric and viewpoint on the e-learning phenomena and where it's heading.

The stock market is currently rewarding businesses that are deeply focused on the alignment of learning with e-business. They like phrases like portal, B2B, supply chain, and other digital age terms. Unfortunately, they are not necessarily as happy with investments in authoring tools, growth of custom development capabilities, or organizations that see learning change as cultural and evolutionary. I have sat with the CEOs of several e-learning companies as they have expressed their frustration with what they need to do to keep the stock market analysts happy, which often conflict with what their customers are asking for and willing to buy.

The vendor marketplace knows the "dirty little secret"—that we are just at the beginning, not the middle or the end, of the exciting era of inventing e-learning. It is not a simple or off-the-shelf process. They know that organizations want to find ways of blending their classroom offerings with e-learning. Their customers are telling them that they are all moving toward e-learning, but they are not paying major amounts of money for e-learning content, *yet!* The vendor marketplace is also struggling with a weak level of differentiation. Every week we hear of new e-learning companies, with very similar names, business plans, and often several million dollars to spend on marketing in anticipation of a rapid IPO. But customers (that's us!) are confused, and this is resulting in longer selling cycles and a disconnect between the hype and reality of e-learning.

Weak Numbers. Be careful of those large numbers and predictions that you hear. Every day someone calls The Masie Center and asks for our prediction of the size of the e-learning industry. I don't have a good answer and I don't really understand the industry sizing numbers that are kicked around. When I hear that a large percentage of classrooms are going to be shut down and replaced with e-learning, I want to understand the basis for that number. Most organizations are already delivering a large amount of learning outside the classroom, through informal, action, on-the-job, reading-based, CBT coaching or nontraining. My experience tells me that e-learning will probably have more of an immediate impact on those styles of instruction than wiping out large numbers of classroom offerings in a single swoop. Sure, classes will get shorter. Many people will be able to learn with fewer visits to the classroom. But the magic is in the mix—we must not let our embrace of e-learning turn into "techno-arrogance" with respect to the proper and important role of the classroom.

The "E" in E-Learning Stands for WHAT? Probably the most confusing aspect of this moment in the learning industry is about the meaning of a single letter. What does the *e* in e-learning mean? The standard definition would be that it is all about "electronic." Add technology to a process and it becomes an *e* process. I think that is a way too simple answer. What if we offered several alternatives for the *e* letter:

- *e is for Experience.* The business drivers for e-learning are about changing the character of the experience of learning in the corporation. A learner in an *e* learning offering would have the options of time-shifting, place-shifting, granularization, simulation, and community support, to mention a few. These are not necessarily all electronic, but go to the heart of evolving and increasing the experience level.
- *e is for Extended.* With e-learning an organization should be able to offer an extension of learning options, moving from an event perspective to an ongoing process. The footprint of the e-learning experience would be larger in terms of time and would linger with the learner throughout their work life.

- *e is for Expanded.* The opportunity to expand training offerings beyond the limitations of the classroom is incredibly exciting. Can we offer learning to all employees globally? Can we offer access to an unlimited number of topics? Can we not be constrained by our training budget when it comes to meeting an employee request for knowledge?

This is what *e* learning is all about. We need to make sure that our suppliers and funders understand that the easiest part of implementing e-learning is the technology. That is like picking a good video camera or receiver. The toughest part is to *invent* and *innovate* the content to create new models of experiences for delivery with this technology. The interesting part is how to blend the classroom and e-learning in appropriate and supercharged ways. And, the ultimate marketplace that we have to look at is the learner. If we build it, will they come?

So, as I look at my own journey through the ups and downs of learning technology, and turn to my navigator to see if we have reached the "hyper-jump point" for e-learning, I get a confusing look. There is a lot of talk about us being at that junction, but on closer inspection, it is just a very fast superhighway. We will have to travel those miles, at a rapid rate, but there are no hyperleaps to be found. I am actually relieved, for creating e-learning element by element will be honorable work. The e-learning revolution is coming, but it will not happen overnight. It will take a bit more time than the stock market hype suggests. It will take more cycles, since we will have to deal with the heartbeats of organizations and the basic human nature of people. But there is no turning back—our journey is still just beginning. If we apply our craft well, the future will be full of opportunities.

Scotty, let's go explore . . . warp factor one!

Elliott Masie *is President of The Masie Center, an international think tank focused on learning and technology (www.masie.com).*

PART II

New Approaches for E-Learning

3

Why Most CBT Doesn't Work and How It Can Be Better

"In order to do things differently, you have to see things differently."

Paul Allaire, CEO, Xerox Corporation

"If we don't change our direction, we'll end up exactly where we are headed."

Ancient Proverb

WE'VE GROWN UP WITH the classroom—an institution that's been around for hundreds of years. Before the classroom, before schools, people learned at the foot of the master. One expert, one apprentice. You were taught, and you demonstrated your skill. Eventually you were deemed ready to practice your trade and you took on your own apprentice. But as the amount of and demand for knowledge grew and outstripped the capabilities of the masters to teach one-on-one, and as the concept of universal access to education took hold, classrooms and schools were established. Teaching one-to-many was certainly more efficient, and we've strived ever since to equal the quality of the original tutorial model. We've come close; we've even discovered new benefits of group learning. But we've always known that schools were mostly an economic response to managing the delivery of an ever-increasing volume of information to an exploding population of learners, and that it is not necessarily a better response from a learning perspective. There's no one who at one time or another hasn't wished to simply be alone with a master, to have his or her undivided attention, to learn from the best there is.

That's essentially what the promise of computer-based training was—to allow us to go back to the expert-learner model, with a patient, all-knowing electronic teacher that would serve all of our growing learning needs.

This vision remains elusive. Most of us have tried computer-based training. And most of us have been, at one time or another, frustrated with it. Perhaps boring, ineffective, slow, unmotivating or just plain bad may be better words to describe many of our experiences. While there have been some great successes, most CBT has been disappointing, not only to learners but also to those who built the programs. Why? Following are eleven possible reasons.

1. The content wasn't any good. Sometimes, the CBT content was just plain incorrect, inappropriate for the audience and purpose, or just out of date. This might have been the result of the supplier/author building the product to appeal to multiple audiences. For example, a CBT program on computer maintenance built by the computer manufacturer might not include modifications that one company made to its systems. The generic nature of the program left learners with huge holes in their knowledge of how to maintain *their* machines. Other problems may come from the fact that the CBT is dated. If non-networked media such as disks and CD-ROMs are used, there is a danger that an older version of the program will be used—and then the dated information presented will be the basis for action. One obvious example is the salesperson relying on an old CBT course on a product that has since been revised, repriced, or even discontinued!

Stand-alone CBT developers were aware of these issues. Their response, to improve productivity so new versions of the program could be cost-effectively released on a regular basis, would appear to make sense. But the solution created a new and bigger problem—version control—keeping on top of all the iterations of the product and making sure users have the most up-to-date releases. Over a short period of time, this could not be managed and the system started to degrade.

I often ask members of an audience how many of them have purchased at least 100 online CBT programs from a commercial supplier. Lots of hands go up. Then I ask this same group if they or any staff member ever evaluated *all* of these programs. Most hands go right back down. Amazingly, most training people do not assess the online training they buy. No wonder they're blindsided when users complain of incomplete or inaccurate content.

2. The learning wasn't authentic. Closely related to content issues are issues of authenticity. Like teenagers who identify with television programs that portray what their lives are really like, instructional authenticity is about people *identifying* with learning programs that reflect what their jobs are really like. Accuracy, comprehensiveness, and even relevancy may not be enough to draw people to the program if it is not believable. A program on how to supervise problem employees, for example, may be accurate, with all the steps and procedures that are appropriate. It may also be comprehensive, covering all of the situations that might be faced and answering most of the questions that might be asked. And it might be relevant—well matched to the experience of the manager group for which it is targeted. But if it isn't authentic, that is, if the learner doesn't *believe* that the steps, procedures, situations, problems, and questions contained in the CBT are *real*, the program is in trouble. When a learner comments that a program "has lots of good information, but it reflects an ideal world, not what actually happens in the real world where I work," the program will die.

3. Form over substance. The rush to internet-based CBT has produced some great-looking, yet awful training. Despite a history of disappointment with learning technologies, IBM's Tony O'Driscoll suggests that many trainers are still obsessed with "technolust," which drives them to try the latest technological gizmo—the Internet just being the latest iteration.[1] Ignoring the tenets of instructional and information design amidst fervor over technology usually results in lots of Web wizardry that often doesn't teach anything of value. This can be a costly lesson.

4. One size didn't fit all. While early CBT developers did take advantage of the nonlinear branching capabilities of the medium, they often had a problem with those who would learn faster by skipping material they already knew. Programs provided questions to learners and, based on their response (correct or incorrect), took them along different paths that might have included remediation of some of the instruction, or skipping some of the training that wasn't needed. Some programs included diagnostic tools up front that assessed the learner on specific competencies or learning requirements and then configured the training path to meet those requirements. But for many learners, this just wasn't enough. They had little time to sit through the diagnostics or to plow through instruction they didn't need in order to get to what they did need (if they actually knew what they needed in the first place). Modules or lessons that must be taken in a specific order frustrated some people who wanted to skip around, and programs that allowed learners to explore on their own frustrated others who needed structure. Ultimately, it became difficult to always find the right pace and the right level of flexibility, let alone the right content (see reason number 1, above). And offering multiple modes often ate up most of the development budget, raising the cost of the program to prohibitive levels.

5. The technology was a barrier. With virtually no standards, CBT was often at the mercy of rapid changes in technology. The first problem, platforms, should have been enough to deter most people—every program had to have multiple versions: for PCs, Macintoshes, UNIX machines, and the various mainframe operating systems. Then there was the problem of storage (hard drive), memory (RAM), and operating system version compatibility (e.g., having the correct version of DOS or Windows). Every CBT program had different requirements, and because users' machines were as varied as they could be in this area, hardware/software compatibility and support became a nightmare. In addition, as new technology came and went, it left literally hundreds of orphan programs in its wake. For example, in the late 1980s and early 1990s many CBT programs were produced on the IBM InfoWindows format, a system that used pizza-sized laser disks and proprietary touch screens. As an early attempt to employ full multimedia capabilities into CBT, this approach demonstrated great potential. But within a few short years the investment that companies made in InfoWindows became almost worthless, as the technology moved to CD-ROMs with content that could be displayed on standard PC screens. With all these technical hurdles, it's no wonder that many CBT programs never made it out of the box they came in.

6. It was useless after the initial use. Unfortunately, like the new car that depreciates in value the minute you drive it off the lot, most CBT programs lose a lot of their value after the very first use. Let's say you've just finished a fourteen-lesson, full-day CBT program on the features of an entirely new product your company is announcing and you're going to be selling. The program had about 800 individual computer screens of information, exercises, etc. Now, a month later, you are about to call on a customer who has asked you a pretty specific question on the product. You can't recall the answer, but you know it was in the CBT program. How do you find that bit of knowledge? Most traditional disk-based CBT programs did not support a good way to search for specific information. At best, you might find the appropriate lesson and retake it until you found what you were looking for. At worst, you might have to retake the entire course—if you didn't already pass the program on to your colleague! And if you did find what you were looking for, is it still accurate? Remember, a month has gone by, so even if you found the information, should you rely on it? (See number 1 above, *again.*)

7. The learning wasn't reinforced. Reinforcement is one of the most powerful tools for learning. Some ways to reinforce learning are: applying what you've learned on the job, having follow-up training (either classroom or more CBT) referring back to what you just learned, and having your manager review with you what you've learned and how you might use your new knowledge. For many people, however, the CBT program was often viewed as a separate activity rather than part of a broader learning scheme. If your manager didn't take the program, how would s/he be able to help you? If the CBT program was considered secondary to the "more important" classroom training, what message does that send about its value? In the end, many people quickly learned that while there was CBT "out there," some of it good, it was not to be confused with any *real* training. Nor was it to be considered a substitute for the classroom. The result was that people quickly concluded that the CBT might not be worth the effort.

8. There was no support for it. Related to reinforcement is the issue of support. From front-line managers to senior executives, support is critical to the success of CBT. Programs often failed because no one, especially those in role model or leadership positions, actually cared about them. Even within training departments, CBT programs took a back seat to classroom training from a budget, communications, and value perspective. I recently took a tour of a major residential corporate university. I saw sleeping rooms, exercise rooms, classrooms, and dining rooms. I saw technology in the classrooms (mostly for systems training) but could not get anyone to tell me much about their CBT efforts, even though I knew they had done some good work. It just wasn't valued. Bottom line: In everything you do, the support you have or give to an initiative has an impact, and it shows!

9. It went against the culture. Here are some statements heard, either overtly or covertly, far too often in many companies:

- "Learning takes place at the training center, not at your desk—now put down that training and get back to work."
- "It's sure cold up here—I wonder what the Florida training center is offering this month?"
- "I have no time to learn—I'm too busy with work," or, "My people have no time to learn—they're too busy with work."

- From the training organization's perspective: "If we send a CBT program to Joe, who ordered and paid for it, and he gives it to Mary and Steve when he's done with it, how will we get paid for those other two users?"
- Also from the training organization's perspective: "If people take this CBT program instead of coming to class, how will we fill our seats?" Or, "If we send a CD to John, how will we know if he's even opened it?"

Many of us have heard these statements or observed behavior that reflects them. In spite of its quality, authenticity, usefulness, and value, CBT programs fail if they are smothered by an unsupportive organizational climate. Leadership support and a positive culture are so powerful that all other challenges pale beside them. In fact, they are the primary reasons why e-learning strategies fail. So important is culture and support that we'll look at them in more detail in subsequent chapters.

10. It was just plain boring.   Sometimes the material wasn't very interesting. Perhaps there were pages upon pages of text that didn't seem relevant, or exercises that didn't challenge us. Perhaps the layout wasn't stimulating. Or the program was too long. Whatever the reason, we often balked at much CBT because, frankly, it didn't excite us.

11. It was "shovelware."   Alistair Fraser of Penn State University uses this interesting term to reflect classroom training that is merely being moved to the Web without consideration of how it must change for the new technology.[2] Recognizing that the first thing we do with a new technology is try to deliver the same material in the same way we used to deliver it in the older technology, Fraser argues that this approach will never allow us to truly benefit from new innovations. The problem is that many courses don't make the transition too well. They reach more students, but are instructionally poorer for the effort and not likely to be sustainable. His recommendation is that we stop focusing on the Web only as a way to provide better administration, distribution access, and delivery speed of the same old stuff, which he refers to as "shovel-ware." Instead, we need to focus more on how we can redesign the learning episode itself.

> **"The test then, is to imagine moving back to a more con-strained medium. If you are successful in moving back-ward, you have been unsuccessful in moving forward."**
>
> **Alistair Fraser,**
> **describing a simple test for Web-based "shovelware"**

The Road to Better Online Training

Of course we can build better CBT—it remains a vital component of an e-learning strategy. But simply being "computer-based" is not enough. For CBT to be effective going forward, it must be *online*. And so, for the remainder of this book, the terms *computer-based training*, *Web-based training*, and *Internet-based training* will be *retired*, and *online training* will be used in their place.

Leaving technology, support, and culture aside for the moment, we can avoid shovelware online training through better instructional design that leverages the distinct attributes afforded by new learning technologies. Too often we move to an online training environment carrying our paradigms of classroom training. The result is programs with lots of lessons and lectures (manifested in text or "talking heads") followed by electronic forms of traditional paper-and-pencil tests. We've changed the delivery strategy but not the instructional strategy. Yet today new approaches to effective online training are emerging.

Goals that are meaningful and motivational. If there's one part of traditional instructional design we've learned to always do, it's write instructional objectives. Courses that may have little else in the way of applied or thoughtful instructional design have them. But we often don't write these objectives very well—they often are irrelevant to the learner.

Let's look at one example: training new front-desk staff for a hotel (or any service business). Objectives such as, "At the end of this course the student will be able to demonstrate the major steps for resolving hotel guest problems," or "At the end of this lesson, the student will be able to name the steps for effective hotel guest relations," do not always reflect the real job situation. Learners are far more concerned about what they'll be able to do on the job rather than what they'll be able to do after the course. And they want to go further, to know *why* they have to do it and how it will benefit *them*. They want to know the impact that their new capabilities will have on the business, on profitability, and on the success of their unit. So we might tell hotel front-desk clerks that the training will give them the ability to solve guest problems in ways that build a better, more valued relationship with the guest, resulting in greater customer loyalty and retention.

Traditional instructional objectives remain important guideposts for developers, but they are hardly motivating for learners. All training must have specific and measurable statements of desired learning outcomes. This is *not* an argument against objectives, but a plea to focus on the right learning outcomes and do a better job of writing these statements in ways that are extremely meaningful to the learner. In the learning program itself, by replacing (or augmenting) instructional objectives with these types of statements, centered on business justification and benefits, we help learners see the value of devoting their time to the program, and we enhance their motivation to learn.

> **"All genuine knowledge originates in direct experience."**
> **Mao Zedong**

Learning by doing—the power of simulations. There is nothing wrong with providing information in the context of online training, just as there is nothing wrong with using lectures in the classroom. There are also times when well-designed tutorials are effective, efficient, and motivating, especially when the need is to teach declarative knowledge and well-structured procedures.

But there are other times when the learning requires more direct immersion in a problem or situation. Just like the classroom that transforms itself into a lab for role-plays, experimentation, and practice, online training must also engage in more interactive activities. Quizzes and tests are one form of interaction, but by no means the only form. Whether we're teaching computer programming, sales skills, or supervision, we can use technology to simulate an application and give learners great opportunities to practice. In fact, the creation of realistic business simulations, made possible by new learning technologies, offers opportunities to enliven online training in ways that were just not possible before. Simulations help increase the authenticity of the learning program, thus making it more transferable and motivating. Through simulations, we can immerse learners in situations that truly test what they know, what they can do, and how they think. We can use simulation techniques and other challenging approaches to motivate learners by allowing them to experience learning rather than just read instructional text, and to see their progress throughout the program rather than just getting a test score at the end. In addition, we do not always have to follow the traditional model of providing instruction first, followed by practice and a formal test. When done well, putting learners into an experience almost at the start of the program provides the kind of situational involvement that makes the online training real from the start. Instead of telling the new hotel front-desk clerk the steps involved in handling guest problems, we can simulate those problems and allow him/her to derive the steps from the interactive learning experiences.

Learning from mistakes. Sometimes there are risks associated with a lack of readiness to deal with a real work situation. For the hotel desk clerk, the risks may be too great that inappropriate behavior would cost the hotel dearly. Even if the risks were less severe, it can take a long time for every type of scenario to present itself in a real work environment. But within the confines of an online simulation, we can allow the learner to experience all types of challenges, and fail in some of them, where "safe failure" can be one of the most powerful learning opportunities imaginable. Within the program, the front-desk trainee can try a variety of approaches and revise his/her strategy so as to be more successful the next time. At each of these points, the program provides feed-back and coaching to build confidence as well as provide guidance. And, through each inappropriate action taken in the training, and each subsequent adjustment, the learner builds a cognitive strat-egy, or internal knowledge base for solving the problem. This now becomes an ingrained part of his/her behavior repertoire. The result is a much more effective learning experience, where new skills and knowledge actually "stick."

Safe failure is not appropriate for all situations, as when you are dealing with low learner self-confidence, but it is a useful tool in many situations. Without the option to experiment, great oppor-tunities for learning can be lost. I was once involved in the design of a classroom program to teach new employees about the business strategy of their new firm. We began with an elaborate activity (learning by doing) that simulated the sales and manufacturing aspects of the business. Some students portrayed customers, while others played various roles within the business. The simulation was specifically designed so the business would fail. It would then be followed by deep discussion as to why it failed, with the result-ing lessons learned becoming the basis for the rest of the course. But the client was unhappy with the design. She didn't think it was appropriate for students to "experience failure," and asked that the simulation be revised so they would succeed. She saw it as demotivating and didn't recognize the important role that learn-ing from mistakes played in creating some of the most powerful and motivating "teachable moments" in the course.

Robust coaching and feedback. Online training programs run the gamut in the quality of the coaching and feedback they provide. I began this book with a story of my first professor, Dr. Phillips, who, more than 25 years ago, was thrilled to get his now-antique CBT program to respond with Correct, Incorrect, and Try Again responses. It's surprising how many programs today still provide little more than this. We all know that incorrect responses should be accompanied by reasons why the response is incorrect and clues that may help the learner respond appropriately when she/he tries again. We also know that correct responses should be reinforced with explanations as to why the response is right. But quality online training programs do much more.

Our hotel clerk-in-training, in the context of a simulation, not only selects a single response, but in doing so dictates the next stage in the simulation. So if the response is incorrect, the result may not be immediate feedback, but the opportunity to see the consequences of that response. If the hotel clerk did not deal appropriately with a disgruntled guest, for example, his/her actions could result in that guest canceling a future reservation, but that consequence might not be apparent right away, giving the learner opportunities to recognize the consequences of a prior action and rectify them. Feedback is sometimes given when the *learner* recognizes that the response was incorrect, *not* when the program recognizes it. When the clerk understands that his/her action resulted in lost future business, the resulting feedback is much more powerful.

In addition to feedback, the system also provides coaching that reinforces learning at critical moments, provides additional insights and perspectives, and engages the learner in a dialogue about why the selected choice was right or wrong. Our clerk receives additional advice, and perhaps some modeling on how to deal with unhappy guests that will benefit him/her going forward. When programs miss the opportunity to provide coaching in addition to feedback, they miss the opportunity to reinforce learning.

Expert modeling and stories. Technology offers a wonderful opportunity to reinforce learning with the sage advice of experts and the reality of stories. Our hotel clerks can see and hear how an expert would have handled the situation. They can see demonstrations of different approaches to dealing with unhappy guests and select one or more as their own. Stories are a little different. Our clerks can learn about how people, just like them, thought about similar situations or how they developed new ways to approach the problem. They can *relate*. Some of these storytellers may be experts, but others may simply be peers who have had similar experiences. Our learner begins to understand that she/he is not alone in solving these problems, that others have mastered the same skills and have contributed their real-life experiences to help him/her. And who knows? Because Internet technologies allow easy and quick updating (a key tenet of e-learning), one day she/he too may have the opportunity to contribute stories to the learning of others. By bringing experts and peers (or customers!) into an online program to model behavior and tell of their experiences, we reinforce learning in ways that are both powerful and long-lasting. And by using technology to keep these elements vibrant and current, we maintain the authenticity of the program.

Authenticity.   Each of the previous approaches to better online training contributes to the authenticity of the program. The effect is both cumulative and iterative. Using all of these approaches well builds a greater level of credibility in the eyes of learners than using just a few of them well, or using each one alone. But as the marketplace, content, customers, products, competition, and technology change these components must be updated. It would be disastrous for our hotel clerk-in-training to hear stories based on an outdated situation, such as a story of how one guest was successfully referred to the local commercial copy center down the street without mention of the business center recently opened inside the hotel! Good online training programs are constantly being revised or else they lose their authenticity. Internet technology, the backbone of e-learning, makes this possible.

Reuse after learning.   Our hotel front-desk clerk has finished her/his online training program. But she/he can still refer back to it because it was designed to support her/him on the job (perhaps using a "random access" capability). It has a search capability for finding information quickly, and the content is continuously being updated through the hotel's intranet. She/he also makes use of several job-related tools and databases that the program taught her/him how to use. In a sense, the online training now serves as a portal or gateway to a host of resources that enable continuous learning long after the training is over.

Building great CBT that encompasses these key features is certainly more complex and challenging than building the more traditional, less effective CBT we've grown used to. It takes great content knowledge and cutting-edge instructional design expertise. And it takes money. That's why any e-learning strategy must deal with the "make vs. buy" decision—do we build the program or do we buy it? And if we build it, do we build it ourselves or hire someone to do it for us? We'll deal with these decisions in more depth in later chapters, but for now, here are key questions to ask your team if you are building a new online training product, or to ask your vendor if you are buying one:

Is the content complete and accurate for the users and the purpose? Does it reflect what's going on at your company, not at a "generic" company (and if it is generic, can you live with it)? Review each and every program you buy or build. Don't take the builder's assurances at face value. If the content is not accurate, do not use the program until it is! The learner may not recognize inaccuracies, and therefore act on the information, believing it to be true. The saying "garbage in . . . garbage out" should really be rephrased as "garbage in . . . gospel out."

"Don't underestimate learners' willingness to try e-learning, but don't think for a nanosecond that they will tolerate a bad learning solution just because it's web deployed."
John Howe, General Physics Corporation

Have you designed the program to take advantage of technology? If you're converting classroom training to the Web, be careful of the shovelware problem. Web-based learning offers a wealth of new design opportunities—use them.

Is it technologically compatible—will it run on your corporate network? This is essential for your e-learning strategy. If it requires different technology from what your firm uses, or if it requires major adjustments to your infrastructure or standard platforms, think twice about using it (more on this in Chapter 6).

Are learners involved in their learning, and involved from the start? Is the level of interactivity commensurate with the goals of the program and not simply questions and answers? Meaningful active involvement reinforces learning. If your people are simply and passively plowing through "page turners," little will be learned, much less retained, and your investment will be marginalized. Do learners have an opportunity to try things out, to experiment and perhaps fail in a safe environment? Does the program take advantage of these "teachable moments" to reinforce learning? Find out how well the program handles failure and how it capitalizes on those key learning opportunities.

Is the coaching and feedback robust and comprehensive? Do learners always understand the consequences of the actions they take? The guidance that the program gives to learners about their actions is critical in helping them internalize new skill and knowledge. Press hard for the best coaching and feedback features you can get.

Are the experts and stories that are provided credible and up-to-date? Can the learners relate to them? These wonderful teaching opportunities can quickly turn learners off if they do not believe what they are reading, hearing, and seeing.

Is the program authentic—real in terms of the working world the learners actually live in? Inauthentic programs are ineffective programs. Enough said.

Where appropriate, can the program accurately assess learning? That is, does the program assess how well the learner mastered the essential skill and knowledge elements that were conveyed?

Does the program have value and usefulness after the training is completed? Leverage your investment by assuring that the program becomes part of the learner's performance "tool kit" back on the job.

Does Multimedia Enhance Learning?

No discussion of learning, or e-learning, would be complete without considering the impact of multimedia. Media elements—graphics, animation, film, audio, and video—have been used in training situations for years. Now, computer technology offers opportunities to combine different media technologies, i.e., *multi*media, *and* enable learners to interact with them. When we refer to *multimedia-based training*, we are referring to how media are used to support learning—an instructional design issue. But when we use the term to reflect an upgraded form of computer-based training technology, we are confusing design issues with hardware issues. What matters more than the technology is how we use multimedia for learning. This is an important distinction.

The instructional efficacy of multimedia has been debated for a long time. Multimedia can add value, but simply adding multimedia to a bad learning program won't improve it. Worse, when we confuse multimedia design and development with instructional design and development, we may be in for programs that look great but don't teach. If we pay close attention to instructional design, the match-up between media and the information to be conveyed will be tighter. The richness and the interactive nature of multimedia is important in allowing learners to be immersed in their learning, to experience situations that add real authenticity and impact. However, all the multimedia in the world can't fix an inherently bad learning design—in fact it may make it worse.

So how much attention should be paid to multimedia? Probably a lot, but the attention must be directed appropriately. When CD-ROMs became generally available, trainers believed they had finally found *the* technology, one that would allow them to incorporate both instruction and multimedia on a storage device that could hold so much data they would be free from the limitations of floppy disks. Unfortunately, in many cases the rush to add as much media as possible often left little room or budget for instructional content. Many CDs were filled with so much gratuitous video, such as "talking heads" and jazzy media-laden introductions, that even a 650 megabyte CD couldn't hold all the content that was needed.

Access and download speed is also a problem for multimedia. Some would suggest that we need to wait before we jump into Web-based multimedia learning until the Internet has enough bandwidth to carry all the media elements that are now possible on CDs. But in many ways there will never be enough capacity and the Web will never be fast enough. The expression "bandwidth breeds sizzle and sizzle breeds bandwidth" has a lot of truth to it. When we get more capability, we'll find ways to use it, and as soon as we fill up the pipe, we'll find new applications that will need even more capacity. What we will do is burn up lots of budget and production time, which can make even good CBT cost-prohibitive, or sacrifice good instructional design.

To deal with this problem, there have been attempts to marry CDs (and now, DVDs) and the Web (often referred to as a "Web-CD hybrid") in a way that allows the CD to generate the bandwidth-intensive multimedia elements, while the Web generates more text-based content. Some of these efforts have been successful, but version control, shifting Web addresses, and added technical complexity can be real management and logistical problems. The key decision is whether the need for the media elements outweighs these challenges, or whether lower bandwidth solutions can be used and then upgraded as plug-in (now) and broadband (future) technologies are deployed. This is a technology *and* an instructional design decision.

When used carefully and properly, it is possible to incorporate the richness of multimedia in the learning experience without degradation in access, quality, or speed. We can simulate experiences more realistically, bring the world to the learner and create interactions that are more reflective of real work. An example of learning-oriented Web sites can be found on the "Specials" page on CNN's Web site. Go to www.cnn.com/specials and select "Cold War," "China," or "The Twentieth Century." Look at the interactivity and the learning opportunities built into these sites and see how the Web and the broadcast programs complement each other. Technologies like Web-TV and various synchronous Web tools (to be discussed in Chapter 5) will provide further opportunities for similar integration.

Injecting good multimedia into e-learning doesn't eliminate the need for solid content behind it, or the critical value that instructional design plays in shaping how the media will be used. Great instruction without multimedia may be more effective than great multimedia without solid instructional design. When considering multimedia, perhaps the best word that comes to mind is *balance*. Balance between production values and instructional values. Balance between glitz and authenticity. Balance between cost and return.

And, above all, balance between "edu-tainment" and learning. Multimedia can be a great tool in enhancing learning and motivating learners. But, like technology, multimedia is not in and of itself an e-learning strategy.

Online Training at U S WEST*

How do you deliver critical messages to employees across dozens of states? How do you assure that key information is communicated quickly and consistently to tens of thousands of employees? That's the challenge U S WEST faced when market forces caused the giant telecommunications company to redefine its business and its business strategy. As competition loomed in its territory, the company knew it had to instill in its people an urgent sense of competitiveness. Of course, the company understood that this was a radical change from the old telephone monopoly days, and that in the age of the Internet, simply selling plain old telephone service wasn't going to cut it anymore. So in addition to providing the technical, product, and sales training necessary to execute the business plan, the company wanted to prepare its managers to help their people with the change. It wanted to be sure that this key group clearly understood just what it meant to be competitive and how U S WEST was going to meet this challenge, so that they, in turn, could communicate this important message down the line.

Clearly, bringing people to a centralized training center was out of the question, not only because of the prohibitive cost, but also because it would just take too long to get the message out. U S WEST turned to its established intranet to deliver the learning program. Developed in a matter of weeks and deployed throughout the company instantaneously, *Managing in a Competitive Environment* (Figure 3.1), a two-hour online training program, was on every manager's computer screen within a couple of days. Using case studies and scenarios, the program conveyed the importance of competitiveness and the manager's role in helping the business stay competitive in a way that was both quick and

*U S WEST is now part of Qwest Communications International, Inc.

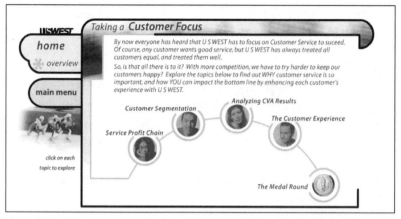

Figure 3.1   An interactive exercise from U S WEST's "Managing in a Competitive Environment" online program. (© Copyright 1999 by U S WEST.)

engaging. Instead of pages of information, the program focused on simple activities combined with extensive feedback. And, where detailed information was required, instead of re-creating the information in the course, the manager was linked to the original information database on the company's internal web. In this way, the manager also learned how to find critical competitive information from a source that would be continuously updated (a feature of knowledge management discussed in the next chapter).

Once this program served its purpose, its use declined. That was to be expected, even welcomed, as managers had new things to learn. In today's world, knowledge is fleeting and the half-life of courseware is shrinking. That's why quick, strategic online training programs can have a greater impact, in less time and with less cost, than traditional classroom instruction.

Moving a Highly Successful "Soft Skills" Classroom Course to the Web: A Case Study

Converting a very popular and effective course to the Web can be an opportunity to take your training to a higher level, if you do it right. If you don't, you can loose a great deal of credibility. How do you maintain that credibility, keep enthusiasm up, retain the best features of the program, and bring your learners along with you rather than pushing them away by creating something they don't want? After all, it wasn't broke, so why fix it? That was the challenge Ken Blanchard (www.blanchardtraining.com) faced as he looked for a vehicle to transform his popular commercial course, *Situational Leadership II®*, to e-learning. Whenever you have a well-designed classroom course, converting it to the Web is fraught with difficulties. Can the learning be as powerful? Could the concepts of leadership, a "soft skill," even be taught on the Web? And in Blanchard's case, could the conversion fit into the company's business model and remain profitable?

Ninth House Network (www.ninthhouse.com) knew that creating effective online training requires a different, experiential perspective on learning that allows for total immersion in the learning experience and opportunities to practice in a safe environment. They were already looking for key thought leaders in several business fields as the focus of their e-learning development efforts. This melded nicely with Blanchard's need and so a partnership was established between the two companies to bring *Situational Leadership II* to the Web. As successful as the classroom program was, simply replicating that success on the Web would be a recipe for disaster. So the team followed some of the new thinking in Web-based instructional design to reinvent the course.

First, the goals of the program were focused on benefits for the learner. With desktop learning there's no instructor to reinforce or reinterpret the objectives of the program, so they had to be motivating and extremely authentic on their own.

In the classroom program there's a qualified instructor who introduces concepts, responds to questions, evaluates performance, facilitates role-plays, and provides quality feedback. The Web-based version had to have all of these components built in or the program would be rejected as boring or unrealistic. An instructional design model was used that centered on concept awareness, knowledge acquisition, and application through practice. For the awareness component, Ninth House converted the instructor's role from "teacher" to "coach," providing short instructional "nuggets" (often featuring Ken Blanchard himself) that can be used prior to the learning and as a refresher after the program is concluded.

The knowledge acquisition element of the program came through story telling and rich media presentations. To allow learners to apply and practice new concepts, they are placed in simulations where they assume a variety of leadership roles and have to respond to a multitude of leadership challenges. Learners see the consequences of their actions and get the skills they need to apply what they've learned in the workplace. In addition to feedback throughout the simulation and the rest of the program, interactive games, puzzles, and quizzes also give learners a sense of how they're doing.

The design goes even further by extending the learning back to work. With the classroom version, a company would bring in the two-day workshop, and at the conclusion hope that the skills and knowledge learned would transfer back to the job. But there was often little in the way of support for this to happen (this is usually true for most training, not just for this example). Now, with the primary learning on the Web, the instructors are free to become true coaches and consultants to their clients, focusing more on facilitating that transfer. They can also help local managers learn how to carry the learning into the world of work. They can lead "learning communities" of former students that continue long after the online training program has ended. Thus the live component of the program shifts from formal instruction to an experience-based, post-training application that can be customized for the client.

One might think that putting this popular course on the Web would make little business sense, since demand for the classroom version would likely drop. However, the reverse is true. Putting the course on the Web gave it the scalability it could never have with an instructor-led mode. Now the program could reach thousands of people in a very short time. It also allowed the "former" leadership instructors to transition to leadership consultants, thereby enhancing the program's "value proposition" by helping the organization apply what was taught.

So converting a course to the Web is not about just copying over the content and replicating the way the information is delivered. By rethinking the process and reinventing the course, learning and enthusiasm for the product increased and, despite the significant increase in development costs, the business value of the program soared.

The lessons for corporate training are clear. First, quality and innovation still matter—a lot. Second, although segments of this program require broadband technology (coming sooner than we imagine) and industry-standard plug-ins, it is very possible to teach soft skills through online training. Third, the role of the classroom and of the instructor will certainly change, but likely for the better. And finally, the benefits of e-learning can transcend training to provide real value in business terms.

While this example is provided to showcase some best practices for converting classroom training to the Web, it also provides a preview of some of the other approaches to e-learning that will be covered in this book. These include the importance of communities, the changing nature of the classroom, aligning with your infrastructure, and building a durable learning culture.

Online Training Is Just One Part of E-Learning

Quality online training is an essential part of a total e-learning strategy, but the road to better online training is not an easy one. We need to be vigilant about quality and the best use of the technology. We must be smart enough to know when online training (instruction) is warranted and when it's not. And for those times when instruction is not the best or the only approach to a learning opportunity, we need a complementary knowledge management (information) strategy. The new framework for e-learning, enabled by the Web, is about online training and knowledge management interacting with each other.

CHAPTER

Knowledge Management: When Information Is Better Than Instruction

"Nobody is as smart as everybody."

Tom Petzinger[1]

"Our age of anxiety is, in great part, the result of trying to do today's jobs with yesterday's tools."

Marshall McLuhan on Technology

F OR MANY OF US, the classroom has come to symbolize learning. From our own personal experiences to the way most training is delivered today, the image of the classroom is something we all share. So it's no wonder that we continue to see the Web as the online version of that classroom experience.

The Web: Classroom or Library?

But we know that training online is only a part of e-learning—access to information is as essential for learning as instruction. We've already referred to the Web as the world's library; perhaps this is a better metaphor. Go to any library, anywhere. Even libraries you've never visited. Instantaneously, you'll know how to use it. Why? Because all libraries have the same search engine, the card catalog (either card-based or online). All libraries have the same scheme for identifying each unique item, the Dewey Decimal System, or the Library of Congress System in university and other special libraries. Need help? The reference desk and reference librarian is there for you. In each library the carpeting may be different, the layout and design of the space may be unique, but the essential elements are universal. So, when you enter a library you've never been to before, assuming you remember the library skills you were taught in school, you should be able to find whatever you are looking for—from a book to a videotape, from an old newspaper to the most recent magazine.

Now think about the Web. Want to find something? Use a search engine. True, there are many different search engines to choose from, but they all pretty much function along the same basic premise. Seeking a unique item (i.e., Web site)? Look up its unique URL. Need help? A live reference librarian may not be available (although some Web sites boast that there are actually real people managing their site), but good navigation and human factors, plus site maps, help resources, FAQs, e-mail links, and other design features are there to assist you. And they are getting better each day at helping users find what they're looking for more easily and faster than before. There's a long way to go before we have a search engine as well structured as a card catalog (try searching the Web for the word *training* and see how many hits you get—and then determine which ones are of any value!). We also don't have a standard content hierarchy as universal as the Dewey Decimal System or a help system as "helpful" as a live reference librarian. But these are very worthwhile goals, especially in controllable spaces like a corporate intranet. Yet the metaphor still works. If we think of the Web as one giant networked library, with all its growing pains, we can embrace it as a doorway to a virtually unlimited treasure of resources.

"The paradox of our times is that we are inundated by information yet starved for knowledge."
William R. Brody, President, Johns Hopkins University

While it's true that we go on the Web to be entertained, to shop, and to send e-mail, we are also likely to surf the Internet to access information. And when we do, we're learning. The need to find information—about a product or a customer, a process or a system—reflects our innate desire to learn. Some people argue that information is not training. That may be true, but if we value the information we are seeking enough to find it and understand it, i.e., turn it into knowledge, it may not be training, but it is learning. After all, if people didn't learn from information, why would anyone use a library in the first place?

"Humans are vacuum cleaners for learning."
Jack Gordon and Ron Zemke[2]

There's an argument that simply providing information is an inefficient and unreliable way for people to learn—that's why we need instruction. It's clear that in many cases people must be trained in specific procedures, done in specific ways and within specific time frames. And it's sometimes desirable for people to do things from memory (firefighting, for example). But in many cases we don't have to go through the time, expense, and rigor of formal training; we may be far better off simply providing accurate, well-designed, and easy-to-access information. It's why people rely so heavily on a good travel guide while on vacation, or why books on how to use computer software are such good sellers.

Do we always have to bring the sales force back to the training center every time they need to learn about a new modification to a product? Do programmers always have to go back to school to learn about every new coding procedure? Must managers always take a course to learn everything they need to know about supervision? Do people need to go back to training every time a new version of word processing software is released? In other words, is training, either in the classroom or online, *always* necessary or *always* cost-effective?

What Is Knowledge Management?

We've already looked at online training, so let's now look at online information. Certainly, there's lots of information on the Internet (and on intranets). Some of it is well organized and well structured, but much is pretty chaotic, which creates real problems for people who need and rely on it. If we apply what we know about how to create information that people can use and rely on, we are working in an area that has come to be known as *knowledge management.*

Knowledge management supports the creation, archiving, and sharing of valued information, expertise, and insight within and across communities of people and organizations with similar interests and needs. Many KM systems are facilitated by Internet technologies. Yet despite the need for technology, knowledge management is as much about people, working relationships, and communication. Live teamwork, collaboration and other forms of person-to-person interaction are essential to create the right balance between the information itself and the actions of people. Librarian Sheila Corrall suggests that KM is "a management *philosophy*, which combines good practice in *purposeful* information management with a culture of organizational learning, in order to improve business performance."[3] Today, most businesses use the Web and most large businesses have corporate intranets. By their very nature, these intranets reflect a knowledge management strategy—providing a centralized approach and a common architecture for managing information. But this is *not* a data warehousing strategy. KM is not focused on collecting every piece of information there is and putting it on the Web—which would quickly overwhelm the organization and users, who would eventually abandon it. The challenge is building this capability so that it is flexible and dynamic, easy to understand and manage, valued by people and supportive of a broad-based learning culture. It's the use of knowledge that counts, not just its storage!

Types of Knowledge

As depicted in Figure 4.1, knowledge is more than what a person knows or what lots of people know. It's also what the organization knows—gathered from internal and external sources for years or even decades. Knowledge can be explicit—easily described and specific enough to be codified in documents, practices, and training. Process documentation is an example of explicit knowledge. Sales models, step-by-step procedures for loading software, a perform-

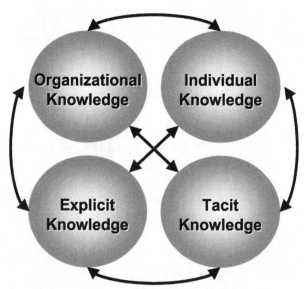

Figure 4.1 Different types of knowledge require different approaches to knowledge management. Each presents unique challenges and opportunities.

ance management system, and business financial requirements are other examples. Or knowledge can be tacit—harder to record and difficult to document or teach to others—heuristics often embedded in people's experiences and life's work, which is often the most elusive and most valuable. While we can define *leadership*, for instance, and even list the characteristics of good leaders, we also know that really powerful and effective leaders are more than what can be documented. They have an inner quality, a combination of factors that's hard to describe or teach—yet we recognize that these tacit characteristics exist. Think about the best salespeople, the best scientists, the best teachers or the best managers you know—the ones who are leaps and bounds above typical performers. What do they know that others don't? Chances are you're looking at tacit knowledge.

The knowledge of individuals and organizations—tacit and explicit—does not sit isolated. More often they interact with each other. Business performance is most likely a result of the mix of the tacit and explicit knowledge of the individuals and organizations that make up the firm. Training is at its best when focused on explicit skill and knowledge delivered to individuals. Knowledge management is more appropriate for group and tacit knowledge.

Knowledge Management Benefits:
The Virtual Corporate Brain

One way to think about the value and benefits of knowledge management is to think about it as a "virtual corporate brain." Figure 4.2 shows six functions/benefits that this brain can have.[4]

1. Learning. Knowledge management can help people and organizations learn and apply information in new situations. It provides links to limitless amounts of company information—information necessary for everything from performing a single job to running the entire business. Information about customers, systems, competitors, budgets, personnel, etc., can be incorporated under the knowledge management umbrella. *Benefit:* Users can access just the information they need, just when they need it, enabling faster and more flexible responses to work and business issues—a competitive advantage.

2. Vision and action. The dynamic nature of knowledge management provides opportunities for the system to "see and react"

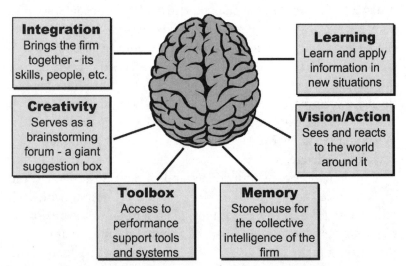

Figure 4.2 Knowledge management can be thought of as a virtual corporate brain.

to the world around it. Knowledge management systems, like human brains, will respond to the changing dynamics of the business environment. If a company merges with another business, the knowledge management system will begin to reflect the synergies or the conflicts of the two businesses. If the company is doing well, the knowledge management system will reflect it. If the company is in trouble, you can be sure the problems will be predominant within the system. New tools and information databases emerge to deal with new business challenges, while legacy or unnecessary features fade away. Like a newspaper, knowledge management brings important issues to the surface, akin to a front-page headline, and relegates lesser information needs to the "back page." *Benefit:* The ability to "push" the most important information to users who need it keeps employees current and aware of what's going on—an "inclusiveness" that is highly motivating. Message consistency assures greater likelihood that the firm can act in more unison.

3. Memory.   Because of the low cost of adding storage to the Internet (or intranet), a knowledge management system can serve as the storehouse for the collective intelligence of the firm. Best practices, standards, and procedures, even company history, can be stored online. For example, the business can preserve the expertise and insights of people who have left the firm, or provide a single source for product information. *Benefit:* Instantaneous access to information, experience and expertise that might otherwise be unavailable to employees (or customers), plus the ability to grow corporate memory over time.

4. Toolbox.   Knowledge management systems are not only repositories of information, they can include a variety of tools that enable users to perform job-related tasks or manipulate information to make it more meaningful. *Benefit:* The ability to manage and quickly distribute knowledge and productivity tools to widely dispersed employees and enable work to be broadly shared.

5. Creativity.   By allowing people to collaborate and contribute to the growth of corporate intelligence, knowledge management can fill a brainstorming function—a giant suggestion box that provides opportunities for new ideas and innovations to be generated.

This is a valuable function for capturing tacit knowledge. *Benefit:* Collaboration and community involvement allows new ideas and insights to be shared in a more open environment. This heightened sense of "belonging" can positively impact recruitment and retention as well as learning.

6. Integration. Ultimately, knowledge management opens up information. It also helps organizations understand and identify what they know and what they don't know (or perhaps, what they *thought* they knew). These are essential criteria for getting organizational learning off the ground. By bringing the firm together—its skills, knowledge, people, processes, etc.—KM can play a significant role in building a learning culture in the company. *Benefit:* Knowledge assets are more systematically leveraged across a wider range of users/communities and uses, resulting in more contributions and more interactions.

The Knowledge Management Pyramid

Knowledge management can be divided into three levels: document management (level 1), information creation, sharing, and management (level 2), and enterprise intelligence (level 3). These levels can be organized into a pyramid (Figure 4.3).

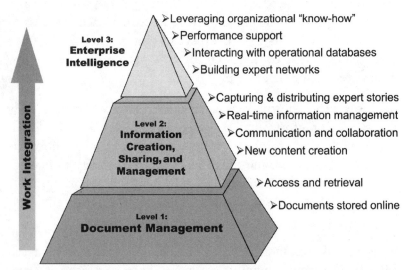

Figure 4.3 The three levels of the knowledge management pyramid. The higher up you go on the pyramid, the more integrated the KM system is with actual work.

Document management (level I). The use of technology to access documentation represents one of the earliest efforts at KM. Today, many companies have put major documents, reports, and forms online. From benefits forms to user manuals and the company's annual report, document access over the Web saves time and money by creating a central repository of information that people need. Access and retrieval is fairly easy; you find the document library's URL and then download the document or form of your choice. But this level is fairly simplistic from a KM perspective, as it only supports the distribution of information, but not the creation, organization, or management of content. And, because the information is downloaded, accuracy going forward cannot be guaranteed.

Information creation, sharing, and management (level 2). This is the level of knowledge management where people actually contribute information to the system, creating new content and growing the knowledge database. Instead of printing documents, people are encouraged to read them online. Instead of downloading forms, completing them, and then faxing them to appropriate destinations, they are completed online. The advantage of this approach is that the information can be continually updated, going a long way toward eliminating the version control problems inherent when documents were downloaded.

Here's an example from the telecommunications industry, but one that is true for almost any business with lots of technical information. The total amount of information necessary to maintain a sophisticated telephone switching system, organized in binders, took up more than *six feet* of shelf space. Looking up the solution to a problem often took more time than actual repair time. Updating became a terrible problem and was extraordinarily expensive. Moving the information database to CD-ROM solved the storage problem and enabled engineers to more efficiently search the information, but updates still depended on the next release of the CD and there was no efficient way for users to contribute on a regular basis. Now, with the same information on a secure intranet site, information is updated in real time, engineers regularly contribute what they know to the database, access has become universal, and distribution costs have fallen dramatically. As the technology got better, so did the effectiveness of knowledge management strategy.

This level of KM enables the organization to capture and distribute expert stories and other knowledge presentations. Imagine the benefits to pharmaceutical researchers around the world who can access a presentation by someone who just found a new use for a lifesaving drug. Or for a brewing company to create a lasting, digital storehouse of the expertise of a brewmaster who's about to retire after forty years. Or for generations of art students to access the craftsmanship of a world-renowned sculptor.

Enterprise intelligence (level 3). The holy grail of knowledge management is the development of a KM system so robust and so interactive as to truly represent the "know-how" of the organization. At this level, the actual operation of the business depends on the expertise embedded in the system. People rely on it in the performance of their jobs, and the resulting experiences are captured and added to the system in a way that grows the collective intelligence of the firm, almost (but not quite) organically. One important approach to KM at this level is through performance support. It is worth discussing further.

Performance Support

What if you could do a job or perform a task better, faster, and with less cost without having to learn it directly? What if the tools and systems you used in your work actually helped you do your work better? What if you were able to do something that you could not do before, simply by using a system that coached you through it? That's the concept behind performance support. Today, many knowledge management systems also include a variety of tools that enable significant productivity improvements. This is a very powerful combination for e-learning, because it directly integrates knowledge and performance, significantly increasing the value of the total system.

One major goal of performance support is to bring individuals up to speed in their work as quickly as possible and with minimal support from other people.[5] Essentially, performance support provides the means for more efficiently accomplishing jobs or tasks, or for accomplishing a specific task directly without necessarily having to learn the intricacies of the performance.

Performance support has been around for a long time, especially in the form of checklists, forms, reference cards, and other types of "job or performance aids." What is relatively new is using computer technology in this way. Electronic performance support tools (EPST) are usually delivered as stand-alone software or independent tools on the Web. Electronic performance support systems (EPSS) are much larger, often fully integrated with larger organizational or enterprise systems.[6] Either way, performance support is differentiated from other forms of software by an intense focus on enabling people to be more productive with less effort. This is referred to as "performance-centered design." It places the needs of the end-user at the center of the development process. In reality, most end-user software, either stand-alone or systems-based, has elements of performance-centered design, although some do this very well while others only scratch the surface.

Consultant Gloria Gery[7] has identified three levels of performance support: external, extrinsic, and intrinsic.

External support.   This is the most basic type of performance support, provided externally to the system or process. Job aids and documentation dominate this level, as do the help desks we all call when we're having a problem with our computers, or fixing the dishwasher, or assembling a bicycle. Characteristic of all of these approaches is the need for the user to stop work in order to get the support. In many cases these interventions were developed after the work system or process was deployed, often to help people cope with a deficiency in the system or to improve their performance with the system. Early word processors often came with keyboard overlays to help users with complex, nonintuitive commands. Call center representatives often consulted massive binders of information to respond to customer inquiries. Today, many of us carry a wallet card around with instructions on how to access our answering machines, and many of us (still!) need a manual to help us program our VCRs.

Extrinsic support.   Almost all software in use today comes with help systems, wizards, cue cards, templates, and other online job aids that enable users to perform tasks they could not have done before, or to improve their ability and the ease with which they can use these tools. These tools do not necessarily require the user to stop working, but they do require the user to decide how to use these features. The user has to determine how and what to look up in the help system, or how to conduct an efficient search. Think about search engines on your Web browser. They help you find what you're looking for on the Internet—maybe. If you don't know how to specify your search, it will take you far too long to find what you're looking for, if you ever do. Wizards, cue cards, and templates can be very supportive, if you know how to use them. Here, keyboard overlays turn into online help, call center manuals become online databases, and answering machine job aids are replaced by natural language system prompts delivered by the voice mailbox itself.

Intrinsic support. The most important characteristic of intrinsic support is the system's ability to anticipate and adapt to the user's needs. The help resources and toolbars of many Microsoft 2000 products can adjust to frequency of use, presenting the most requested help first and placing the most used functions on the toolbar automatically. A true knowledge management system, where usage patterns define how the information database will evolve, is an example of how systems adapt to the requirements of the people who use them. Expert systems and artificial intelligence hold the promise of systems actually "learning" what the user needs at any particular moment and providing it, ideally without the user even being aware it is happening.

This book was written using Microsoft Word. In earlier versions, Word came with numerous CBT lessons (external support) on how to use it. For the most part, they were ignored and users often stripped off of the hard drive to free up additional storage space. Now, instead of CBT, Word has a knowledge base of information in its help system and a little character we've come to know as "Mr. Paper Clip," who pops up at interesting times asking you if you need help and often offering assistance to show you how to do something (extrinsic support).[8] It even will do some tasks for you if you want. Now, Mr. Paper Clip often pops up at the wrong time when I don't need assistance (always asking me if I need help writing a letter), and I sure wish he'd learn to recognize the type of support I really do need (for me, that's making "styles" work). I suspect in future versions of Word he'll learn to *adapt* to my needs (intrinsic support), but the news here is that Microsoft made a major transformation from online training to performance support in much of its product line.

> "Performance support is a goal, not a technology. The goal
> is to generate immediate work performance by people
> with little or no experience in what they're doing.
> Technology enables you to achieve that goal."
>
> **Gloria Gery, Consultant**[9]

Not every task or job can make use of electronic performance support. Some tasks have too many variables that change too often or that are situationally based. For example, a flight attendant's decisions and actions relating to helping passengers during a flight emergency might not be appropriate. Too many things happening too quickly require a high level of training that results in the right decisions and actions taken on an immediate and instinctive basis. Other tasks do not yield the benefit or are simply not worth the cost or effort and can be more easily improved with a better sign, a simple Post-it® Note, a job aid, or just the office manager coming around to suggest a better way to do something.

Is Expertise Always Required?

Ask people who are looking to improve the performance of their people if they truly want their job performers to be experts, or would they be satisfied if their customers *perceived* them as experts. This is an important question. At first, there is usually a resounding response that of course they want people to be experts—*to know everything* about what they do. Many would like to go further—to fluency, in which the performer not only can do things better and faster, but can do them "without even thinking about it." But training people to have that much knowledge or skill is very expensive and can take a lot of time and an enormous amount of practice. That's why it costs so much to train doctors, astronauts, athletes and pilots, for example. But there are many jobs where all expertise does not have to be internalized—it can be supported with knowledge management. We can teach people to be experts at *finding information* when they need it and then using it correctly. Do airline reservation agents need to know flight schedules? No, they consult a system that gives them the information they need to book our flights. Are we concerned that they have to consult a computer system? No again, we expect that they will use this tool; furthermore, we expect that the information we receive will be more accurate because it came from a system that *supported* the agent's performance. So agents don't have to know the flight schedule, but they do have to know how to use the system. And, because less training is needed once they have mastered the system, valuable learning time can be shifted elsewhere, toward customer care and sales, for instance.

Do new managers have to know all the HR policies in a company? In many corporations HR information on the firm's intranet can coach the new manager through a variety of supervisory tasks, like performance appraisal, and, as a bonus, ensure that appraisals are carried out more or less uniformly, a key legal consideration.

Do mechanics have to know everything about a car in order to fix it? Most of today's modern automobiles are so computerized that tried-and-true methods such as "listening" to the sound of the engine is no longer adequate. Furthermore, information changes so much from model to model that it can be dangerous for service technicians to trust their memory. Airline mechanics are trained to always work from the manual, not from what they learned in a class taken weeks or months ago. These manuals are constantly updated based on service experience with the planes as they are used. In each of these instances, and so many others, we use information and tools to augment our expertise and, in many cases, actually perform tasks that we used to do. This frees us to focus on more complex and more challenging issues.

Integrating Performance Support Into Knowledge Management

The advent of knowledge management has had great influence on performance support, and performance support capabilities have added a lot of value to knowledge management systems. All performance support systems operate, at least in part, on a database of information that tells them what to do, or provides information to users to guide their performance. Most knowledge management systems exist to enhance user performance by giving them the information they need to accomplish a task, complete a job, etc.

Now, users find information and tools side by side. Quicken software has information on how to manage your money and also has tools to help you plan and track your investments. Any number of travel-related Web sites offer rich information on resorts, sightseeing, hotel prices and amenities, etc. But of course, they also have tools to let you find and book your travel online. On many corporate intranets, you can access the latest HR information as well as change your 401(k), adjust your deductions, and select your benefits. Invariably, knowledge management and performance support systems will often merge into a combined resource.

The combination of training (classroom and/or online), knowledge management, and performance support is a powerful force for learning. But as much as they can work together, to use them appropriately it is still important to understand some ways these approaches differ (Table 4.1).

Table 4.1 Comparing Training, Knowledge Management, and Performance Support

Training	Knowledge Management	Performance Support
Purpose is to instruct	Purpose is to inform	Purpose is to guide performance directly
Requires the interruption of work to participate (even online)	Normally requires less work interruption than training	Least interruption from work (ideally integrated directly into work tasks)
Program dictates how the user will learn	User determines how s/he will learn	Task at hand defines what the tool will do.
		Learning is secondary to performance
Goal is to transfer skill and knowledge to user	Goal is to be a resource to user	Goal is to assist performance (or do it completely)

(Continued)

Table 4.1 Comparing Training, Knowledge Management, and Performance Support *(Continued)*

Training	Knowledge Management	Performance Support
Sales Example #1: Teaching selling skills	*Sales Example #1:* Accessing customer information in preparation for a sales call	*Sales Example #1:* A tool to help create a sales proposal
Technical Example #2: Training technicians to fix a computer system	*Technical Example #2:* Accessing an interactive troubleshooting database on a particular piece of computer hardware	*Technical Example #2:* Using a diagnostic tool to pinpoint a failed component in the computer
Characteristic user expression: "I know what to do, and why (but adding information and tools will help me do it better and easier)."	*Characteristic user expression:* "I can get the information that will help me do it (but I still need to learn how to find the information I need)."	*Characteristic user expression:* "I don't need to know how to do it—the system does it for me (but I still need to learn how to use and monitor the system)."

Community and Collaboration in Knowledge Management

To be successful, knowledge management must provide a way for the people who use the content to be involved in its creation. It thus distinguishes itself from information-laden Web sites by its focus on collaboration and community. From business performance to employee services, intranet-based knowledge management can create a communication and collaboration network that links everyone in the organization.

> **"A learning community is a trusting group of professionals united by a common concern or purpose, dedicated to supporting each other in increasing their knowledge, creating new insights, and enhancing performance in a particular domain."**
>
> **Eric Vogt and Diane Hessan,**
> **Communispace Corp.[10]**

Information exchange goes on in every organization, even those where the climate is hostile to knowledge sharing. However, a positive climate makes the process more effective and more comfortable for all. This is where communities add value. Knowledge management fosters the growth of knowledge communities, learning communities, or communities of practice (these terms are used interchangeably). Where needs assessment in the training world often focuses on a precisely defined target population that needs specific training, KM focuses on broader communities that have common interests or goals. Communities can be built around content or disciplines, such as engineering and sales. They can also be project, process, or product specific. So engineers would be members of the engineering knowledge community, but also members of the community around the products they support. The entire sales force might constitute a knowledge community, but all the sales teams that service an existing account might be another community. Multiple community membership is common as people join both vertical and horizontal groups. Also, within these and other groups, smaller knowledge communities can emerge. For example, within the programmer community there might be a knowledge community of C++ programmers and another community of practice focused on Java. A knowledge community of corporate lawyers might be subdivided into staff attorneys and litigators. A community of technicians might be subdivided into practice areas of computers, telecommunications, systems, etc. The key organizing schemes might be based on the work to be done, the customers served, or the products supported. In addition, people can also join (or be assigned to) knowledge communities based on their personal or professional interests.

Here are some examples on the Internet. In the medical arena WebMD (www.webmd.com) is subdivided into knowledge communities for consumers, physicians, nurses, and office managers; and Mediconsult (www.mediconsult.com) does an excellent job at helping people form and participate in communities that are meaningful for them. BabyCenter (www.babycenter.com) provides long-term community involvement primarily for mothers. BigChalk (www.bigchalk.com) and LightSpan (www.lightspan.com) provide communities for kids, parents, and teachers in support of K–12 education, even allowing people, as well as individual schools and classes, to create their own Web sites in a particular subject area to share what they know with others.

Although people within a community of practice have similar interests and are focused on closely related goals, they may not have the same level of expertise or experience, and they may have different needs for the knowledge management system. So a good KM system will allow members of a community to explore content at different levels of breadth and depth, depending on need. To do this well is a great challenge for those who design the knowledge structure and navigation strategies for the KM application.

The importance of community cannot be overstated. It helps the "right hand" know what the "left hand" is doing, reducing the possibilities of reinventing or making the wrong move. When well structured, its members form a strong bond that contributes to a climate of openness to new ideas and to learning. The motivational influence of being a "member" of a community helps people forge a stronger identity with their peers, and with the firm as a whole. While it is common for training programs, especially classroom programs, to also create a sense of community among the students, the force of that bond is rarely maintained after the training has ended. But if supported correctly, communities that focus on work and common interests tend to endure and, in turn, build strong learning communities. And the members are much more likely to be contributors to the system. A collaborative environment emerges.

There has been a great deal of research on the value of communities in support of learning. At the Institute for Research on Learning, in Palo Alto, California, now a part of the research group WestEd (www.wested.org), work over many years has reinforced the social nature of learning, that people learn best when they can interact with other people as full members in communities of shared interest. From a knowledge management perspective the implications are clear: Access to the right information at the right time *and* membership in a knowledge community are *both* required for the most learning to take place.

The real power of a knowledge community is that it creates opportunities for people to go beyond interaction with content to contributing information and sharing it with other *people* as well, like a community of patients focusing on a common ailment. Here are some other examples. Sales organizations are moving quickly to KM to allow account executives, spread out across the country or around the world, to input competitive intelligence and other insights they gain by talking with customers. A new practice successfully employed by one salesperson can be made available to the rest of the team instantaneously. Marketing managers in different countries can collaborate on products that will be sold worldwide, allowing for adjustments and considerations that are necessary for differing cultures. Information technology specialists separated by distance can still contribute their special expertise to an enterprisewide IS project. The project can be split up among different groups of programmers who may reside across the country or across an ocean, and then reassembled upon completion.

Even more dramatic is the amount of knowledge that's created when people can collaborate online. Contributing and accessing reliable content is just one side of the coin (albeit an important side). Combining content management with cross-organizational online collaboration, at all levels of the business, can help unite a company and give it greater insight and perspective. And online collaboration can contribute to the growth of the corporation's intellectual capital far beyond what's in the firm's databases, especially in the area of tacit knowledge.

One of the great benefits of communities is that they tend to be incubators of future best practices. Community members try new approaches and ideas, and then, when proved out, integrate them into the knowledge base of the firm.

Managing the Information

Collaboration requires a means for people to contribute to the KM database as well as a way for them to access and distribute its content. This contribution side of KM—the collection, structuring and archiving of content—is actually more difficult than the distribution side, and is worth considering further. There are three key functions that must be carried out in order to assure that the contribution aspects of knowledge management work well.

Inbound information management. Of course, knowledge management won't get off the ground if no one knows where the high value information is in the organization. So the first step is to identify knowledge sources. Then there must be a way to manage all the information that's coming in, including a way to prioritize it. Not everything should be published on the site; to do so would quickly overwhelm the user. This is a very difficult process to do right. Too much management will stifle contributions, and too little will invite chaos. Policies should be established that create enough control to ensure that information is written, *tagged*, and published in a systematic and usable way, but care should be taken that too much control doesn't limit innovation and usefulness.

Tagging is of special importance. Various chunks of content, in courseware or knowledge management systems, can be identified by adding labels, or *tags*, to describe them. Tags are used to describe the type of content, the level of detail, who should have access to the content, who developed the content, etc. Tagging allows specific content to be presented to target users automatically. It is a key to making the knowledge management system more dynamic (discussed in more detail in Chapter 6).

Despite all the technology, the best KM systems use people (as well as tools) to edit and filter incoming material. In addition, a set of standardized templates, formats, and a cataloging scheme let contributors develop content according to the design parameters of the system prior to sending it in. A great metaphor for information management in a KM system is to think of a newspaper. Each day, reporters create stories using standardized formats and file them in specific categories (e.g., national, international, or local news, sports, and business). Editors review all stories to assure consistency and relevance to the readership, and then place the story in the newspaper based on importance, interest, etc.

Purging dated information. It is important to have a procedure for removing dated material. Just as libraries replace out-of-date resources with newer resources, KM sites must also be sure that this is done. If dated content is left on the site, users may continue to rely on the inaccurate information without the benefit of more recent knowledge. And the growing content clutter will soon make the site unmanageable. Again, editors have an important role to periodically scan knowledge databases and remove dated material. In addition, good KM systems identify the life expectancy of content before it goes in. Some content may be in the system for a day or less, while other content may be in the system for a year. KM systems should identify each contribution with vital information such as the contributor and/or subject matter expert—they are not always the same (name, title, phone, e-mail, etc.), date published, and expiration date. This gives the user a "heads up" as to the validity and recency of the content, as well as a person to contact about the information. The system may also notify the contributor to "pull" the content on the expiration date, or do it automatically, depositing the old content into an archive and replacing it with newer information.

Benefiting contributors. The benefits of contributing must be clear to the knowledge providers. Why would someone want to contribute to the knowledge database or replace a "comfortable" process with something strange and new? If it is difficult or punishing to contribute, a KM site, even with all the technological bells and whistles, will still lose its robustness and its value will diminish. Whether you use monetary incentives or other perks, recognition of contributors as experts, or appeal to people's sense of obligation to contribute, you must ensure that those who share what they know find the experience both personally and professionally rewarding. And, you must be consistent in how you administer these benefits. In some firms, contributing to a knowledge management system is a recognizable component of compensation—people are appraised and rewarded for sharing what they know. KM expert Tom Davenport suggests that the best way to encourage worker participation in the creation and dissemination of knowledge is to "bake it into the job." Davenport makes a lot of sense when he notes that KM must be a part of the "fabric" of their work—importing knowledge when it's needed and exporting it to the rest of the organization when it's created or acquired."[11] Great KM systems are not just "bolt on" additions to work, they are *part* of the work.

In the end, the culture of the organization must support participation in KM activities. If people are discouraged from sharing what they know, if they see only penalties for the effort, you can be sure that they won't participate, either as contributors or users, and the system will die.

Knowledge Structuring Is Key

Many companies have discovered that when information is well structured, accurate, and easy to find, learning occurs. But for this to happen, information must make sense for the user. Posting information in a haphazard way will be very frustrating, and people will quickly avoid using the KM resource because it has become more trouble than it is worth.

Many corporate intranets suffer from a form of information anarchy. Thousands of pages might be posted without any way to find what is needed or to determine the value of what you could find. There is no way to prioritize information or structure it to assist people in finding what they need. Current, important information might be stored alongside trivial, out-of-date pages. And in many cases the user might not know which is which. Although content will change all the time, as new information comes in, old information may or may not be removed.

Without a structure for classifying knowledge—just focusing on distribution—everyone will drown in useless data. How you organize, label, tag, and manage content—by job functions, topics, products, steps in a process, etc., is critical. In addition, the linkage between content pieces is just as important. For example, product information might be linked to application examples, competitor product comparisons, a pricing database, companion products, etc.—all from the same product page. The various automobile sites on the Web do this quite well, as does Amazon.com with books and other products.

Setting up the search parameters is also important. There is a delicate balance in search strategies. On one hand, you need to provide a robust search capability that will enable the user to find information—any information—quickly. But it can't be too comprehensive as to provide literally hundreds or thousands of "hits" for each search. In other words, balance knowledge "order" and knowledge "chaos." Develop a way for the search engine to prioritize or filter the search results in a way that benefits the user.

Many commercial search engines continue to work on improving this capability.

Going further, don't just rely on the search engine to help people find what they need. That's where the knowledge structure comes in again. The way you organize and tag your pages, the design of your hyperlinks, and the number and detail of your navigation aids all contribute to helping users find what they need without endless searching. Which is why knowing the content domain, as it pertains to your audience, is *job one* in knowledge management. Once your knowledge structure is tested and set, it should be as stable as possible so people become comfortable and self-assured about using the resource. But you should not be deterred from carefully evolving your knowledge structure to accommodate new users and new needs.

Knowledge Management
for Sales Executives at AT&T Global Services

How do you keep a professional 3,000 member high-tech sales force constantly informed about changes in the business, customers, products, and competitors? How do you do this when most team members work out of their homes most of the time? How do you do this when the team is dispersed throughout the country? That was the challenge faced by the AT&T Global Services organization, whose account executives are charged with selling a wide array of telecommunications services to large corporations.

> **"I've got 3,000 sales people on the street touching customers every day. How do I get market intelligence from each of them to the rest of them before that information is useless?"**
>
> **AT&T Senior Sales Executive,**
> **prior to the development of IKE**

Training wasn't the answer, at least not the total answer. For years AT&T maintained a centralized, state-of-the-art sales training center. But over time it became apparent that the company couldn't afford to continuously bring the sales force in for training every time a new product was launched or a new competitor was identified. It wasn't just the cost of travel and other traditional training costs; it was also the risks incurred when the account executive had to leave his/her customer to attend class. And while classroom programs have been retained in some key areas, and online training has been introduced in others, it was clear that a new approach was needed to convey the bulk of the information these people needed to do their jobs well.

So AT&T turned to knowledge management, developing the Information and Knowledge Exchange (IKE) to support the sales force.

The company recognized that no individual could be an expert in all of the telecommunications services that were being sold to customers who sometimes knew more than the sales executive did. So it established knowledge communities around products and technologies such as *data, Internet, wireless, voice,* and others. People were assigned to a knowledge community based on their expertise and interests, but could also learn about and support teams in other knowledge communities. The IKE home page is shown in Figure 4.4.

You would expect a company like AT&T to have a sophisticated and well-deployed intranet. So building IKE was not an issue. In fact, so much business is run over the company's internal web that the inclusion of IKE did not add a great deal to the cost of running the system. And the cost savings from the reduced need to travel to the training locale and, more important, the savings from having to take a talented salesperson out of the field for training, more than makes up for IKE's development and management costs (more about building a business case in Chapter 8). Speed was the second most critical requirement of the system, next to content accuracy, of course. Because there is a lot of distribution to homes, where access speed can be a problem, the site is designed with minimal graphics (except where necessary to convey key information) to facilitate faster uploading and downloading.

Prior to establishing knowledge communities, the company's marketing and product managers were talking to the entire 3,000 member sales force. To each marketing or product specialist, *everything* was important. In addition to overwhelming salespeople, information was conveyed differently from one product to the next.

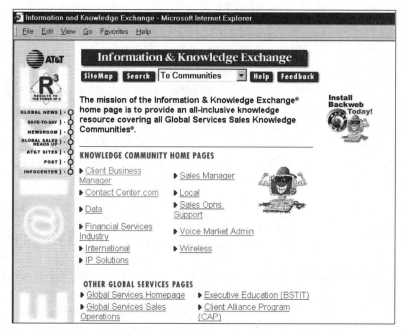

Figure 4.4 AT&T Global Services knowledge management home page. (Copyright © 1999 by AT&T.)

Too much information is no better than no information at all. By segmenting the sales force and the marketing staff into knowledge communities, the groups that had to speak to each other were smaller and more manageable. Additionally, each knowledge community is led by a facilitator who works to make information sharing easier and more valuable. Using a "market sensing" strategy, information flows in from field salespeople and internal specialists to central knowledge community facilitation teams of five to seven employees that link the groups and ensure that all communications are in a standardized format that has "clarity and perspective." The teams sort, prioritize, format, and publish the content according to a well-defined and well-tested process, of which turnaround speed was one of the highest priorities. So while content changes every day, the navigation and knowledge structures are consistent, making the system comfortable, familiar, and reliable in the eyes of the user. Finally, everything published includes the source information, including how to contact the author.

Today, IKE provides a variety of resources to its knowledge communities. In 1999, the site received more than 114,000 hits each business day from 12,000 unique users. It is the source of real-time product information (specifications, pricing, feature, benefits, etc.), competitive intelligence (competitor's offers and how to counter them, etc.), business planning and strategy information, proposal development tools, success stories and case studies (submitted by field salespeople), customer satisfaction data, new R&D insights, and information about training (to be discussed in the next chapter). There are also many common features you'd expect on such a site, like phone and e-mail directories, organizational charts, company news and announcements, online newsletters, etc.

Knowledge Management
for Customer Service at U S WEST

Customer service is one of the toughest jobs in any business, especially if it's call-center-based. Working with customers on the phone to solve their problems or sell new products and services can be a real challenge, especially when the number of calls taken per hour is a critical measurement of productivity. With one eye on the clock and the other eye on a myriad of computer screens, how can customer service representatives stay on top of all the changes in products, promotions, and pricing, not to mention all the information coming in on the competition? On top of this, honing sales skills and concentrating on customer satisfaction can also take time.

At U S WEST, knowledge management was the only way to be sure that call center representatives had the information they needed, when they needed it. Relying on print documentation or a supervisor's directive did not ensure cross-company accuracy or even that the information was delivered to all who needed it. KM was the only way to ensure that support would be available for every conceivable situation, and that the information was accurate and complete. U S WEST has had an online procedures database for quite some time, but it was just online documentation. Each document looked different. Design was in the hands of the individual author, and there were lots of authors. Compounding the problem, authors had their own view about the content and the appropriate level of detail. Generally speaking, they wrote what *they* thought the representative needed to know, not necessarily what the representative *actually* needed to know.

In 1999 the old system was replaced by *InfoBuddy*, U S WEST's knowledge management system. It supports a wide variety of job functions in addition to customer service representatives, including technical repair, installation and maintenance, etc. InfoBuddy is a methods and procedures database with intelligent KM capabilities, such as searching, tagging, and customizable interface. It can reorder the information presentation based on who the user is. When users identify themselves and their job function or role, the system knows how to configure itself to provide information of most value to each person. In addition, users have the ability to personalize the system through the "MyBuddy" feature, enabling representatives to place bookmarks on their home pages to the information they feel is most important. Over time, as users "learn" from the system, they are able to replace learned material with new, usually more advanced information.

In addition, the system "pushes" information to specific users based on their needs. For example, if a new promotion were initiated, specific information—products, pricing, etc.—would appear on the "desktop" of those representatives who are involved in the initiative. A sample home page for InfoBuddy is depicted in Figure 4.5.

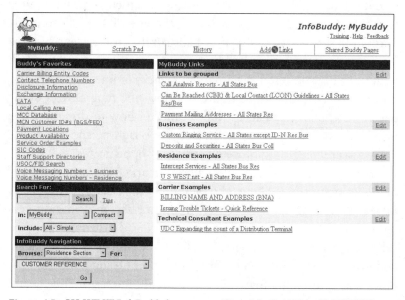

Figure 4.5   US WEST InfoBuddy home page. (Copyright © 1999 by U S WEST.)

Information providers now must adhere to a set of templates that represent standards for authoring and content management. All documents follow the same structure and level of detail, enabling users to move more quickly through the system, finding what they need much faster.

Initially, people resisted InfoBuddy, partly because they had come to rely on older tools. But the transition to the new system was surprisingly quick, partly because older systems were retired and partly because care was taken to ensure that the new way was in fact a better and easier way.

Knowledge Management and Performance Support at Merrill Lynch

Merrill Lynch is the world's largest investment firm, with more than 22,000 financial consultants (FCs) and support staff distributed in the U.S. alone. Serving millions of clients with more than $1.7 *trillion* in assets under management requires huge data and information capabilities, not only to track investments consisting of thousands of companies, mutual funds, and other vehicles, but to meet client needs with a growing number of products and services.

FCs have always been inundated with an overwhelming amount of data that was difficult to manage and keep current. Computer technology helped somewhat, but in the age of specialized computers for specialized tasks, FCs had to rely on different systems for different information. It was not uncommon to see an FC's desk with multiple computer terminals and stacks of unread papers and reports. Often they had to figure out how one type of data influenced another. They had little flexibility in how information was provided even though the nature of the business, and the firm's clients, were becoming more diverse and sophisticated.

In the mid-1990s Merrill Lynch embarked on a massive re-engineering project. The goal was not just to streamline the firm's infrastructure or to build better computerized information systems. Merrill Lynch wanted to provide tools that would dramatically enhance FC productivity, enabling them to better serve clients and grow their business. The firm didn't want to upgrade its technology just for technology's sake; it wanted to focus on people and performance—to enhance the effectiveness of a critically important group of front-line professionals.

The first rollout of a new, comprehensive technology platform to support the FC community took place in 1998. Called TGA, or *Trusted Global Advisor*, even the name connotes a human performance focus. The system, built with significant input from the field, ties together many of the firm's important legacy databases with a host of new applications and a user-friendly interface. Initially, just getting all the data and information onto one platform was the goal. Now the focus is on tool building and knowledge management—finding out what types of specific information databases and support tools the FCs need and deploying them. Another focus is learning—helping FCs make the best and most profitable use of TGA. If you ask Merrill Lynch people about TGA, the most descriptive word you might hear is "evolving." And that's the very nature of performance support—the ability to grow and evolve as a business, and for its employees to do the same.

Moving Problem-Solving and Decision-Making Skills to E-Learning: A Case Study

It's one thing to teach advanced problem-solving and decision-making skills, and quite another to ingrain these new techniques into an organization's way of doing things. That's the challenge Kepner-Tregoe® (www.kepner-tregoe.com) was facing. For more than four decades the company's training programs have been successfully offered as public and in-house corporate seminars. Their rational (systematic) process for decision-making, problem-solving, and project management reaches more than 25,000 people a year. But increasingly, the firm's clients are asking for tools that can "install" this rational process technology into their company in a way that is durable beyond training and can be used directly in the context of work. Even as a highly successful training company, Kepner-Tregoe recognized that training might not be the best solution (especially when used alone) for getting their methodology to "stick" in the organization and getting people to use the process.

Since the 1980s, the company has experimented with computer-based training but found that neither the technology nor the instructional design approaches that were available were robust enough for such complex skills. With the proliferation of PCs and intranets, Kepner-Tregoe reexamined their strategy and came up with a fundamental paradigm shift in how they approached this challenge: If information is the grist of critical thinking, maybe they ought to think differently themselves about how people really do solve problems and make decisions.

This rethinking resulted in a new e-learning strategy that is a combination of knowledge management and performance support. The product, eThink®*, provides a variety of different workspaces that are suited to solving a problem, making a decision, sorting out complex solutions, avoiding problems, or taking advantage of opportunities. Actions that are generated while working in any of these spaces can be coordinated and monitored. The tool provides information and collaboration that models and enhances the Kepner-Tregoe rational process and provides two modes of interaction. The interview mode takes a Socratic approach to help people work through their situation. It asks a series of questions and embeds each user response into the next question. In a sense, it is a personal decision-support adviser. Online information, reference, and help is context sensitive and always available. For those who have more experience, a worksheet mode lets the user define the decision or problem issues more directly. Thus the system provides an option to allow experienced users to enter their own data with less guidance. As with any good decision-support tool, the system provides opportunities to add personal information and notes, manage the access of other contributors to the process (or share their work more broadly through e-mail), and track changes.

The new tools are being introduced with the more traditional Kepner-Tregoe courses. But some clients may use the tool instead of the training. Is Kepner-Tregoe concerned that technology will eat into their core business? Not at all. They see e-learning innovations like eThink as adding a new dimension to their business (perhaps more consultative than instructional). They also see their new focus as helping them change the nature, but not the value, of their services as the world around them continually evolves.

*Patent pending.

Commercial Examples From the Internet

Although it's not possible to explore proprietary corporate intranets to look at their KM capabilities, we can look at a number of commercial Web sites that have knowledge management characteristics. The first thing you'll notice is that most examples have both knowledge management and performance support components. There are several categories of sites worth exploring.

Knowledge Portals

The first areas to explore are knowledge portals (not the commercial learning portals mentioned in Chapter 2). Until recently, these sites—like Yahoo!, AltaVista, InfoSeek, Lycos, Excite, and others—were merely search engines. They still have that capability, but previously that was pretty much it. Users visited these sites, and once they found what they wanted, left. Now portals have taken on new characteristics that provide more value to the user. One of the major enhancements is the ability to personalize the site to meet the information needs of the user. So in one sense the portals offer opportunities for individual users to form basic knowledge management structures based on their interests. Current events, finance, entertainment, sports, and so on are some of the customizable categories that most portals provide, as well as searching. In addition to these "generic" portals, you can now find portals on almost every topic imaginable and for almost every user on the Web. In fact, with more and more sites referring to themselves as a portal, this term will lose some of its distinctiveness over time. However, in understanding its main function as a gateway to related content, it remains a useful concept for e-learning.

Sites like Microsoft's CarPoint (www.carpoint.com), Edmunds (www.edmunds.com), and Autoweb (www.autoweb.com) are examples from the automotive industry. The designers did a good job of structuring information on these sites the way people would use it. Information about the cars themselves—price, specifications, features, and options—are grouped together. Independent reviews, financing, safety records, and other content are also provided. What makes these sites so interesting as a knowledge management example is that we know that the information will change often—new models, new prices, new reviews, etc., but the way we would want the information structured would be quite stable. We still want to compare features, reviews, prices, and the rest, but we expect that the content would be updated frequently. As long as the new content, such as a new review of a new model sports car, is plugged into a knowledge structure we are comfortable with, we find that we can easily assimilate, and in fact welcome the new information. These sites showcase the benefits of a good user *and* content-centered knowledge structure that reflects how people actually use the information provided.

The same is true for the many comprehensive financial Web sites that many of us use to access investment information. Some examples include Quicken (www.quicken.com), Clearstation (www.clearstation.com), and Motley Fool (www.fool.com). We expect new information almost in real time as we watch the performance of our portfolio and scan for business information that might influence our investment decisions. We also expect that however many times the sites are updated with new information, we'll continue to find it in the same place. If the content was accurate but hard to find, if older, out-of-date content was not removed from the site, or if we had to constantly relearn site navigation, we'd find another financial service pretty quickly.

In the consumer market, Purina (www.purina.com) is more than just a product site—knowledge management plays an important role in providing a wealth of information, tools, and other e-learning resources to help people learn about pets and select the pet that's right for them (try the "breed selector").[12]

KM features are also prevalent on Web-based medical sites, such as WebMD (www.webmd.com) and Medixperts (www.medixperts.com). These sites focus on helping people get information about treating illness, taking medication, health and lifestyle concerns, and choosing a physician. Other examples include Medscape.com, the Mayo Clinic (www.mayohealth.org), and the National Library of Medicine's "Gratful Med" search engine for the Medline database (igm.nlm.nih.gov).

LRN—the Legal Knowledge Company (www.lrn.com)—is a legal knowledge management portal that can be customized for individual companies and industries. One of the reasons why the medical and legal fields have taken a leadership role in knowledge management is because the knowledge base and codification systems of medicine and law are pretty well standardized at the professional level, and at least fairly well standardized at the consumer level. So industries and disciplines that have existing knowledge structures are early leaders in the KM arena.

Encyclopedia Britannica (www.britannica.com) is an excellent example of content organization. (Who knows better about content than an encyclopedia?) Not only does the site have internal content, but an excellent system of links to prescreened and rated Web sites on the same subject area. Britannica doesn't just give out URLs—it recommends them (this may be an advantage or a limitation, depending on your perspective).

Agillion (www.agillion.com) provides KM and performance-support capabilities to small businesses that don't have intranets or the resources to do it themselves, allowing users to configure productivity and communication tools and information resources in personalized ways. The interest here is the myriad of choices and the flexibility of customization available to subscribers. My SAP (www.mysap.com) provides similar services plus the ability to join any number of business communities. The more freedom users have to personalize the knowledge they receive, the more value they'll find in the site. Amazon.com (www.amazon.com) goes even further. Once you register with the site, it tracks your activity and tries to recommend products it believes you are interested in. In other words, it is constantly repersonalizing what the user sees, based on past usage.

My Help Desk (www.myhelpdesk.com) is a computer help portal that allows customers to create a personalized page based on the computer equipment they own. In a sense, they tell the site what equipment they have and My Help Desk delivers e-learning specifically for that equipment. Categories labeled, *get help* (knowledge and information), *get productive* (tools), *get connected* (community), *get smart* (online training), *get support* (human contact), and *get technical* (specifications and other resources) work together to provide a variety of ways to solve problems (not all of them as robust as some users would prefer). Since users have predefined their areas of interest (by specifying their computer equipment), the system limits what they see based on these specifications. It also uses these specifications to continuously update the support databases. Dell Computer (support.dell.com) also uses this approach to support its customers, making it easier for them to get information and learning directly related to their computer configuration.

In the business services category, Smart Age (www.smartage.com) and All Business (www.allbusiness.com) provide a variety of online training and knowledge management (with tools) resources. CNET.com provides similar services, but works in a significantly different way. Unlike My Help Desk, which caters to consumers, CNET focuses on a different community—sophisticated users and IT professionals.

There are also portals for educators that link to thousands of sites that contain e-learning resources, from online training to knowledge management and other resources in between. Some even provide detailed guidance on how to use these sites in a broader learning environment (which we'll discuss further in the next chapter). Education World (www.education-world.com) and Pacific Bell (www.kn.pacbell.com/wired/bluewebn) use a KM/portal approach to link to thousands of educational sites, making it a great resource for teachers (and others).[13]

Now imagine how this might work inside a company. Knowledge gained in building successful business-to-consumer (B2C) sites can be used to create successful business-to-employee (B2E) models. These can be based on portals that provide single, easy-to-use access to corporate content, applications, work processes, and collaboration tools. It brings together disparate information sources and knocks down walls between organizations (essential for organizational learning). Corporate intranet home pages can be constructed as portals to the knowledge of the firm. Some gateways might be defined by the business, such as HR, products, services, etc. Other gateways might be defined by the user, such as links to internal and external Web sites that are meaningful to a particular project or business venture. A regional manager of an "electronics superstore" chain might use a portal not just for information about the chain and its performance, but could also link to the sites of competitors, manufacturers, consumer groups that rate the products, etc. In this way a customized Web site that provides full coverage and immediate access to information will make the manager more knowledgeable and competitive. Of course, the manager could do this on his/her own by using the browser's bookmarking feature. But by having the company set up the initial knowledge structure and maintain the accuracy and functionality of the links and tags, it assures more uniform and efficient coverage. And based on this foundation, the manager can personalize the portal by adding his/her own knowledge structure (links, favorites, etc.).

For another example, a geographically dispersed organization might create a portal around a specific business function. For instance, clothing buyers in California, New York, Chicago, and Miami who work for a national department store might create a portal for exchanging information about fashion trends, competitors, consumer tastes, advertising, and even the price of raw materials to make the clothing. Financial information as well as insights on various suppliers can be shared. Through this linkage, the performance of the total buying community increases and the store's buying process is significantly improved. And the side benefit— that buyers learn from each other and from the information in the system—is icing on the cake.

Information Dashboards

Schwab's Stock Analyzer (www.schwab.com) takes investors through a well-organized path that helps them understand a particular investment opportunity by presenting information in an easy-to-read and easy-to-understand layout. Like many of the automobile sites mentioned previously, the Stock Analyzer allows for comparisons between companies in a similar industry. By taking people through this process, Schwab enables them to better understand a particular stock and the investment process overall.

The federal government's interactive census Web site (fact finder.census.gov) allows people and organizations (businesses, governmental agencies) to access and configure census data to meet both commercial and research needs. Just set the data parameters that reflect your inquiry and the system reconfigures the information for you—both knowledge management and performance support in one.

While these approaches may seem similar to knowledge portals in that they link the user to information resources, there is a key difference. In a portal, the user specifies links that s/he wants to access on a regular basis, so it organizes *Web sites*. An information dashboard is more complex. It is programmed to find specific information from various sources and reconfigure it so that it can be displayed in a common way. So a dashboard organizes *information*. When you ask any of the investment Web sites to profile the performance of a particular stock, you are asking for an information dashboard.

There are many corporate uses for information dashboards. Executives can use them to monitor the performance of the business, from profit and loss to stock price to comparison with competitors. Managers can use an information dashboard to assess the backgrounds and skills of the people in their organization. For example, an IT manager can scan a personnel dashboard to see how many Java programmers are currently available for project assignment. A product manager can consult an information dashboard to determine how a product is selling in different parts of the country and to better understand what customers are saying about it. An e-commerce business can use a dashboard to gauge the sales performance of their Web site. Through information dashboards, people get the key information they need faster and more reliably than would otherwise be possible. And, through continued use, they will clearly incorporate new knowledge. In other words, they will learn. The creation of an information dashboard is a complex task. It requires programming expertise to make the dashboard work—but the business insight that generates an understanding of what information to display, how it should be displayed, and what performance improvement is expected from the dashboard's use are also key requirements.

Decision Support

You might think that *etown* (www.etown.com) is just another consumer electronics e-commerce site, selling everything from camcorders to televisions. In many ways, it is. But the site has some interesting knowledge management and performance support features. Its *knowledge book* provides detailed information not only on products, but on how to use and troubleshoot them as well. Why have knowledge databases on an e-retailing site? Probably because they add value to the consumer's experience and create site loyalty and repeat visits. But etown also provides innovative performance support features. *Ask Ida*, its "expert advice service," asks a series of questions of the user. With each question, Ida provides information designed to help the user make the right purchasing decision. Based on each response, Ida formulates either additional questions or zeros in on a recommendation. The etown example shows how valuable a combination of information and performance support can be. Of course, the purpose of the site is to sell cameras and VCRs, but there's little doubt that consumer learning is an integral part of the etown strategy. Another decision support strategy can be found at PersonaLogic (www.personalogic.com).

Many companies are making use of similar strategies on their Web sites, especially in the area of customer service and troubleshooting. Computer and software companies ask customers a series of questions designed to pinpoint the solution to their problem. If the problem can be addressed over the Web rather than having the customer contact a call center (and most likely wait on hold for a while), the company saves money, and consumers learn how to fix the problem themselves.

How can the decision support model be used inside corporations? In companies where there are cafeteria benefits or multiple 401(k) options, decision support can help employees make better selections that are right for their needs. Salespeople can input customer requirements into a system that will help pinpoint the best product solution. Copy machine repair personnel can input responses to diagnostic questions designed to help the technician locate and fix the problem in much less time.

Task Enablers

Task enablers have the most performance-support-like features. They take people to a higher level of capability than they would reasonably be expected to demonstrate based on their existing knowledge and skill.

> **"I don't understand the technology. But you don't have to. You have to understand what it can do for you."**
>
> **Rupert Murdoch**

As a task-enabling performance support tool, Ask Jeeves (www. ask.com) is a performance support approach to finding information on the Web (i.e., performance support for knowledge management). It represents an effort to improve user performance over other search engines through a natural language, question-and answer-technology,[14] rather than the traditional key word or search string approaches, which are seen as more cumbersome by many users. And the system creates an ever-expanding knowledge base of questions and answers, in a sense growing smarter every day.

Other good examples of task-enabling performance support systems are the various travel sites, such as travelocity.com (www. travelocity.com) and expedia.com (www.expedia.com). Like a dashboard, they search databases to find flights, hotels, and car rentals that meet the requirements of the traveler. But these sites go beyond merely finding the right information and displaying it in a user-friendly way. Travel sites simplify a process and enable performance. Instead of multiple calls to different airlines, hotels, and other travel services, everything is combined, the itinerary creating the process. In effect, these sites replace many of the services of a travel agent—customers are doing the work themselves. In e-commerce this is referred to as "outsourcing to your customer." But from an e-learning perspective, tools like these enable people to do things (like book flights) they would not have otherwise been able to do. And from this, they retain more control over the task and learn more about schedules, pricing, trip planning, etc.

Financenter (www.financenter.com) is a financial services site with over 100 performance support tools (called *ClickCalcs*) and knowledge pages (called *ClickFacts*) that enable people to test scenarios on almost any financial topic (e.g., loans, retirement). Direct Advice (www.directadvice.com) uses an interview metaphor to help users develop a financial plan, which they might not have been able to do by themselves.

By working with the tools, people become more knowledgeable; they use the tools to better understand the choices they have around their particular financial situation. This personal focus is a very strong motivator for learning. In fact, playing "what if" scenarios is akin in many ways to an online simulation (thus bridging KM and online training).

How might task enablers work in a business? Sales teams are being equipped with customized tools to improve their productivity and "win rate." Proposal generation tools, linked to information databases, enable faster, more timely responses to RFPs. One particularly good example of a blend of knowledge management and performance support can be found on Siebel's (www.sales.com) online sales account management system. To the knowledge databases on customers, competitors, the economy, and other information areas of the user's choosing, Siebel has added performance support features of account planning, contacts, opportunities, and other customizable and updatable tools. Learning is enhanced because of the tight linkage between performance and information, enabling users to have a much clearer and more accurate picture of their total work environment.

Almost every mid- to large-size company has automated its expense and voucher process, either by building a performance support tool or purchasing one. Applying performance support to this typical business activity resulted in several benefits. First, individuals had a record-keeping system that helped them track their expenses and made it easier to submit them on time. Second, the business has a uniform process that lowered the overall costs of managing the expenses. Third, the information from the system enabled more accurate expense tracking, providing further cost-saving opportunities. So not only did this performance support solution make the end-user's work easier, it made work easier for the accounting department as well. Equally important, the output of this task enabler can be directed toward an information dashboard on expenses, cash flow, etc.

Many companies have converted their quality or TQM training curriculum into a knowledge management system that provides extensive and consistent process information and enables teams to use a variety of business improvement tools in a more collaborative mode. As these systems are put on the company's intranet, people from diverse locations form communities that contribute to a project without meeting in the same room or shipping files around the world. At the same time, the software guides the teams in a standard process and reporting format that enables easier comparison and collaboration across projects.

All of these sites try to incorporate knowledge management capabilities (some better than others), including a rich database of information, familiar navigation, updated content, performance support tools, and well-devised knowledge structures. Some sites go even further, allowing the user some level of personal customization, collaboration beyond e-mail (threaded discussion, chat rooms, etc.), and, in a growing number of sites—education offerings. Of course, since these are commercial ventures, you should expect advertising and e-commerce. Some sites do a good job of separating advertising from content, while others create situations (purposely or otherwise) that confuse advertising with content, so be careful. Today, there are knowledge-oriented Web sites on just about any topic, reflecting once again the library orientation of the Internet. Every day more people are drawn to these sites. One of their primary goals is to *learn*—about cars, or stocks, or health, or any other topic.

As knowledge management solutions are adopted, changes in the way people learn and work together are clearly evident. First, the demand for traditional training declines, especially after some introductory, "how to use" training is completed. One major company, having moved to a cafeteria benefits plan, was concerned that employees would not complete the online enrollment system correctly. Hundreds of classes were scheduled in work centers across the country. But because the system had good, built-in knowledge management and performance support capabilities, almost everyone was able to correctly complete his or her enrollment the first time. The system enabled performance without the need for training, and most of the scheduled classes were cancelled—a great savings to the business.

Collaboration also increases as more people and teams use the same resources, especially if knowledge sharing is encouraged throughout the various communities. Users contribute ideas and suggestions based on their experiences, thus creating new knowledge that can be shared by all. And finally, the overall cost of performance is reduced as use of these systems and actual work become one and the same, with less time away from the job for training (a productivity factor).

Building a Knowledge Management Solution

If knowledge management sounds like something worth trying, it's important to pick a project that will succeed. The project doesn't have to be huge—creating a KM system for the entire corporation is a worthy goal, but if you don't have the resources or the support, don't try. Instead, go for smaller communities and smaller projects. Small successes are much more desirable than big failures. In initiating a KM project, here are 18 key points to keep in mind.

1. Determine if the effort makes sense. Don't build solutions that do not meet real and important needs or that cost more than the problem they are attempting to solve. It's far better to build a small solution that meets a critical need, gets used, and results in improved performance, than to build a larger one that tries to do too much. This often results in people returning to the original, less efficient but more "comfortable" way of doing things.

2. Understand the community you are addressing. If you can't define the knowledge community, or the community of practice, your KM project is in jeopardy. Look for situations where the community is self-apparent, even self-identifying. Then identify the specific roles and jobs performed and the most important needs that should be addressed. Also, work to understand the prospective user's current knowledge level, vocabulary/frame of reference, and motivational state. It makes little sense to develop a KM system to tackle a trivial problem—work on a knowledge domain that's truly important to both the community and the company. In many situations the most important issues will be apparent, but check them out anyway. Needs assessment techniques are very appropriate here.[15] Don't shortchange this step. Identifying the key needs of the community is essential to building a KM system that people will want to use. Also remember that not everyone can benefit from knowledge management all the time. Aside from true instructional requirements that call for a training solution, problems with access, computer skills, readiness to learn independently, internal motivation, and even language issues can inhibit KM's effectiveness. Keep in mind that the KM technology is a tool to be used by people and is not a replacement for human interaction and collaboration. Finally, remember that sustaining a community is hard work. Ongoing facilitation is essential.

3. Know what you know. Identify existing experts and knowledge repositories so that you know where to get the knowledge the firm needs. In a sense, knowledge sources either already exist in the firm—you just have to harness them—or the information is missing, in which case you have to find it externally or build it. Identify any knowledge gaps and work on closing the most critical gaps first.

4. Master the content. This is probably the most critical point, and tightly linked to your understanding of the community. Avoid the temptation of putting in just what *you* think is important. But also avoid the temptation of putting in everything *everyone* thinks is important. There's also information that's *unimportant*—be sure you have the means to filter it out. Don't rely on subject matter experts or the R&D staff exclusively. Get input from all system stakeholders, including the users and the "owners" (the people who are paying for it).

5. Employ the technology of the enterprise. Using technology for KM seems like a blinding flash of the obvious, but it's important you use the *same* technology everyone else is using. This is a hardware and a software issue. For KM to be successful you need to remove as many barriers to its use as you can. This means that you don't want people to learn a different technology than they are using for their other work. Work closely with the IT department and the CIO as partners, but don't let the systems people drive KM (users are much better drivers). It goes without saying that the system should work in the real world. It shouldn't take forever to download files or pages, links should go where they're supposed to go, and all users must have the access and display technology to take advantage of the system. In other words, don't add a feature, such as streaming video, if the infrastructure can't support it.

6. Develop a knowledge structure and test it. Then test it again. Be sure you create a KM system that creates logical links and tags between content elements, which allow searching and navigation that follows how the content is naturally structured and how people naturally think about it. In addition, content should be structured so users get "just enough" information "just in time" for their needs—novices, experts, senior managers, etc., might get different views and different levels of detail according to their particular profile. Your knowledge structure should make the level of detail easy to discern and navigate. Unfortunately, experts who can tell you exactly how information should be structured cannot always write it in ways anyone else would understand, nor is the expert knowledge structure necessarily the right one for the user community. It needs to be both at the right technical level and written with the intended users in mind. If the users think that the way you've populated the KM system makes no sense, it probably doesn't, and if they can't understand the information you've provided, they won't bother to use it. And they won't come back. Use tools well, but don't rely on them totally. There are many search engines, authoring tools, expert system and advisory tools to help build the KM system (discussed more in Chapter 6). However, be wary of claims that knowledge management can be totally automated or that anyone, from novices to experts, can author the content.

7. Prototype. Prototyping allows you to build selected components of your system, even components without all the desired functionality, in order to test each piece with end-users and with the infrastructure. This is a common practice in manufacturing, product design, engineering, and software development and has been shown to save considerable time, money, and rework.

8. If you include performance support, it should make work easier, not harder. We often try to make work easier and inadvertently make it more difficult. For example, if a Web-based time reporting system replaces a paper-based one, it may make the work easier for the accounting people. But if employees have to wait a half-hour for the online forms to download, or if they are asked to provide redundant information (e.g., if they have to enter identifying information every time the tool is used), they are not likely to use the system. Bottom line—success depends on performance improvement *and* work simplification. If you give as high a priority to user benefits as you will to system features and functionality, you're more likely to hit your target.

> **"It is a simple task to make things complex, but a complex task to make them simple."**
>
> **Meyer's Law**

9. Plan for the running of the KM system, not just the building. Ensure that you can grow the knowledge base, keep it current, and get information out to the community quickly. Many KM systems have died because although there was money to build them, there were no funds or resources to run them. When making the business case for knowledge management, be sure to include cost-benefit justification for the life cycle of the system, not just the rollout. If you don't have the support to put the people and technology in place to fulfill the information collection, archiving, editing, prioritization, and distribution functions *every day*, you're in trouble.

10. Work to generate the support you'll need going forward. That's why small demonstrations of success mean so much. Beyond showing that the system works, demonstrate that it has worked and creates value for the business. This will generate the support you need. Without leadership support, the sustainability of your knowledge management system will be tough. With the right support, you can provide the technological and design leadership that will energize others to follow.

11. One portal. Knowledge can be unmanageable if every organization wants its own system or site. Once you have defined the community—enterprise or organizational—create a single top-level gateway to all the information databases and other resources. Within the hierarchy of the portal, you can provide opportunities for subgroups to differentiate themselves, but not at the expense of a single, universal access point or a common navigation/ search strategy. This may be one of the biggest political and cultural hurdles you will face.

12. Don't stop at document distribution. If you build a system just to allow people to post and access documents, you've still got a long way to go before you have true knowledge management. There's no question that document archiving and distribution has value, but if it's not managed, on both the input and the output sides, you will ultimately end up with an overwhelmingly massive database of disjointed and outdated content. And you cannot solve this problem with just a better search engine or adding a chat room. You must focus on the *management* part of knowledge management by establishing a knowledge structure, processes for content contribution *and* content removal, formatting guidelines, prioritization rules, community definitions, editorial roles, and other key functions that are essential for KM. This can require an oversight group, composed of all the KM stakeholders, who set policy, guidelines, standards, and practices for the system, and a core team of specialists that implement them on a daily basis.

13. Understand the value of time. "I want it now" is no longer an unreasonable demand. The work of business has reduced cycle times to bare minimums, and nowhere is this more apparent than with information. The inability to manage critical information can be a major barrier to a successful KM system. Don't shortchange this requirement. Provide the resources, including staff that can stay on top of the system to meet the information needs of users in the most *timely* manner possible. When an e-business can't deliver products to customers on time, it's a disaster. When a knowledge management system can't deliver content to users on time, it's a disaster as well.

14. Establish key KM roles. No KM system can run on technology alone—people are still a core component. While good knowledge management systems encourage everyone in the organization to participate, there are some key roles that should be filled. These roles have direct responsibility for running the KM system. Each company may define the roles (e.g., scope and duties) differently, but in general, in addition to KM managerial and technical resources, there are some unique functions that should be covered by one or more people (depending on size and scope):

- *Information Architect:* understands and manages the overall knowledge structure and tagging system (usually centralized and serves the entire system).
- *Editorial and Publishing:* manages the incoming information stream and assures that the content is appropriate for the system; prioritizes (and reprioritizes over time) the information based on community requirements and business needs (usually centralized and serves the entire system)
- *Online KM Librarian:* assures continuity and accessibility of all information resources
- *Knowledge Owner:* responsible for a specific knowledge domain, and assures that it is up-to-date, relevant, and complete (usually decentralized and serves a specific content domain)
- *Content Contributor/Author:* creator of the specific content that will be entered into the knowledge database and "published" on the system (usually decentralized and serves a specific subject area; can also be the knowledge owner).
- *Community Facilitator:* encourages and facilitates the interaction between members with and across communities, and assures that insights, recommendations, etc., are captured and communicated through the system (usually decentralized at the community level).

15. Build in collaboration. Provide ample opportunities for people to interact with each other. The use of discussion groups, instant messaging, and expert exchanges (i.e., matching knowledge seekers and knowledge providers) are just some of the techniques that are available.

16. Balance codification (explicit knowledge) and collaboration (tacit knowledge). Determine what types of and how much information can be codified into databases and delivered to users and what types of and how much information should be based on people-to-people collaboration and idea exchange. Both are valuable components of KM.

17. Incent and reward participation. Encourage information sharing and incent people to volunteer their expertise. Building a great Web site may not be enough. You'll need to build in the right incentives and rewards (from recognition to compensation) for using and contributing to the system.

18. Finally, don't be afraid to "hang" online training from your KM system. Online training and knowledge management are not mutually exclusive. They are more yin and yang—mutually compatible. You'll find that using both tools wisely and appropriately creates enormous power for your system. But don't force users into a training mode; let them go there only if they need to.

Implications for E-Learning

The implications of knowledge management for e-learning are huge. Rather than simply relying on instruction, we can use well-structured information as well as productivity enhancing tools to help people learn and improve their performance. We can differentiate between skills that must be performed automatically from information that can be accessed or referenced when needed. For example, we may not have to teach people the steps in a sales process; we may only have to teach people where to *find* the steps. And while we may have to use instruction to teach heating and cooling technicians how to repair an air-conditioning system, we may not have to retrain them when a new model comes out. We can simply reference the new information and have confidence they can learn it—*if* they know how to learn, and *if* we've provided the information in ways that make sense to them.

> **"If you have great skills training but don't have access to information, you won't look good in front of the client."**
> **Brad Hall, Human Resources Director,**
> **AT&T Global Services**

Here's an example. Figure 4.6 depicts a hypothetical e-business centered around cooking that focuses on all aspects, from planning to inviting guests to a dinner party. The site has numerous knowledge management resources, including a detailed recipe database. However, sometimes people need more help than a text-based recipe can provide. When the directions call for beating egg whites until you get "stiff peaks," people may not understand this

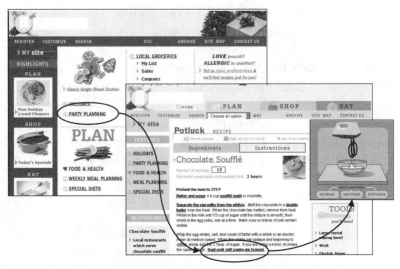

Figure 4.6 This prototype e-commerce site has knowledge management (the recipe) and a training demo (beating egg whites).

point. So, at their option, they can access a short animation that clarifies the point. This combination of access to information plus an instructional demonstration adds great value to the overall e-business site.

Why is this important? First of all, accessing KM systems is much more efficient than relying solely on training, even online training. We can keep knowledge databases accurate and available, and keep key people in the field rather than having them stop work every time training is needed. Secondly, we can provide a much broader range of information and performance support tools, and allow users to self-select what they want or need. So one KM system can serve the needs of a much wider community of practitioners. Third, we can use the collaborative features of advanced knowledge management to engage people in the learning process. Although well-designed, highly interactive online training programs and simulations do a good job of involving learners, the ability of good knowledge management systems to create an *expectation* that "everyone's a contributor" is an immensely powerful motivation to learn. Fourth, through communities, we can extend a continuous learning process beyond the end of the course and move it directly into the workplace. Finally, with KM added to online training, we have another tool in a growing arsenal of approaches to creating a more effective and efficient environment for learning.

A sound e-learning strategy recognizes when it is appropriate to teach or instruct, when to provide information and tools, and when it is best to do both. But this broader view of e-learning does not exist in a vacuum. It's important to position e-learning in the larger context of a total learning architecture that still includes the classroom.

An E-Learning Journey

by Barry Arnett, IBM Education (retired)

Why Companies, Even Large Technology Companies, Have Difficulty Exploiting Learning Technology— An IBM Example

DURING THE 1980S AND 1990S I worked in various education departments in IBM and learned how difficult it is for companies to successfully exploit learning technology. My assignments ranged from managing education departments, leading the development of corporate learning strategies, and being the executive in charge of external education consulting with Fortune 500 corporations in the U.S., Europe, and Asia. IBM's long history of pioneering new methods of using technology in learning provided a rich environment for trial, which resulted in numerous successes and some less than fantastic examples. Over the years, several themes emerged in this work which I will try to share with you here.

My own educational background and experience are in mathematics and technology management so I was always very optimistic that technology inherently offers the potential for "improving" any situation if reasonably applied. This bias led me to repeatedly seek out and attempt various ways to use technology in the learning process.

Even though I was positively inclined early on, I was extremely impressed when I first discovered what were then called "Electronic Performance Support Systems," or EPSS. Although a little simplistic from an educator's point of view, an EPSS *embeds* any needed "learning" directly into the software tools that the learner uses in performing his/her job. A simple example might be an order entry system that tells a user that a particular entry is invalid but offers the opportunity to "learn" how valid entries are composed. Another example might be a "pop-up" window in a word processor that tells the user that a word has been misspelled and suggests alternatives.

The first EPSS I saw was "prepared" by a young technical programmer in IBM working in a marketing headquarters support department. He was trying to assist dozens of sales people to sell products to the financial community. They frequently did not understand the industry, the local financial community, or how the products offered value. The programmer did not have the time or experience in training to offer classes, so he developed an online system within a few weeks that was proactive in providing specific information, advice, and other support to the field sales force. For example, small tutorials were available, online databases were linked from external sources to internal systems, local contact information was listed, and suggested sales procedures were suggested and monitored (in a friendly way). This system was extremely successful.

Success was impressive enough, but the big shock to me was that this particular group of sales people *no longer needed ANY classroom training to learn about this aspect of their work*. For an educator, this was incredible competition. I had just discovered the only known competitor that could completely eliminate the need for a training department! Rather than panic, I quickly adopted this new technology which had far exceeded even my most wildly optimistic hopes for how technology could be applied to learning. In addition, it was now obvious that learning included a lot more items than I had previously thought. It involved help in looking up reference materials, it involved making helpful procedural suggestions, and it didn't all have to happen in a classroom.

But over the years (and including that original EPSS) it became disappointingly clear that early success in demos or even early initial success on a broader scale was most often followed by low and declining usage as well as frequent failure or discontinuance. This paradox of how success seemed to lead to future failure became my passion over my remaining years of corporate work at IBM and later at Citigroup.

I came to understand that in most corporations it doesn't really matter if something is good (or in this case learned), it only matters if the new thing (or learning) can be successfully applied to business objectives. Furthermore, it was clear that the complexity of long term success in applying technology to learning was much more involved than I had initially imagined. Almost any professional can complete a successful demo, but few can sustain strategic success.

Out of this understanding came three major areas of focus:

1. *Whole systems approaches.* Rather than consider just the learning event, one must understand the entire environment that contributes to success of the learner on the job, and one must somehow prepare the learner to thrive in that environment. This means that how the learner is managed on the job, what tools are used, what reward systems are used, and many more items must be considered when formulating a "solution" that leads to learner success on the job. In other words, addressing only a part of a performance need was insufficient to bring about sustained change or performance improvement. At IBM a model was developed in my organization that attempted to guide education professionals through the application of this concept. It was (and is) called the Human Performance Model. It included training but also the other aspects that supported eventual performance/success. This model was applied in hundreds of situations within IBM, in other companies, and in government agencies. For the record, we did not invent this concept, which had been in use in the profession for thirty years or more, what we did was successfully apply it on a large scale in environments in which it was unknown at the time.

> *Learning:* A wise educator once said to me "the reason trainers don't measure the effectiveness of their training programs is that when they do they often learn they didn't achieve the real objectives of the training—to bring about real change." As a trainer in a business setting, this always bothered me. Using the Human Performance Model greatly improved the effectiveness of any training that we did and therefore was a major personal lesson for me during my career.

2. *Business cases.* While every major corporation endorses the need for training and development loudly and proudly, almost no company will sustain this commitment unless it can be shown to be financially sound in supporting the company's business strategy—especially the financial strategy or objectives. If a corporate executive

is forced to choose between funding a training initiative and any other business imperative vital to short-term business success, then training almost always loses. This means that a training executive that does not become fluent in marketing the value of learning, and how it leads to successful business performance, will not be successful over the long term or even over the short term. Specific facts, financial commitments, and fully integrated learning and business plans are mandatory. This is not easy to do and varies dramatically in different corporations, but one avoids the subject at his/her own peril. If you make no "sales" of any learning proposals, you go out of business personally.

> *Learning:* Earlier in my career (when I first believed that I knew how to "do training"), I spent most of my management time trying to convince other managers that if they would only listen to my wonderfully brilliant training strategies they wouldn't have so much trouble. It took a while, but eventually I learned that the only way to make real progress was to involve myself in their business strategies and respect their right to make business decisions. Business drives corporate training, not the other way around.

3. *Leadership.* In applying technology to learning, there are so many variables that contribute to or detract from success that a very high degree of leadership is required to manage the whole system in order to attain long-term success. This was learned the hard way at IBM and elsewhere. It didn't do any good to have excellent technology or learning design if the learners' managers were not supportive. It didn't matter if 100 percent of learners benefited if administrative procedures for usage were incredibly obtuse, thus discouraging completion. It will not work if short-term financial objectives are incompatible with needed learning funding, even if learning time is decreased by 80 percent. There are six to eight factors that influence learning technology success, and they must be managed together and in balance. If one is ignored or slighted, doom will shortly follow.

> *Learning:* Flexibility and openness to new ideas are core competencies for a corporate training leader. If you believe classroom training is the *only* way that certain learning can occur, you will miss opportunities as shown in my earlier EPSS example. If you believe lack of funding for a training pro-

posal always means management doesn't support training, you will tend to withdraw from the business process rather than fully engage it. If you believe learning only includes a finite number of methods or techniques, you aren't thinking broadly enough.

In spite of the difficulties, why am I still profoundly optimistic that technology will increasingly play a major role in learning in corporations? It's simple—there is tremendous value potential. There is money to save, time to save, and quality to improve. Those that figure out how to do this will be honored and rewarded.

Technology cannot address every learning need completely, but I strongly believe there are very few that it cannot contribute to significantly.

Barry Arnett *retired from IBM and then worked for Citigroup through 1999 as their Vice President of Organizational Development and Training for the global Operations and Technology function. He is now fully retired, so he says.*

CHAPTER

5

Integrating E-Learning and Classroom Learning

"Personally, I'm always ready to learn, although I do not always like being taught."

Winston Churchill

"I've always thought that technology could solve almost any problem. It enhances the quality of our lives . . . lets us travel across the galaxy . . . even gave me my vision. But sometimes, you just have to turn the whole thing off."

Chief Engineer Geordi LaForge
Star Trek: The Next Generation

IN THE PREVIOUS TWO CHAPTERS we discussed two forms of e-learning: online training (instruction) and knowledge management (information). The power of these approaches is magnified when they are used in combination. But they are even more powerful when properly integrated with more traditional classroom training programs. In following this path, you will move from building single learning programs, courses, databases, or tools, to building a *learning architecture*.

A learning architecture is the design, sequencing, and integration of all electronic and nonelectronic components of learning to deliver optimum improvement in competence and performance. In other words, it is how you structure and integrate *everything* that contributes to that goal.

A learning architecture is not the same as a curriculum, which generally refers to the organization and relationship of courses to create the appropriate learning sequence. Curricula are important but insufficient to define a complete learning architecture or system. From e-learning to classroom training, independent study, mentoring, work experience, and more, a learning architecture goes beyond training curricula to detailing the entire plan for learning and performance.

Within the context of e-learning, you have a number of choices and decisions to make about the types and combinations of online training and knowledge management to deploy. Moving up one level to a learning architecture, you have additional questions to answer, including:

> *Where is e-learning* not *appropriate?* Not everything can or should be delivered electronically. Determining where e-learning should be deployed and where it is not appropriate is one of the most important decisions you'll make. How should classroom learning be used to supplement e-learning? One way is to use the classroom component as a sort of "graduate school," following the "undergraduate" learning that takes place on the Web. On the other hand, in some cases the initial learning may require a classroom environment, and once people know how to learn on their own, the online component can be introduced. Or, the Web can simply be a gatekeeper, ensuring that those who attend a classroom program have the prerequisite capabilities to be successful. This can be done with Web-based introductory or remedial material with an associated assessment. The prospective classroom participant must first master the Web-based content before being allowed access to the classroom component. Since a great deal of variance in learning performance is accounted for by differences in the readiness of incoming learners, this can be

very important in making your learning architecture more efficient and effective.

How should e-learning be used to supplement classroom learning? There are many opportunities, especially for enrichment and follow-on learning. The Web can serve as a "community wrapper" of sorts, keeping those in the knowledge community in touch with each other and with the content, either after the formal learning is concluded or between learning events.

How should the e-learning and classroom learning components be sequenced? E-Learning tends to be short, targeted, task-driven, and episodic, while classroom learning tends to be longer, less well-targeted, and programmatic. For some learning tasks the former is ideal; for others the latter is desirable. Sequencing for efficiency and effectiveness may often produce conflicts. There may be some pressure to combine all the classroom programs into a single, short, but intensive experience, to reduce travel and downtime. But the best learning plans usually call for more distributed classroom experiences so that application, mentoring, online learning, and the integration of new knowledge with what's already known can take place between events. Experience and skill in designing learning architectures will help determine the best approach.

How much time should there be between each component? Again, experience and the nature of the content, plus an assessment of the needs of the business and the ultimate performance requirement, will help make this determination. If you push too much together, there may not be enough time for practice or experience to integrate what was learned. On the other hand, if your architecture is spread out over too long a period of time, the linkage between each component could be weakened and the overall costs of the program could go up. In addition, until learners have completed all essential parts of the program, they will not be as productive as the business might need.

How can on-the-job experience be integrated into the architecture? This clearly involves a transition to on-the-job learning. Sometimes we are so involved with formal learning events that we forget how much learning takes place on the job, through experience. With the right mentoring and support, this can be very powerful. The success of such efforts depends primarily on the extent to which a true learning culture is established in the organization. We'll explore this in a later chapter.

How will the effectiveness of the total learning architecture be assessed? It is vitally important that data on the impact of the learning architecture be gathered and interpreted. As we'll see in Chapter 8, assessing the effectiveness of e-learning and the overall learning architecture of the organization is much more than "testing" the learners.

The New Role of Classroom Training

With all the potential of e-learning, it might be easy to dismiss traditional classroom training as completely antiquated—of no value down the road. Although e-learning has a great deal to contribute, it does not mean the end of classroom learning. In fact, classroom learning will fill a unique role within a learning architecture, but it will be a different role than in the past. Group interactions, business problem solving, performance evaluation, expert observation, culture building, and teamwork are all critical attributes of an overall learning system that, in many cases, is still best suited for classroom experiences.

"What is emerging most clearly from the technological explosion is, ironically enough, a refocusing on people."
Laura Winer, Nick Rushby, and Jesus Vazquez-Abad[1]

With e-learning becoming a significant part of your learning architecture, there will be a number of changes in classroom-based learning strategies (Table 5.1).

Table 5.1   How the Web Will Change the Classroom

The classroom will no longer be the default delivery system.	In many situations in the past, the development of classroom training was almost automatic. If you wanted to go an alternate route, you sometimes had to go to extreme measures to justify your position. In some cases overt and covert barriers were put in place to keep technology-enabled learning at bay. In the future the reverse will be more likely. As e-learning systems

Table 5.1 *(Continued)*

	are established, the use of classroom learning is where more justification will be required.
However, the synergies between e-learning and classroom learning will become more refined.	As e-learning capabilities are deployed, organizations will find new uses for classroom learning. Granted, the amount of classroom training will likely decrease, but the importance of classroom experiences that remain will certainly grow. Creative combinations of the two will become central to a successful learning architecture, each contributing its unique value.
There will be less teaching and more facilitating.	As classroom learning moves from teaching facts to applying concepts, and from reviewing procedures to generating new ideas, the role of the instructor will change from the all-knowing "sage on the stage" to more of a "guide on the side." In addition to the instructor/facilitator, knowledge will come from a greater variety of sources, including the corporate intranet (every classroom should have Web access), the learners themselves (as they form knowledge communities), and outside experts (either live or via technology).
There will be more reliance on original source materials.	With content changing all the time, it is becoming problematic to rely on "student guides" that quickly become dated. At the very least, these guides will be Web-accessible so they can be updated easily. But some courses will drop student guides altogether, in favor of corporate information on the Web, organized to meet the needs of the learners. This has two major benefits. First, it is much more likely to be accurate and comprehensive, and second, through the use of these materials in the classroom, the students will learn how to use and value them on the job.
Course start and end dates will become increasingly irrelevant.	With Web access, learning can begin prior to the class and continue long after the class is over. This is especially true for community building among the students and for follow-up access to updated content and expertise. Furthermore, because of the increasing differences in the backgrounds, knowledge level, motivation, and availability of people, it will become increasingly difficult to find enough people who are ready at the same time for the same classroom course.

Building a Learning Architecture

Let's look at a high-level design for a hypothetical sales curriculum to see why building a learning architecture is so important. Assume that the curriculum covers five major areas: orientation to selling, key products, sales systems, advanced selling skills, and a practical application of selling skills. What should the learning architecture look like? An evolving learning architecture for sales might be depicted in Figure 5.1.

In the first scenario, each class sequentially follows the last and they are equally distributed across time. There is no e-learning component. But simply adding e-learning is not as easy as it may seem. Where should e-learning be used? Which course is a good candidate for e-learning? Which competencies are best supported with e-learning? Perhaps you determine that e-learning should be used for orientation because people can get the big picture of the sales process and the sales organization before they come to class. You might also determine that the sales systems training could be Web-based, perhaps because you know a vendor that has a good course in this area. So your architecture morphs into something akin to the first iteration in Figure 5.1.

Wait a minute! Wouldn't putting all the product information into an online training format be better? After all, there'd be a lot of updates, and the Web is ideal for content that will change. And wouldn't orientation be better in the classroom, so sales teams can meet for the first time and forge the first stages of their community? And the sales systems are so new, perhaps we need an expert to help everyone through the complex screens and commands. And, just when you think you've got your architecture nailed, a colleague suggests that the advanced skills be conducted in the field with an experienced salesperson as a mentor and coach. You think this is a great idea, and further discussion and research leads you to conclude that the practical application component also belongs in the field as a unique work assignment. So now your architecture looks like the second iteration in Figure 5.1.

You do more research, including an extensive needs assessment, and you find that there's a greater requirement for practical application earlier in the program, so you'll have to add another component. Plus, you find that competitive knowledge is far more important than earlier anticipated and needs to be included as well. But because of the instability of this information, it is unsuited for any form of fixed learning event. And, because the required performance of users of this information is hard to antic-

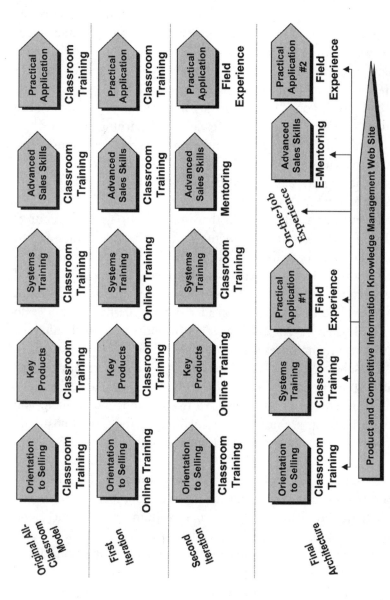

Figure 5.1 The hypothetical sales curriculum evolves from all classroom to a more complex learning architecture.

123

ipate, formal training of any kind could be artificial, at best. So you determine that competitive information is best delivered through a knowledge management Web site, which will now also contain product information enabling you to eliminate the product course. And that mentoring program you implemented—perhaps you can do it online (electronic mentoring). Also, through discussions with experienced salespeople, you determine that a different distribution of the program components across time is needed. Now, your "final" learning architecture, as shown at the bottom of Figure 5.1, has a wide variety of learning elements.

Think this is the right architecture? Maybe; maybe not. Are you sure you've put the right learning in the classroom and the right learning on the Web? What if you could help develop a performance support tool to make it easier for the sales team to use the new systems? How would that impact your systems training? What if the sales vice president wants to include a message to everyone in the organization—in person? What if your company is hiring both college graduates and experienced salespeople? Should the learning architecture be designed to accommodate different entry-level skills? Have you considered what salespeople should do *between* learning events, or how long the entire process should take so that these employees are "on the street" as quickly as possible?

The answer is that whenever you are looking at curricula or learning architectures, flexibility and adaptability are key. Generally speaking, however, here are twelve guidelines to help you build a learning architecture that will stand the test of changing content and changing business requirements.

1. Conduct a thorough needs assessment. This includes analyzing the targeted learners and the communities they associate with (entry-level knowledge, structure/frame of reference, and motivational profile), and understanding the performance gap you're trying to close. Don't make erroneous assumptions about the content or the learners—be certain. By fully understanding all the learning requirements, you'll be in a far better position to determine and recommend what is appropriate for the Web and what is appropriate for the classroom. There will absolutely be situations where Web-based "anything" will not be appropriate. For example, laying a foundation for a house is probably best taught on the job by a skilled craftsperson. But if a construction worker someday wants to own her/his own home-building business, she'd/he'd better learn a little bit about architecture, accounting, and small business management—clear candidates for e-learning.

2. Base your architecture design on the competencies you wish to build. You have probably developed a competency model that reflects the needs and characteristics of users and the business. Now your task is to ensure that the competency—the learning, practice, and demonstration of performance—is matched to the right delivery vehicle in the right place in your learning architecture.

3. Keep the business need in mind. Understand how long you have to develop the required skills and competencies within the targeted groups. The more people in these groups and the more geographically dispersed they are, the more attractive e-learning will be. This is especially true if your time frames are short. If the company is gearing up to meet a new competitive threat next month, having the sales force trained by next year won't cut it. The less time you take to reach the performance goals for your program, the lower your costs and the sooner the students can become productive.

4. Test your architecture assumptions with all stakeholders. Key stakeholders would include:

- Those who will teach/facilitate classroom components
- Developers of each of the e-learning and traditional learning components
- Organizations or leaders sponsoring the initiative (in this case, perhaps the sales vice president and/or branch managers)
- Managers of the employees who will experience the learning
- The learners themselves

Using a rapid prototyping strategy, involve the stakeholders as early as possible in the design/development process. See how willing each group is about helping you launch the system. Find out what will motivate each stakeholder group to be active contributors. Ask them to review the content from all angles—relevancy, accuracy, completeness, authenticity, clarity, fitness for intended use, etc. Get their input on overarching governance of the entire learning effort (a governing body that deals with long-term policy, financing, advocacy, and other strategic issues). This will assure that your learning architecture design is on the right track. More often than not, if you leave out a key stakeholder group, it's likely that the group you've omitted will be the group that will complain the loudest.

5. Start by associating classroom learning with application and teamwork, and e-learning with content and tools. This general rule will help you position the learning requirements appropriately. In most cases you'll have better results by first moving as much knowledge and information to the Web as you can, and focusing your classroom time to the application of that knowledge, especially in team-centered scenarios. You will undoubtedly find exceptions to these guidelines (such as simulations, which can cut across all approaches), but it's a good one to get you started.

6. Use existing source materials, if available. Don't reinvent the wheel. Most training materials are obsolete within six months of the learning event. If you've developed tools or other resources that will be useful significantly beyond the learning event, consider integrating them into your firm's mainstream intranet resources and direct your students there. Besides, you cannot count on students even being able to *find* their training materials a half year after the course, unless they're integrated and maintained within an ongoing knowledge management system.

7. Use the Web to link all learning components. The Web can be the main source of learning information, including prerequisites, access to coaches and mentors, testing and assessment, program evaluation, communication between students and with instructors/facilitators, posting and sharing course work, scheduling learning activities, etc. In other words, use the Web as a unifying portal for your learning architecture.

8. Help people learn "how to learn." Look at intranet resources as on-the-job resources, not training resources. This means that if you have knowledge management and performance support components, be sure that employees learn not only how to use these resources now, but how to continue to use them as they evolve. This will help employees become independent learners. I was told a story of a trainer who was so impressed with a small knowledge management site being run by a technical division in his company that he printed each page and put it into a binder for his students. How much better would it have been if he had taught his students how to access and use the original source material in its original form!

9. Think "precision learning." People don't always make the right choices when it comes to their own learning and development—they often don't know what they don't know. Some are unable to identify the gaps in their own skills. Others may select a learning path inconsistent with the needs of the business; for example, enrolling in a project management program when there are already too many project managers. Even when someone has identified a real need within the company and is inclined to build her/his skills in that area, she/he may not know where to start. Your learning architecture should have a way for individuals, and possibly entire work groups, to assess themselves against their own needs and those of the business (including self-assessment, manager assessment, knowledge testing, coaching, etc.). Then, it should be able to prescribe a precise learning plan to achieve their goal. This competency assessment strategy enables the right learning and information to reach the right people at the right time (more on this in Chapter 6).

10. Create and maintain a community on the Web. This will be especially useful between learning events and after the major learning components are completed. As we've previously discussed, communities can be one of the most powerful forces for continuous learning and growth. They also contribute to a feeling of belonging, which will be important as individuals seek help from their peers. But community development does not end with the Web.

11. Use the classroom as an extension of your online learning community. Although your online training programs and your knowledge management systems were (hopefully) built around the needs of the various communities of practice, bringing people together, face-to-face, can accentuate membership in the community and reinvigorate a shared purpose. This is a much more valuable use of expensive classroom time than delivering simple instruction, and although not all training is transferable to the Web, the more that can be moved there, the more "face" time can be devoted to community building.

12. Engage learners every step of the way. Keeping employees involved in e-learning is a challenging situation. And keeping them engaged between learning events is even more challenging. You don't want them to abandon your learning programs. Here are a few ideas:

- Keep the communications up, especially between events. Use e-mail, synchronous technology (described later in this chapter), and other formats to keep employees informed about the program and to put learners in touch with each other (i.e., provide early and continuous support for the community of learners and make communications two-way).
- Communicate the value of the program, especially WIIFM ("What's in it for me?") and YCDI ("You can do it!"). Help users see benefits of continued use.
- Provide incentives for sticking with the program. In addition to benefits and building intrinsic motivators, such as making the program engaging and valuable, extrinsic incentives, such as more pay, certification, promotion (see Chapter 7), or the possibility of new or desirable work assignments, can coax reluctant learners to stay with it.
- Create opportunities for employees to use the program in a way that fits their availability. This means creating smaller "bites" or "chunks" of content that can be completed in short periods of time. Users can easily bundle many of these pieces together if more time is available, but if time is short, having to wade through too much content before finding a natural break can be a turnoff to future use.

- Keep the technology at bay. Don't let problems with technology cause potential users to sense that it just isn't worth it.
- Allow opportunities for problems to surface—from boredom and worthlessness, to bad systems or not enough time—and be responsive to the concerns that are raised.

A Learning Architecture for Sales Development at AT&T Global Services

AT&T Global Services, the sales arm for the telecom giant's largest customers, had gone through a number of organizational changes over the last ten years as the company retooled for an ever-changing marketplace. As noted in Chapter 4, their traditional residential training center was drastically downsized during this time, and ultimately eliminated, with most of the responsibility for learning transferred to the branch offices. While this was a successful cost-cutting initiative, the decentralization of learning created a number of problems, from inconsistent allocation of funds for training to a significant divergence from recommended curricula. The result was a learning program that could not meet its obligations across the business, and complaints from employees and managers that the skills of the sales force had degraded.

Instead of reconstructing the central training organization, the leaders of the business set about to look at learning differently. Using a large dose of e-learning, combined with some classroom-based courses, they developed a new learning architecture.

The first thing the business did was to define all the competencies that typified the sales executive's job. Fifty-six competencies were identified, but no one was sure which were most important to the success of the business. To get at this answer, all sales executives were tested across the competencies and their scores were compared with their sales performance (as reflected in the compensation plan). Out of the 56 competencies, only 6 were statistically correlated with performance. The rest of the competencies were deemphasized. Then a specific learning plan was put in place for each of the six competencies, plus three additional competencies that the knowledge communities felt were important, especially for the future. The ongoing goal was to compare sales performance to competency assessment, year over year. The assumption was that competency would be highly correlated with performance.

When training was cut, the belief was that, because of an extensive investment in e-learning—computer-based training for the most part—sales executives could train themselves. In a sense, learning was put on autopilot. It didn't turn out that way. Money assigned for training was often spent on other priorities. Different sales centers purchased different training on the same subject. So, for example, there would be different programs on selling skills or project management.

To correct this problem, money for training is now controlled centrally and allocated only to sales centers that would spend it on the specific learning plans associated with each competency. If the organization wanted to buy a course outside the learning plans, they could do so—out of their own budget. The learning plans are changed each year based on the changing competencies, which reflect business requirements. Business leaders' compensation is tied to the extent to which every sales executive was assessed on a Web-based competency instrument every year. If assessments were missed, the leader's bonus was affected. Needless to say, participation in the program is almost universal.

The performance support element of the program includes an organizationwide, Web-based competency tool that allows individuals to easily and quickly participate in the assessment, and allows management to get hard information on compliance and workforce competence that were guessing games before. Assessment included knowledge testing, self-assessment, and manager assessment.

Assessment scores were aggregated and sales centers were ranked from most to least competent. The rankings were then shared with the sales center leaders. The fact that competency scores were not tied to pay did not in any way decrease sales leaders motivation to get off the bottom of the list. Who wants to be considered the "least competent" sales center in the country?

Individual assessments were electronically linked to specific learning plans. The prescribed learning plans were tied to competency gaps rather than specific interests (although in many cases these did overlap). Most of the components of the plan were online training and some independent study with a few key classroom components; about 20 courses remained in all for the entire organ-

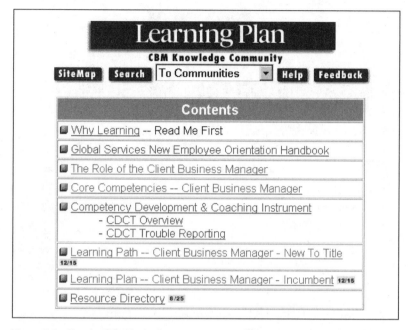

Figure 5.2 For the AT&T sales team, competencies were directly linked to learning plans. (Copyright © 1999 by AT&T.)

ization. These courses were all outsourced and delivered in company meeting rooms, hotels, etc. AT&T Global Services did not use any of its own classrooms—it didn't have any. Figure 5.2 shows a page from the competency and learning plan development tool.

A competency assessment database was created to aggregate scores and analyze whether employees improved performance year-over-year on the target competencies. It also provided a vast amount of objective data to make adjustments to the learning plan and programs. For example, there was a good correlation between competence and sales results. Each learning program has a pre- and posttest. If performance on the posttest did not correlate with measure of improved competence, the course was killed. Individual posttest scores were also aggregated in the database. If an individual consistently performed poorly on classroom posttests, she/he would not continue to be invited to the training.

All of this effort came from a strategy that had four major elements to building the competence of the sales force (see Figure 5.3). First, access to comprehensive, real-time information was critical. This component was the fundamental force behind the

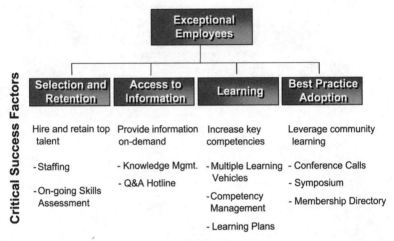

Figure 5.3 AT&T developed a four-component framework to developing exceptional employees. (Copyright © 1999 by AT&T.)

development of the IKE knowledge management system (see Chapter 4). Second, skill development was critical to job performance. Here online training and some very specific classroom programs were used to enable sales executives to attain competence, as measured by a competency assessment tool (performance support). Third, even with all of this learning, AT&T needed to attract and retain the right raw talent that could make the best use of the skills and information at their disposal. And finally, the organization sought to measure the adoption of best practices. Did the sales force get smarter? Did they have to relearn over and over? Or were new insights freely shared and integrated into the business?

The results of this integrated approach to learning are encouraging. On a standard employee satisfaction survey, satisfaction with learning and development went from 39 to 70, seven points higher than the norm for high performing companies. And the competency improvement system (they don't want to call it training) was cited by entering and exiting employees as the second most impressive aspect of the company (people was first). All of this was done in a significantly shorter learning time, allowing sales executives more time on the job.

In the end, AT&T Global Services created and deployed a learning architecture that included online training, knowledge management, and performance support, combined with appropriate classroom training and a comprehensive competency assessment process. The result: lower costs and improved performance.

A Learning Architecture for Financial Consultants at Merrill Lynch

Merrill Lynch has a tradition of learning and education that dates back to the founding of the firm. At their residential training center near Princeton, New Jersey, thousands of employees have received training in the basics of financial planning right through the most advanced concepts of investing. With the deployment of its new front-line platform, *Trusted Global Advisor* (TGA), to more than 22,000 financial consultants (FCs) and client associates (CAs, who support the FCs in the branch offices) nationwide, the firm was ready to build a learning architecture that leveraged the best of classroom training with a state-of-the-art e-learning delivery system. Because of the integrated and universal nature of TGA, the firm found itself with a natural launching pad for its online learning efforts. Other delivery alternatives, such as CD-ROM, were tried but eliminated early on in favor of using TGA as the single delivery system for both business processes and learning.

With about 1,000 new CAs coming into the branches each year, the firm couldn't bring all of them to Princeton or send trainers to each location fast enough to make them effective in the highly competitive investment and financial planning industry. In 1998, as TGA was being rolled out to the field, work was under way to build the first Web-based program, *Skill-Builder for CAs*. Launched in December of that year, this course focused on initial training for the CA community. The success of this program led to other programs for CAs and for the 1,700 new FCs that were being hired at the same time.

As is typical for any new and promising technology, Merrill found that e-learning trials were under way in various parts of the firm. After all the work that went into creating TGA standards, there was a concern that without some controls, Web-based learning would be introduced in a variety of competing standards. And so, in 1999, the Merrill Lynch Learning Network was born with a single link on the TGA main screen.

Within one year the firm had over 150 learning products deployed on the Learning Network. Not just online training, but databases of stories by successful FCs who share best practices with the rest of the firm. A variety of resources, online job aids, and performance support tools are also accessed through the Learning Network portal. In addition, the ability of individual FCs and CAs to personalize their Learning Network home page greatly enhances the system's ability to "push" a customized learning plan to each user. Standards for look and feel, navigation and access, are maintained throughout the firm so that wherever FCs or CAs are located, after they experience the Learning Network for the first time, their ability to access additional e-learning programs does not require relearning the interface. This created a sense of comfort, and although the capabilities of the Learning Network and the interface are upgraded from time to time, care is taken to assure that people move with the transition and are not blindsided by it. In addition, the Learning Network standards have created development efficiencies and a better use of development resources. The portal Learning Network is shown in Figure 5.4.

The ability to deploy e-learning across the firm has fundamentally changed how the classroom component of Merrill's learning architecture is run. Previously, live training was stand-alone—all the content was delivered in the classroom setting. Now the Learning Network provides prerequisite training for almost every classroom session. Furthermore, the design of classroom and e-learning components is coordinated, often by the same team. This assures little redundancy between the two, and that employees who attend the live program have the background they need for a successful learning experience.

Merrill Lynch's e-learning experiences have resulted in a clear differentiation *and* a clear coordination between its role and that of the classroom. Today, e-learning is used to provide fundamental information, examples, best practices, stories from the field, and firmwide key messages. The associated classroom components focus on application, practice, and personalized coaching from very experienced practitioners who serve as instructors and facilitators. And, for those FCs and CAs who cannot make it to the live class, the Learning Network provides additional content, assuring that no one is left behind.

In the near future the Learning Network will be augmented with a synchronous option (discussed later in this chapter) that will enable live and archived presentations to be delivered throughout the system. Better search capabilities will be able to find related content beyond the Learning Network, anywhere in the firm—in other Web sites and TGA itself. As the Learning Network evolves, it may look more like knowledge management than training. Already each online course is broken down into small pieces of content (often referred to as *objects*, to be discussed in Chapter 7). With the personalization of the Learning Network under way, it's likely that future e-learning products will be built for each user, on the fly, from an ever-growing knowledge base.

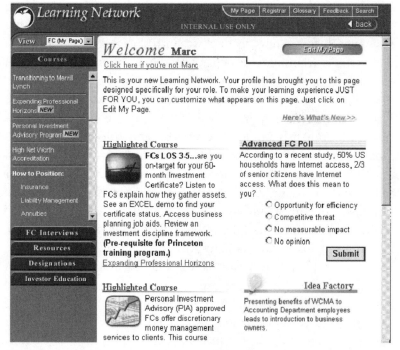

Figure 5.4 The entry portal for the Merrill Lynch Learning Network includes the ability for learners to customize the page, submit ideas, and access nontraining resources. (Copyright © 2000 by Merrill Lynch, Pierce, Fenner & Smith Incorporated. Reprinted with permission.)

A Learning Architecture for Initial Call Center Training at U S WEST

At U S WEST call center representative training is an expensive proposition. New hires could spend their first three months in training to learn the job. Each year more content was added, reflecting the increasing technological and competitive nature of their business. And because the company's service area was so large and regionalized, deviations from the prescribed curriculum were common.

To combat the regionalization problem, the company decided to use a self-paced format, primarily print. But updating the content became a nightmare. Turnaround times could never be short enough. Version control and distribution costs got out of hand. With about 600 people trained in 1997 and more than 2,200 trained in 1998, the company knew it had to change direction.

The solution was to reorganize the curriculum to reduce redundancy. It wasn't necessary to reteach the product ordering system each time a new product was introduced. Product, process, and systems training were separated. Then different elements of each system and process were introduced into each product module, dramatically reducing training time. Basic knowledge came first. Then, as fluency increased, increasingly complex information, comprehensive practice exercises, and role-plays followed. Eventually the students were able to practice with live customers.

Another part of the solution was to move to online training for much of the content, leaving synthesis activities, like exercises and practice, for the classroom. The Web-based system enabled stand-alone training modules to be consistent across the company, and allowed for instant updating of the content and continuous monitoring of student performance. The learning architecture of the program meshed online training of products, processes, and systems with classroom practice and discussion. An instructor-led sales training component was also added. The result was greater consistency and a further reduction of training time, now 40 percent fewer training days than under the old design. This made it easier to add important new content.

But U S WEST's learning architecture also includes knowledge management. InfoBuddy, the company's knowledge management system (see Chapter 4) was integrated directly into both the online and classroom training. Recognizing that the nature of the business would require continuous updating of the training, the most volatile content was accessed through InfoBuddy and not through any of the course materials. With InfoBuddy continuously updated, the training group had high confidence that the information the students accessed would be current. Special elements were added to the course that required students to solve problems by using InfoBuddy. This resulted in the added benefit of the students learning how to use and rely on the InfoBuddy system before they went "on the floor." Finally, a training management system (to be discussed in Chapter 6) managed all the modules. Different people in different roles received a different combination of modules. For example, a representative who services customer billing issues would receive all the training modules on billing, but might only receive overviews of products, whereas a representative in a sales role would get in-depth product training but perhaps only receive an introduction to billing.

In the end, U S WEST created a learning architecture that included classroom training, online training, and knowledge management, each intricately woven into the others. Results of the new learning architecture for initial customer care representatives have been encouraging. In addition to reduced delivery costs and a reduction in training days, graduates of the program who are in sales jobs appear to be reaching their goals significantly faster than those who were trained under the old design.

Creating a Learning Architecture for Executives

Getting executives involved in learning has always been a challenge. We often express frustration that company leaders do not attend courses, even courses that were designed for them. And if they do, they often can't participate fully, sometimes leaving early due to the pressing nature of business. With little time to spare, executives say they don't have the luxury to take time to learn—it's not something they seek out to do. Instead of trying to find the right course that would attract executives, perhaps it's time to rethink the approach—to develop a learning architecture that's designed for business leaders from the start.

That's what *nMinds* (www.nminds.com) is doing at a commercial level, focusing on providing business leaders with leading-edge business knowledge. Instead of asking executives to change their work and lifestyle to learn, nMinds is changing the learning architecture to fit into the work and lifestyle of executives.

The first component of this executive learning architecture is knowledge management. Following in-depth needs assessment of typical business executives, nMinds engages subject matter experts in areas such as digital business, making alliances, and product development. These experts are videotaped in an interview format, which is then "chunked" into episodes of stand-alone information of about ten minutes each. The executive learner can view each episode independently or look at the entire series at one time. In many cases, the information presentation is customized for executives based on a profile they each complete when they enroll. This makes the learning experience more personalized and valuable. And, to ensure that each interview or series offers relevant, "actionable" insight, every episode offers diagnostic tools, some online and some printable, to help leaders better understand how they and their company can use this new knowledge. Checklists, questionnaires, short simulations, ideas to think about, feedback, and coaching are all part of this interactive environment. The result is that executives are involved in the content, not just passive viewers. The system also provides alternatives to the broadband video presentations, including "key take-aways"— major points that can be printed and reviewed anytime and anywhere, and visuals which can be incorporated into personal presentations to aid in communicating these new ideas to a broader audience.

The second part of the architecture involves community building. Studies have shown that executives want to understand how their peers—even those in other companies—are dealing with the business issues they are facing. The system provides opportunities for executives to create personal profiles that will enable them to be placed in communities of other people with similar backgrounds and interests. Great care is taken to ensure privacy of community members and to make sure that communities consist of qualified individuals (only CEOs are allowed in CEO level networks, etc.). More than just centered on message boards, these communities can be content-based (allowing participants to learn more about a subject), practice-based (enabling dialogue around solving a common business problem), or strategic-based (helping participants generate new ideas and content that can be fed back to the larger community).

The power of face-to-face interaction should not be discounted, even with executives. So the third part of the architecture is networking. If members are interested in a face-to-face dialogue with an expert, they can be placed in conferences or even workshops where that expert is presenting. If enough members are interested, a special seminar with the expert can be arranged. This is not a return to the original course paradigm that wasn't successful with business leaders—there is a major difference. In the old paradigm, programs were created for executives and then they were encouraged to attend. In this new model, it is the learners themselves who specifically ask for the live interaction, and who also set the parameters of the meeting (length, subject matter, etc.), gaining their support for e-learning.

The implications of this example for e-learning and organizational learning are important. While there are many ways to engage executives in learning (including other approaches not mentioned here), treating them like other employee-learners is probably not one of them. Despite their busy schedules and perceived short attention spans, executives *will* take time to learn. But the learning architecture you design for them must recognize their unique needs, constraints, and interests. And getting your leadership involved in learning, as we'll see in Chapter 7, will go a long way to gaining their support for e-learning.

Can You Put Classroom Training on the Web?

Much of the e-learning approaches and examples mentioned up to this point are characterized as *asynchronous*. Asynchronous delivery refers to programs that are independent of time ("prerecorded"). In other words, anyone can access the program at any time and as many times as desired. There is no "live" component, and in most cases nothing has to be scheduled. Communication between people does not take place in real time. *Synchronous* programs, on the other hand, are time dependent. Communication takes place in real time. The delivery is live—if you miss it, that's it (unless it is repeated live again, or recorded, which would then make it asynchronous). Learning programs on CD-ROM are asynchronous, as are most Web-based online training and knowledge management resources. Performance support, by definition, is asynchronous, as is this book you're reading. The most obvious form of synchronous learning is classroom training or other forms of live group experiences, but some Web applications, such as chat rooms, are also synchronous.

If you put live classroom training on the Web, it's a synchronous event. It is scheduled, and all parties—students and instructors—must be present at the same time, just like any classroom event. But on the Web they don't have to be in the same place. Web technologies now allow synchronous learning at a distance. But is this a good idea?

There's a great deal of interest in Web-based synchronous training and a lot of products are in the marketplace.[2] The main argument is that it will dramatically reduce travel costs and time. Several of these products offer combined synchronous and asynchronous features, as well as learning management capabilities. Some companies position themselves in the learning business, but many focus on business-to-business services, such as live, Web-enabled collaboration, meetings, conferences, and presentations. The technology is not prohibitively expensive or unreasonably difficult to use, so why not use it for training? Isn't this a good way to utilize instructors in an e-learning environment? Is this a good foundation technology for your e-learning strategy?

The answers are not so simple. While there are times when a synchronous class is appropriate, saving on travel costs alone is not enough justification. While the technology does offer teacher-student and student-student interaction, it's not as personalized or as casual as it might be in a regular classroom. So if high levels of interactivity or teamwork is critical, relying solely on a "Web-ized" class may not deliver all that you are looking for. In addition, the number of students that can participate in an online class and still have some level of interactivity is often lower than in a face-to-face situation. So some of the cost savings are mitigated by a potential increase in the number of times the program must be offered.

Asynchronous programs require a much deeper understanding of instructional design, and are more costly to develop than synchronous programs, which also have important design considerations, but tend to concentrate more on delivery. Nevertheless, if this is done at the expense of design, i.e., simply transferring classroom courses to the Web, you're likely to end up with shovelware (see Chapter 3).

> **"In short, many training departments today are merely using the Internet to increase the rate at which they 'spray' training at employees and 'pray' that organizational performance will improve as a result. For many training departments, the Internet is simply a bigger hose with which to deliver training"**
>
> **Tony O'Driscoll,**
> **IBM's Institute for Knowledge Management[3]**

There certainly are times when moving a classroom course to a synchronous solution is desirable, but the benefit of this approach is enhanced when the class is redesigned to take best advantage of the new delivery technology, rather than simply broadcasting the original course. More important, there are other innovative ways to use this technology to enhance the learning experience rather than just saving travel money (Table 5.2).

Table 5.2 Uses for Synchronous Delivery Technology

Quick applications or process training	If your business changes a process or introduces new software, synchronous delivery can deliver a short instructional program quickly. In an ideal situation, this could be followed by a more permanent and cost-effective asynchronous solution.
Create greater access to key events	When there is one and only one opportunity for people to have access to a person or an event, use this technology to enable more people to participate. A special event in your company, like a speech by the CEO, the announcement of a new product, or the impact of an outside event on the business are all examples where synchronous technology can be used. While this may be less "instructing" and far more "communicating," there is value in enabling more people to be exposed to the original content than otherwise possible.
Learning management	Synchronous systems can be used to coordinate and manage learning experiences, perhaps providing just enough struc-

(Continued)

Table 5.2 Uses for Synchronous Delivery Technology *(Continued)*

	ture to assure that learners "show up" and continue to participate. Short, scheduled live presentations, online chats, or other synchronous events can introduce subjects, and the instructor can assign work and set expectations. Most of the actual learning takes place asynchronously, using online training, knowledge management, and other resources (including books!). The synchronous class might resume with discussion and feedback regarding what was learned. UNEXT (www.unext.com) is an example of an e-learning Web site that follows this model. Pensare (www.pensare. com) and University Access (www.universityaccess.com) are other examples.
Community building	The technology can be used to reinforce communities of practice, especially between other learning events or after the formal training is over. Community meetings and special presentations can take place without people having to leave their work sites. There are a growing number of synchronous approaches that support community building and growth. Threaded discussion, online chat, news groups, online conferencing (see next), instant messaging, and personal Web pages are just some of the techniques (beyond e-mail) that make the vital online community experience work. But getting people involved requires that: • Participation is seen as worthwhile to the community member. • There are a significant number of members participating (i.e., participation is seen as worthwhile to a *lot* of people). • Participation in an online community is easier than alternative approaches, such as face-to-face meetings. • There is a well-founded assumption that something beneficial, for the members as well as the firm, will result from participation.
Online conferencing	Synchronous technology can help facilitate meetings by people who are separated by distance. The technology offers many enhancements over traditional conference calls, including the capability of combining voice, graphics, audio, live video, and the sharing of software applications.

Table 5.2 *(Continued)*

Rich media delivery	The technology allows more media options to be delivered than may be possible with just a browser. Through the use of specialized plug-ins, full-motion video and presentation slides can be synched to a speaker's voice to allow a presentation to be delivered as if it were live. Eloquent (www.elequent.com) is an example of a company that specializes in this service.
Preservation	Key events and other unique situations can be recorded, then accessed and played back. This ability to archive actual events and make them available to anyone, anywhere, and at any time is a boon to knowledge management. Want to hear and see a presentation by a distinguished researcher who has since retired? How about a feel for the company's history by seeing the major events over the last few years? An industry briefing, an analysis of a competitor, or a major report on the state of the business that you couldn't see because you were with a customer is now available to you at your convenience.

Many of these features can be combined for more complex applications, and you may have noticed that of these seven uses, the last two are really asynchronous applications that use the synchronous technology. So it's probably not the best idea to think of synchronous and asynchronous learning as separate. They are more like points on a scale of interdependence between the expertise (instructor or the content) and independence (e.g., individual control) in learning. If thought about this way, synchronous technology has a key role to play in your e-learning strategy. If simply used to create a different way to deliver classroom training, especially if this is your *primary* e-learning application, you really haven't cracked the potential or the promise of e-learning at all.

> **"The truth is that, properly used, technology can extend education beyond the four walls of a classroom and help students collaborate. But merely using [technology] to broadcast lectures is a bogus approach that lacks the social richness and interaction of the classroom experience and will never be a substitute for it."**
> **Mohanbir Sawhney, professor of e-commerce, Northwestern University[4]**

Killer Apps in E-Learning

Which brings us to the ultimate opportunity for e-learning—to create *killer apps*—those e-learning applications that are so effective and innovative that they redefine e-learning in your organization by setting the bar higher and raising the value that e-learning delivers.

The original justification for e-learning was to make learning better, faster, and cheaper. These are still noble reasons for building and deploying an effective e-learning strategy. Certainly you want people to learn more, and to learn it faster and at less cost than before. This improves productivity. Using technology to deliver the same classroom training that you've always delivered may meet this criterion, but is this all you want to accomplish?

Everyone is working toward similar goals, including your competitors. Breakthrough applications—killer apps in e-learning— give you a quantum leap in learning and in competitiveness.

The development of performance support in the late 1980s was an e-learning killer app. So is the development of knowledge management solutions. The ability to create totally absorbing and authentic simulations changed the nature of online training. Building learning architectures that leverage all of your e-learning and traditional learning assets can result in killer applications if you ensure that each component works seamlessly with the others and that the sum of the combined architecture is significantly greater than the individual parts. No doubt new technologies and new thinking about learning will result in killer apps we haven't thought of yet.

You don't have to reinvent learning to create a killer app. You just have to create a solution that fundamentally changes the game and raises the bar—inside or outside your organization. You will not succeed every time, but just by thinking "killer app," you'll find yourself aiming higher. In order to accomplish this goal, you'll need to look beyond the applications themselves to the environment in which they'll be used. Infrastructure, culture, support, organizational design, talent, change management, and other issues must be addressed. We'll do that next.

An E-Learning Journey

by Maddy Weinstein, Merrill Lynch

Where We've Been Says a Lot About Where We're Going with E-Learning

IN THE MID-1970S I HAD THE PRIVILEGE of beginning my e-learning journey at Control Data Corporation working on courseware designs for the new PLATO system. I didn't know much about using technology to deliver training at the time, but I was in good company since few people, back then, had the experience of using computers to enhance learning. While there were a few notable successes and a fair amount of experimentation in the works, it really was an industry in its infancy. There was a great deal of excitement for the potential of technology's role in radically altering learning paradigms, and my colleagues and I knew we were on the bleeding edge of the way things would be done in the future. We weren't exactly sure how things would turn out, but we knew we were onto something big. Now, with the advantage of over twenty years of hindsight—even with our grand dreams—we underestimated how much the future of education and training was impacted by new technologies.

By the time I arrived in the Merrill Lynch Training Group in 1979, the firm had just begun experimenting with PLATO and there was a sizable commitment to using new learning technologies to address the training needs of employees in several hundred locations around the U.S. We had several courses in development and had built a small learning center to house our terminals. Distributed, remote-access training would come a few years later. While small in number, we had an incredibly talented, enthusiastic, and passionate group of instructional designers and developers who were dedicated to redesigning the delivery and experience of learning. With a couple of years of computer-based training (CBT) under our belts, we knew that technology would be a big factor in learning. We experimented with student response systems, innovative classroom environments, new approaches to instructional design, and other emerging ideas. Our first project provided the perfect opportunity to build a program that was different than the traditional lecture-based and drill-and-practice formats. The results of our efforts were two terrific self-contained courses that engaged the learner in an interactive manner. The program was "gamelike" in format, and learning shifted from a passive experience to a proactive one. Of course, by today's standards the level of interaction was minimal, but we were thrilled. We went on to introduce CBT into the mainstream business; into environments where people already used computers for work—but this was the first time they used them for learning. We could see that people really liked learning this way, and deployment across the firm quickly became our next challenge.

Because our initial program required CBT in one room of our training center, our first attempts at deployment called for custom-crating the system and shipping it to our branch offices. The idea was decent but our deployment plan was shaky—the hardware took a beating. In the end we learned a lot about influences on learning—namely, *how* environment affects learning, and *what* it takes to fully engage the learner. We envisioned that technology would evolve to take learning to the desktop; so we began to think not only about the learning program, but the learning environment and the integration of technology with traditional training methods.

When we conducted live classroom programs, we worked very hard to create value for our employees who left their workplace and came to the training center to learn and develop new skills. We also understood that many of our classroom courses were strictly fact- and information-based, and that live training alone is generally an inefficient way to learn this type of material. Without level-setting participants' knowledge, learners are frequently not a homogeneous group—they have various levels of knowledge and skill set. The good news is that technology can be leveraged to present information and prepare people for more skills-focused, live training. It also enables us to raise the bar on the base-level knowledge of our employees before they come to the training center. Afterward, by gathering information from employees on *how* they're using what they've learned, capturing all of the additional learning that's going on in our branch offices, and enabling them to stay in touch with each other, we can create an online learning center where everyone shares what they know. This extension of the learning experience is very important for us.

Although our financial consultants have a very sound foundation of knowledge in financial services, some products and services for specific client needs are extremely sophisticated and may not be used often. When financial consultants meet with clients who have these specific needs, they should be able to go online and get the latest information that's of particular value to those clients. Information on the intranet enables us to better meet the needs of our employees and, in turn, our clients. If a financial consultant is meeting with a client and the topic of discussion is related to material covered in a program that he or she attended several months ago, the key concepts may be remembered, but most likely some of the finer details may have been forgotten. We need to provide online access to the information in our training programs long after the programs are over. Consequently, a lot of what we're dealing with is the structure and classification of information, and we're getting much better at that. It's not just a learning issue; it's a knowledge management issue as well.

Ultimately, however, leveraging our long-held belief that continuous learning is critical, creating a real environment for that to happen is our biggest challenge. Financial consultants and client associates are our competitive advantage, and we need to provide them with leading-edge capabilities. To do this they must have robust remote-access training so they can learn wherever they are, whenever they want. Within the last several years we have built a technology platform that delivers information to everyone's desk, and leveraged that platform to deliver an intranet site called the Learning Network. This Web site offers our employees hundreds of interactive courses, information, resources, interviews with successful peers and colleagues, and quick tips, so that they can access information "just in time," at their convenience.

We also need to deal with the fast-paced nature of the job and the fact that taking time out for learning is often difficult. Our employees believe that continuous learning is critical, too. We're getting more and more requests for learning opportunities, especially e-learning, but we need to do more to help them take advantage of it. As we continue to grow and hire increasingly technology-proficient employees, e-learning will become second nature.

Due to continuous changes in the financial services business, we need e-learning capabilities that enable us to respond instantaneously and appropriately to changes in the marketplace, government regulations, and other events. It's not just about effectiveness; it's about efficiency too. We developed a good balance between the human interactions so essential to our training center and the e-learning programs we delivered to everyone's desktop. Equally important was that we used these new capabilities for our own learning as well. While classroom training, featuring "talking heads," can be inefficient, it is very effective if you take the learning to the next level. Online training can offer prerequisite information prior to

coming to a classroom program. During the live training, participants can then practice what they learned in role-plays and facilitated discussions. Selecting the right delivery strategy and media and
matching them to learning needs is key. There are times when it's
important to get away from the workplace to learn, but it's also exciting to learn in the environment you're working in. Finding the right
balance in terms of location is critical.

Over the years, we experimented frequently and learned a
great deal. Sometimes what we learned was very powerful, and
sometimes it was not always necessarily what we were looking for.
So we've come a long way in making our training center a true
learning environment—now we have to do the same for all our
branch offices.

For organizations that are in the early stages of their own
e-learning journey, here are some basic operating principles that
have worked well for us. First, begin with a solid understanding of
who your learners are, what they need to know, and what they
need to be able to do in order to excel. Second, work hard to have
a solid understanding of the strategy, direction, and goals of the
business—all the time—and reflect the learner and the business in
the programs that are built. Third, understand your role as a culture builder. A learning culture is essential for success. And finally,
be mindful that the training organization must be a learning organization. You have to practice what you preach.

Merrill Lynch is an organization that has valued learning from its
earliest days, and we are committed to hiring the very best people
and training them well. Designing programs to meet the needs of
employees and businesses is a key part of our legacy, and every single
person here recognizes that we are only as successful as our people
are excellent.

Madeline A. Weinstein *began her career as a junior high school teacher.
She spent the last two decades at Merrill Lynch in positions including
instructional designer, director of training, and most recently as senior vice
president for Merrill Lynch's Business Innovation Group, which develops the
integrated resources necessary to implement the business strategy of the firm
and directs the development and implementation of Merrill Lynch's training
programs and technology-based learning platforms. Her current position is
director of corporate marketing for Merrill Lynch and Company.*

PART
III

Organizational Requirements for E-Learning

CHAPTER

6

Building and Managing an E-Learning Infrastructure

"On the Internet, content may be king,
but infrastructure is God."

Tom Kelly
Vice President, Worldwide Training,
Cisco Systems, Inc.

"Yes, God is alleged to have created
the world in six days, but He didn't have
an installed base to work with."

Don Tapscott[1]

U P TILL NOW THIS BOOK'S EMPHASIS has been
on expanding our notion of what learning—and e-learning is—and
how it can be made better. Following this chapter, we'll concentrate

on organizational issues that can make or break an e-learning initiative. But for all that's been said about e-learning, or will be said, the fact remains that none of this would be possible without the Internet. So while it's not possible to go into great depth on every aspect of e-learning technology, there are some important technical and infrastructure issues that must be considered. And now is the right time to consider them.

You Cannot Begin Without Access ... or a Strong Partnership With IT

Of course, no e-learning strategy will be viable if people can't get to the Web. At its basic level, access simply means everyone (or at least most people) can get online. If people do not have basic access, nothing else matters—you cannot move forward until people can actually get to your programs. This is not just for the Internet, but the corporate intranet as well. Access must be reliable. If you can get the Web to everyone, but your infrastructure is unreliable (always going "down"), or you're using an unreliable Internet service provider (ISP), your users will become very frustrated, very fast. Going further, access must be available where the workers are. In large corporate buildings with a sophisticated infrastructure, access is usually not a problem. In smaller facilities some network architecture is necessary to connect people to the corporate web. But if people also work from home or on the road, access means enabling them to log on as well.[2]

If the level or speed of connectivity is different for different groups of people (e.g., broadband vs. dialup), the content (e-learning, knowledge management, or any business resource, for that matter) will have to be adjusted for the level of access available to a particular user (or you'll have to improve the level of connectivity). If connectivity can't be upgraded at least in the immediate future, you may have to create two versions of the content, one with richer media and greater features, and one that is simpler and more text-based. Or it may mean just creating the simpler version (focusing on the "lowest common denominator") until the access bandwidth improves for everyone (the deployment of broadband technology is speeding up). The challenge for e-learning developers is not so much building products for the high-bandwidth users, but rather, building effective programs for the low-bandwidth users. An in-depth understanding of instructional design and the proper use of multimedia are essential in making the right decisions here. But it is very possible to build a rich and rewarding instructional or information experience in a low-bandwidth environment.

Enabling access is not the function of the training department—it is the function of the information technology (IT) department and the CIO. It is their job to see that the Web reaches everyone, and it is their job to build a reliable technical infrastructure that makes connectivity possible and easy. While training departments should have enough technical expertise to talk to and work with the IT department, it is wasteful for a separate infrastructure to be built for e-learning; the costs for maintaining the expertise, technology, and other aspects of a separate delivery system would quickly overwhelm it. Given a choice of using the mainstream corporate infrastructure for e-learning—even if there are some restrictions placed on that usage or some controls imposed by the IT organization—or building separate e-learning infrastructure components, it is almost always better to leverage the corporate technology infrastructure.

A particular issue around access is how to support the e-learning needs of employees who don't use a computer on the job—people who are in the field, on an assembly line, in an installation, a technical or maintenance mode where they move around a lot, etc. As the Web becomes more portable and wireless and as Internet connectivity is built into systems other than familiar computers, this issue is lessening. But still, some people (e.g., retail sales, food service) may need access through special kiosks, workstations, or learning centers located as close as possible to where they work, perhaps supplemented by access at home. The degree to which a company responds to this problem depends on how many employees are impacted and the degree to which Web access (and e-learning access) is necessary for the work they do.

Related to the infrastructure issue is the platform issue. When Merrill Lynch wanted to launch its Learning Network, the training professionals who managed this e-learning component had a fundamental decision to make. They knew that if they launched within the firm's primary platform, TGA (see Chapter 4), there would be some limitations on the types of Web-enabled features that would be available.[3] But they would have immediate reach to the entire community of FCs and CAs, and they would be integrating e-learning with the firm's primary business tool. If, on the other hand, they launched the Learning Network as a separate Web-enabled service, they would either have to force users to leave TGA in order to access training or provide a separate PC simply for e-learning which *they* would have to administer. Their decision: place the Learning Network on TGA and live with some limitations for a while. In this way they accomplished a very important goal—the integration of the learning platform into the work platform. In the end, the common platform/common infrastructure argument made the most sense for the firm.

Using the corporate platform rather than building a separate e-learning delivery system is actually a benefit for the training organization in two ways. First, e-learning can "ride" on the infrastructure practically for free. Since it is relatively inexpensive to add more memory, e-learning simply fills that extra capacity. Second, it drives the resources and focus of e-learning professionals back to their real competency: creating high-quality learning and information programs. But be careful—you don't want e-learning programs placing more demand on the infrastructure than it can handle. For example, multimedia elements take up more bandwidth than text or graphics. If the system is not ideally configured, this could slow down other business processes. So it's important that the capacity be carefully managed. Thus, a strong, compatible, forward-looking, and mutually beneficial relationship between e-learning and the IT organization is absolutely essential for e-learning to be deployed and to thrive.

The Fall and Rise of PLATO: How Advances in Technology Almost Doomed One of the First Real CBT Systems

One of the earliest forms of computer-based training was PLATO.[4] Invented more than 35 years ago by a graduate student at the University of Illinois, PLATO was a mainframe-based system that required its own proprietary hardware and software. The educational programs on the system were good enough that, in its earliest years, it become a dominant CBT platform. In the early eighties, the system quickly became commercialized under its new owner, Control Data Corporation, which at the time was a major supplier of mainframe computers, so the PLATO system seemed a natural supplement to the mainframe business. Even then some businesses were thinking that learning could be a value-added offer for customers.

But events overtook PLATO's leadership in the market. The advent of personal computers and PC software opened up new opportunities for competition. Soon, CBT on floppy disks were being produced that were, in many ways, equal in quality to PLATO. But they were less expensive and began to take advantage of the new, easier-to-use, customer-friendly (at the time), personalized platform that the PC (and the Macintosh) represented. As a mainframe company, Control Data either didn't see the PC revolution coming, thought it wouldn't last, or assumed that mainframe technology would continue to provide a competitive edge. Perhaps they saw PLATO only as a means to sell more computer hardware. Whatever the reason, they were wrong.

PLATO was near death because it required expensive proprietary technology, both hardware and software, that couldn't be used for other purposes.[5] It was inconsistent with the direction computer technology was taking. It required a proprietary authoring language (TUTOR) that, along with proprietary tools of other fledgling systems, fragmented the market so that no industry standard could emerge. Although it was powerful in its day, TUTOR was difficult to learn and limited in its functionality (remember, it was designed for a mainframe). And because of this platform, PLATO could not offer many of the newer features that gave PC-based software the edge, such as a graphical user interface (GUI), color, graphics, multimedia, etc. Users, both training professionals and students, abandoned the system. Control Data no longer exists, and neither would PLATO if a small company didn't see an opportunity to turn it around.

TRO Learning, Inc.,[6] a small Chicago-based company, purchased PLATO and began a multi-year effort to turn it around. They replaced the closed, inflexible platform with an open system based on standard technologies. Recognizing that legacy code can kill you unless you're aggressive in dealing with it, the company completely recoded the operating software, upgraded all aspects of the courseware, and emerged with an efficient set of object-oriented authoring tools that are compatible with the Web. They created high-quality testing capabilities and a new set of computerized tools that enabled higher-level learning around problem solving, complete with intelligent coaching. And they surrounded the system with a comprehensive training management system. The goal: to reinvent PLATO as a high-quality learning platform that is totally compatible with the same technologies that people are using for every other computer application, and to eliminate technology as a barrier to using the system.

It's also interesting that in addition to an aggressive technological transformation, PLATO was transformed instructionally, benefiting from new advances in instructional design, effectiveness assessment, and quality assurance. This represented a rethinking of the nature of learning, moving from predominately tutorial (drill and practice) approaches to broad-based interactive simulations, with tutorials in a supporting role. In addition, the learning architecture was expanded to include help in curriculum planning, professional support to help teachers, and consultation on instructional design, curriculum integration, and technical support. Today PLATO is a leading educational software supplier for the adult and young adult market (i.e., schools and colleges, with corporations as a secondary market) that is moving quickly to the Web.

This story serves as a good example of how an inappropriate infrastructure almost killed a leading learning system, and how rethinking that technology, and the surrounding environment, rejuvenated it. It's not just the quality of the program that matters. Beyond effectiveness, there's also the "seamlessnees" with which the technology can be integrated into mainstream business and end-user systems, and how adaptable that technology is going forward.

Learning Portals

Once most employees have access to the Web, the next step is to enable them to quickly and easily find e-learning and non e-learning solutions easily. One of the best ways to do this is through a learning portal. A learning portal is a Web-based, single point of access that serves as a gateway to a variety of e-learning resources on the Web (Internet, intranet, or both). Using a knowledge management approach, a learning portal can access and distribute e-learning information, programs, and other capabilities to employees. And, it can bring order and easier access to an ever-increasing array of information and learning choices.

There are really two types of learning portals: those you can buy and those you build. In Chapter 2, a number of commercial e-learning portals were listed (there are many more). These exist on the public Internet as e-businesses, but many can be "installed" inside a corporate intranet. The most important point here is to clearly separate content from infrastructure. Determine if you are interested in the portal's functionality, but not the content (e.g., courses and other resources) that may come with it. If this is the case, work with that firm to separate the two in order to get a complete and comprehensive look at the capabilities of the portal alone. Also remember that portals may be built once but they are maintained forever, so be sure to build in easy maintenance and upgradability.

Learning portals can also be built for a particular internal application: to suit the very specific needs of the business and fit nicely with the emerging e-learning strategy. The portal should be designed with a specific learning management system (discussed next) in mind, so that access (the portal) and functionality (the system) work hand in hand.

New capabilities allow users to personalize either all or part of the portal to meet their needs and interests (to experience this, go to www.yahoo.com or any other Internet search engine and set up your personalized portal, e.g., myYahoo!). This allows users to specify links and content that are important to them, while at the same time allowing the company to "push" required corporate and organizational content to the site. This balance and flexibility is almost always very well received by users. Besides a navigational role, portals can serve as a launching point for business applications, content searching, discussion and collaboration, workflow tools, and other resources and services.

How many portals does the organization need? In the rush to the Web, it's likely that many training organizations and other groups have already built portals, or are in the process of doing so. There might be a sales training portal, a technical training portal, a management training portal, and so on. There could also be multiple portals in the same curricular area. For example, different product lines or business units in a company may have their own sales organizations, complete with their own sales training programs, with each requiring a portal. In some cases this "portalmania" is more of a marketing activity than an access activity, with each training organization trying to get exposure on the corporate Web. It often represents deeper problems, such as multiple (and incompatible) registration systems, redundant content and e-learning products (either internally built or purchased from vendors), and a general suboptimization of the entire learning function of the firm. This is an important issue because the resulting chaos represents not just a lack of coordination, but a fundamental breakdown of a comprehensive e-learning strategy.

The response to this problem, ideally, is *one* corporate learning portal, that can be personalized to the needs of each user. This is done through user profiles that the portal "reads," and then presents instruction, or information resources in line with that profile (many knowledge management systems have this capability). In this way, employees will have one place to go to access their unique learning plan (i.e., "my learning portal"). Sometimes, in large organizations, multiple training organizations will insist on their own portal. This is often more a political than an e-learning issue, but if it can't be avoided, at least these portals should be links off of one corporate site. If the ideal is not possible, then portals related to business units or topical areas can work. However, there must be a great deal of coordination and a central governing body to assure that they all use common systems and tools so that for the user, functions like registration, access to e-learning, online assessments, etc., are universal.

When employees access any one of these business unit-level portals and want to register for a course, for example, they should be linked back to a single corporate system.[7]

Finally, there will be efforts by everyone to get their learning portal link on the corporate intranet home page (which is a portal itself). Because so many groups are vying for "real estate" on the corporate home page, putting all these training organizations up there is unlikely. If the company has a single learning portal, the answer is simple: It gets a spot on the corporate intranet home page and the other learning sites link off of it. If there were no single corporate learning portal, one suggestion would be simply to build a "reference page" to all the training sites and provide that link to the corporate intranet home page. Common tools and resources, like a registration system or catalog, can be in the background, accessible from any of the training portals.

Using a Single Web Portal to Consolidate Employee Orientation at Prudential

Mergers and acquisitions. Downsizing and right-sizing. Recruiting and reorganizing. It seems no company is safe for long from recurring and massive shifts in employees. And with this movement of people—in, out, and across the business, comes the need for more effective, efficient, and timely orientation.

All of these major employee transitions have been a fact of life for the Prudential Insurance Company of America. For a long time the company saw itself as a collection of businesses, each responsible for its own staffing and recruiting. People were hired into one part of the company and oftentimes only received an orientation program unique to that business unit. Often, orientation was simply a short meeting in an auditorium, but just as often it was left to the individual manager. If employees wanted to learn about the overall company, there were inconsistencies—in content and technology. In order to achieve its vision to be a leader in the financial services arena, the company recognized the need to operate as a single entity, "One Prudential." The managers within the learning organization revised the orientation process to support this concept.

Relying on existing orientation programs, even with better coordination, was not the answer. Evidence pointed out that it often took months for people to figure out the whole company, with "word of mouth" the primary, yet often unreliable, vehicle for learning. So Prudential worked with CRK Media (www.crkmedia.com) to establish a single intranet portal, *Essential Prudential,* as the center of a new, corporatewide orientation initiative (see Figure 6.1). A single gateway to orientation information was necessary to accomplish this. And while different parts of the business still have important messages and information to disseminate, the central portal created consistency of information about the organization. Essential Prudential is one of the first online experiences for the new hire. It has links to information and tools about career development and performance management, facts about the company, corporate policies, benefits, administrative services, and business strategy. In addition, the orientation portal links to the company's new single training site, where corporatewide online training about the firm and its businesses will be universally accessible. Finally, in an effort to keep new hires engaged, and to assure that key content areas have been mastered, an interactive, online learning "challenge" guides each new hire in a simulation where she/he is asked to help other people learn about the company. (A good way to learn about something new is to ask the learner to teach it to someone else.) The "challenge" teaches employees how to use the entire Essential Prudential site so it can be a resource long after the orientation is completed.

The company has made a commitment to use more technology-enabled learning as new programs are developed. Prudential also developed two Web-based programs for their Corporate Literacy curriculum as part of their effort to get new employees assimilated more quickly into the company. Through this work, Prudential recognized two important things about the power of its own intranet. First, that it can be an invaluable tool for companywide orientation and corporate literacy education, and second, that to be effective, it must be designed in a way that lessens chaos and strengthens corporate identity. Creating a single orientation Web site and developing targeted Web-based programs are some of the ways that Prudential is leveraging e-learning as an efficient way to develop their employees.

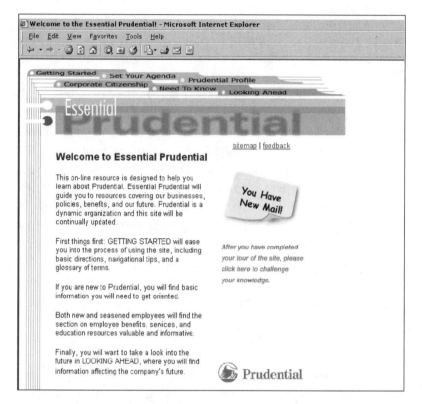

Figure 6.1 Prudential's single portal strategy was instrumental in improving the impact of their corporate orientation initiative. (Copyright 2000 by Prudential, Inc. Reprinted with permission.)

Learning Management Systems

While portals provide gateways to learning resources, learning management systems (LMS) provide the functionality. A learning management system uses Internet technologies to manage the interaction between users and learning resources. Why is this important? As all forms of learning become more costly, both in direct costs and employee time, management will want more information not only on the performance of the learners, but on *who* is learning *what*, how many qualified (or certified) employees are available for any specific assignment. In addition, a learning management system is essential for creating an environment where employees can plan, access, launch, and manage e-learning on their own.

There are many types of interactions and functionality that can be deployed and coordinated by these systems, including these eleven core capabilities:

1. *A common online course catalog.* This catalog can represent all the offerings across the business, organized by business unit, curricula, product, community, etc. Users can search on a number of dimensions and get information about the course, its format (classroom, online), duration, the content covered, target audience, prerequisites, charges (if any), location, etc. The advantage of a global online catalog, in addition to providing access to everything in one place, is that redundancies can be easily spotted, demand better managed, and utilization easily monitored.

2. *A common online registration system.* Registration can be for classroom and online training, and can include selecting specific times or locations, paying fees (if any), seeing a class roster, moving, canceling, or changing a registration, and documenting completed training for credit.

3. *An up-front competency assessment tool.* The system can include diagnostic tools, including pretests that allow potential learners to assess their readiness for a given learning activity. They can also assess their learning requirements against a competency model, and even allow managers and peers to conduct similar assessments (with proper confidentiality safeguards) so that they gain insight into key developmental needs. Such a tool could also generate a personalized learning plan for each employee (who should then review it with his/her manager or coach prior to implementation).

4. *The ability to launch and track e-learning.* The system can access e-learning programs and launch them for the learner, making sure the computer is properly configured (hardware, software, plug-ins, etc.) for the program (and installing selected components if necessary). In addition, the system can track the learner's progress through the experience (see the discussion on interoperability and standards, which follows).

5. *Learning assessments.* The system can provide a robust evaluation component that can assess the level of skill or knowledge (learning) attained by the user—based on participation in the learning experience. It can provide additional developmental feedback, even altering the learning plan, based on this feedback.

6. *Management of learning materials.* Instead of printing instructor and student materials each time a course is offered, the system can maintain a library of these materials that users download right before the learning experience begins. With careful monitoring, this ensures that these materials are kept up-to-date and accessible for current and former students.

7. *Integrating knowledge management resources.* In addition to classroom and online courseware, the system can point users to specific KM resources based on their specific needs. In other words, the system can deploy information as well as instructional recourses. For nonelectronic products, the system can support a fulfillment function; for example, enabling learners to order non-Web materials through the system and having them shipped directly to their work or home location.

8. *Organizational readiness information.* The system can act as an information dashboard on the competence of specific communities or the employee body. When senior management wants to know, for example, how many people have had training in a specific programming language, they can query the system. This helps in strategic workforce decision making. It can alert management to an under- or oversupply of specific talent and where that talent is located (or should be located), and help them decide what additional training or recruiting efforts are needed to ensure that this particular competency is sized and positioned appropriately for the business. The same benefits can be delivered to line managers to help them give better feedback and coaching to their people.

9. *Customized reporting.* The ability to query the system for standard and unique *Web-based* reports related to e-learning,

and workforce development in general, is important if management is to get the most informational benefit out of the data stored in the system.

10. *Supporting collaboration and knowledge communities.* The ability to build, maintain, and manage knowledge communities (member information, recommended learning programs for the community, discussion or chat facilities, links to advisers and coaches, etc.) is essential.

11. *Systems integration.* The learning management system must work seamlessly with the corporate HR and other systems the company uses to run the business. At the high end this would include ERP (enterprise resource planning) systems from PeopleSoft, SAP, Oracle, etc. But it also means working with smaller systems, even home-grown ones. Compatibility with the firm's e-mail, scheduling and other productivity software is also essential.

There are dozens of learning management systems in the marketplace.[8] So many that building one from scratch is not necessary in all but the most unique circumstances. Some of the systems have more limited functionality, for example, focusing more on catalogs and registration, or exclusively on e-learning. Others are more comprehensive (and perhaps more expensive). Most are installed on a corporate intranet, but an increasing number are provided via an Internet-based service that is still secure and designed exclusively for a particular client (an *extranet*). While this arrangement provides a great deal of learning management functionality without committing to purchasing the system, the degree of customization and control is more limited (as response times may be, for example, because the product is on the public Internet). The key is to select a system that's right for the business—its size, deployment, budget, sophistication, etc. When evaluating vendors, here are 23 more technical questions to ask of them and their products (see Chapter 10 for more on generic vendor evaluation). All questions should have a *yes* answer except as indicated:

1. *Authoring tool neutral.* Will the system manage e-learning programs built with any of the major authoring tools equally well?

2. *Vendor neutral.* Will the system manage e-learning programs produced by all of the major vendors, especially if they adhere to emerging standards? (More on this later in the chapter.)

3. *Browser neutral.* Will the system work virtually the same on the latest Microsoft Internet Explorer and Netscape Navigator browsers?

4. *Platform neutral.* Does the system have versions that will run on any common back-end platform, such as Windows NT or Unix?

5. *Client-side software.* Other than browsers and plug-ins, is there any additional client-side software required? (Look for a *no* answer.)

6. *Plug-ins.* Does system use industry standard plug-ins that are readily available without a fee (even better, the system helps the user install the plug-ins)? A plug-in is a piece of software that enhances the capabilities of the Web browser, expecially for interactivity and multimedia use.[9] Examples of plug-ins include Shockwave and Flash (from Macromedia, www.macromedia.com) and RealPlayer (from Real Networks, www.real.com). There are many others. They are normally downloaded from the vendor Web site and then installed on the PC.[10] Some popular plug-ins are now preinstalled with a browser, and in many corporate intranet environments, supported plug-ins are made available through a corporate license.

7. *Scalability.* Can the system easily scale in size to meet the growing demand of users and the increasing number of users?

8. *Firewall.* Can the system serve clients outside your company's firewall, if necessary? Can it import data through the firewall, if necessary?

9. *Interface.* Is the system's interface easy and intuitive for both administrators and end-users?

10. *Registration.* Does the system register all forms of training equally well? Does it do it in real time (confirmation, seat allocations, student notification)?

11. *Tracking.* In addition to launching e-learning programs, what level of tracking of user activity and performance

does the system provide or support? (The more, the better—a minimum of course start and stop, completion, time in course, pre- and posttesting, credit policy.)

12. *Personalization.* How well does the system enable users to customize the interface and their learning paths to meet their unique profile?

13. *Testing.* How good is the system's test development engine? (Look for a more robust test engine, for example, one that has multiple testing scenarios, random item generation, and other features that provide flexibility in test design and administration.)[11]

14. *Speed.* Does the system respond adequately when used in a dial-up mode?

15. *Communications.* Does the system use the Web and company e-mail to communicate with users?

16. *Security.* Does the system have appropriate security protocols to protect users, but, at the same time, can it be modified to seamlessly interface with standard corporate intranet security arrangements (i.e., no unnecessary security "hoops" to jump through)? Does it allow different levels of access based on administrators, users, designers, etc?

17. *Upgrades.* Does the system allow for easy upgrades when new capabilities and modules are announced?

18. *Technology.* What technology or architecture does the system require (e.g., NT, Unix)? Does the vendor provide the server and related technology, or is that the customer's responsibility?

19. *Vendor.* Is the system's vendor stable and easy to do business with?

20. *Implementations.* What other companies are using this system? (Can you speak with them?)

21. *Support.* What is the level of support provided by the vendor? Who handles database repair and maintenance? How are version control and upgrades managed? How long is the warranty, and what are the charges and commitments for nonwarranty support? Does the vendor provide *user* support (or is that the responsibility of the buyer)? Support can be an expensive proposition, with costs often unnoticed until it is too late.

22. *Curriculum planning.* Can the system help design and plan curricula and learning architectures?
23. *Cost.* What does the system cost per user? (Break this down into charges for installation, usage, licensing, maintenance, support, customization, and consulting.)

These technical questions, along with the core capabilities described just before them, should provide a good start in evaluating the right learning management system for your business.

There is also a relatively new field of knowledge management systems that are similar but not the same as learning management systems.[12] They assist organizations with building knowledge portals and structures so information can be systematically created and stored, easily found, and quickly disseminated to the right users. These systems focus on providing ways for people to create and submit information, tracking that information, and organizing it in a manner that can be searched and distributed. Many of these systems also have functions that help support online communities.

The Goal of Interoperability

So you've established access across your business, set up a portal structure that helps everyone find and make sense out of all your learning resources (classroom and e-learning), and installed a learning management system to provide the functionality you need. There's a great deal that can be accomplished just by stopping here, but a progressive e-learning strategy must pursue a goal of interoperability.

Essentially, interoperability describes the ability of your e-learning systems and products to work seamlessly with each other. This is not as easy as it may sound. Many e-learning products have been built with different tools. They are organized in different ways and are often bundled with their own learning management system. Imagine buying online training from three different vendors and adding products that you've built yourself. You might think that learners could take tests in each product and the system would analyze the test results together to determine performance levels. While it is true that most vendor products have a consistency across their own product lines (i.e., tracking across one vendor's products is fairly easy), there is little consistency across multiple product lines. So, what one vendor calls a test may not be seen similarly by another vendor. Or, while one vendor's products are programmed to collect data on start and stop times, another vendor's products may not have this capability. And although all vendors make their products compatible with standard Web browsers, this does not mean they can be managed or tracked easily outside of the architecture that came with the products. Thus, it has been advantageous for buyers to stick with one vendor for all their online learning. And vendors historically embraced the closed system approach as a way to capture a customer because of the huge costs that would be incurred to move to a competitor (it's why razor companies literally give away the razor, preferring to make money on the blades).

The analogy here is Microsoft Windows. Because it is the dominant operating system in use today, most applications are developed to work with Windows in a similar fashion. Non-Microsoft products work as well as Microsoft products. So there is interoperability. But Windows-based products don't work on Apple's Macintosh computers. A lack of interoperability. In the e-learning world, the situation has been more the latter than the former. And since the market is fragmented, no de facto standard has emerged so far.

But change is coming. Customers have begun insisting that using multiple product lines be as easy to use as a single product line. Content vendors have begun to recognize that it is now in their best interest to "open" their architecture so their programs can be more compatible with more of the learning management systems on the market, not just with their own. And the learning management system vendors are working with the key content providers to assure that the e-learning programs work on their learning management system. Initially, this was done through the exchange of the proprietary coding of each system. A learning management system company and a content vendor would make a business deal and would "certify" each other as compatible. The learning management systems that signed up the most content vendors would be in a better market position. Likewise, the more learning management systems that the content vendor was on, the more available their products would be.

Standards

More recently, the industry has been moving to a set of standards that can truly open up the e-learning management and distribution environment. These standards seek to label each major part of an e-learning product with the same tags so they will be universally recognized, and to embed this same tagging system into the tools that create these products so that they will be standardized as they're built.

There are many organizations working to develop e-learning standards. Here is a summary of some of the key groups, along with their Web addresses for more additional information:[13]

> *Airline Industry CBT Committee (AICC).* As the name implies, the AICC started out to create standards for the airline industry, and it was one of the first groups to venture into the e-learning standards issue. Its focus is on standards for online training, e.g., tests, lessons, modules, etc. (www.aicc.org)

> *EDUCAUSE Instructional Management Systems Project (IMS).* A vendor group also working to build standards for e-learning, based on the work of the AICC. The focus here is developing a set of tags that can be used universally to define each component of an e-learning environment, including user characteristics. (www.imsproject.org)

> *Advanced Distributed Learning (ADL).* This group, a federal government initiative, is also working on the standards issue.[14] (www.adlnet.org)

> *Alliance of Remote Instructional Authoring and Distribution Networks for Europe (ARIADNE).* An industry association focusing on European e-learning standards issues. (ariadne. unil.ch)

> *IEEE Learning Technology Standards Committee (IEEE LTSC).* This organization will actually accredit the standards for the U.S. that emerge from the other groups. While many vendors already comply with standards developed by AICC, IMS, and others, look for this body to certify and publish the official industry standards based on contributions by these and other groups. (ltsc.ieee.org)

Much of this standards work is based on using a more advanced Web development language. Currently, most Web sites are written in HTML (Hypertext Markup Language). But the new language, XML (Extensible Markup Language), developed by the World Wide Web Consortium (W3C) provides much greater ease of use by allowing more flexibility in content tagging, among other features. The development of XML should accelerate the standards work.[15]

Standards hold a great deal of promise for interoperability, but there are some concerns. First, awareness about standards is too low in the industry, especially among buyers. It's important for standards to be a key topic in dealing with a potential vendor, and that support for standards be a requirement for doing business. Second, it will require a great deal of work to get everyone (corporate buyers, vendors, etc.) on board with standards, which may require reengineering legacy systems, changing development processes, and altering business models. The transition to true interoperability will not happen overnight. Third, it is likely that when initial standards are published, they will likely center on more traditional training models, characteristic of CBT in many ways. There is agreement that more should be done around simulations, knowledge management, and other advanced e-learning approaches, but that may come later. So when working in more advanced areas of e-learning, there may not yet be suitable standards to use. The forth concern is standards acceptance. There is the question whether standards will ever get enough "traction." Ultimately, the marketplace will have a lot to say about standards—when this will happen is the big uncertainty. Nevertheless, the entire standards movement is important and worth watching closely.

Learning/Knowledge Objects

One of the more promising technological advances on the horizon is the building of e-learning solutions based on learning or knowledge objects. A learning/knowledge object is the smallest "chunk" of instruction or information that can stand alone and still have meaning to a learner. Instead of defining online training as courses, we could break down the course into its component parts—text objects that focus on a specific concept or skill, media (e.g., video, audio) related to a specific fact or topic, graphics and animations, assessments, etc. By creating *object libraries*, different products can use the same material, thus reducing redundancy and lowering costs.

For example, suppose you were developing a course on how television signals are transmitted from the TV studio to the home. Ideally, you might develop animation to show the process, a glossary of related terms, specific content that explains the process, and perhaps an explanation of the process by an expert. Once created, these objects are identified with tags that describe what they are, who built them, how and for whom they should be used, etc. When a learner signs on to a learning management system and identifies him/herself, the system looks for objects that match the needs of the learner and assembles them into a meaningful program. If the learner is new to the field, the number and sequence of the objects may be different than if the learner was an expert.

Now suppose another developer in another part of the company also has a need to explain this process—not in a training course but in a customer presentation. Instead of redeveloping these components, s/he searches the objects library and discovers existing material that can be used. Again, the specific need determines the number and sequence of the objects used.

There are several benefits of using learning/knowledge objects. First, costs are lowered because objects can be shared again and again, even for different purposes. Second, it enables real customization of learning, because the configuration of the objects can be dependent on the needs of the learner. Third, it enables e-learning solutions to be very quickly reconfigured based on changes in users or the business itself.

One easy way to think about learning/knowledge objects is to envision a page you're going to develop on your Web site. You access information on databases and document files and paste the content into your site. To make a point, you go into a clip art file and cut a graphic that highlights what you want to say and paste it in as well. Perhaps you also access a spreadsheet that was completed by a colleague and paste that into the document. You may add an audio or video file, or links to other Web sites. In the end, you've constructed something new with *existing* content objects from one or more repositories. At the same time, other people may be using the same objects for other purposes (within copyright laws). Sounds a lot like knowledge management!

Some companies will use an objects strategy not at the "chunk" level but perhaps at the lesson level. So for online training, each lesson in the lesson database is an individual object that can be called and configured to create *virtual* customized online training. Many development tools and learning management systems are building this capability into their products. Initially, each system will have its own process for creating and managing learning objects, so moving between different systems will be difficult, but like everything else in this industry, as standards and a common tagging model emerge, learning object technology will increasingly move toward complete interoperability.

The advantage of a learning/knowledge object approach can be seen in what Integrated Project Systems (www.ipspm.com) is doing in the area of project management training. After many years of offering a successful classroom-based project management curriculum that was customizable for each client, IPS sought to move some of its programs to the Web, in response to increasing customer demand. In working with e-learning solutions provider Informania (www.informania.com), IPS began to realize that simply putting courses on the Web would do little to differentiate itself in its marketspace. By breaking their project management content down into *reusable* learning objects, IPS was able to use its content for multiple purposes. The objects could be assembled into online training courses, but they could also be used to build knowledge management components or performance support tools. And, by linking the system with a competency model, learners would be able to receive just the content they needed in the format best suited for them. In this way, intellectual property of IPS could be used for multiple purposes and still provide the degree of personalization their clients desired. The flexibility of learning object technology—its ability to select, assemble, and deliver relevant content on terms defined by users—has resulted in a significant addition to the IPS current business model.

Don't Just Throw Stuff Out There!

Building an infrastructure for e-learning is primarily about creating an environment where users can easily access the learning products (instructional or informational) they need, when and where they need them. It is also about making the entire e-learning initiative easier and more cost-effective to manage. This cannot be achieved by just putting a lot of e-learning "stuff" on a server and hoping for the best. As shown in Figure 6.2, the various systems and tools must work together to ensure that e-learning can be deployed to all.

Content, sources, and formats are defined as learning or information objects and then combined into sound instruction or information. Then the material is delivered through a learning portal, either asynchronously or synchronously (see Chapter 5). Depending on the needs of the user/learner (perhaps based on an online competency assessment), the right training, information, performance support, and other resources are delivered to the desktop. The learner is also enrolled in the correct classroom programs, sequenced according to a defined learning architecture or competency model.

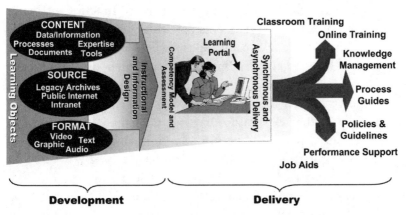

Figure 6.2 A sound deployment infrastructure is essential to manage and deliver traditional and e-learning solutions.

Some Notes About Authoring

There are a host of online training authoring systems on the market (e.g., Authorware, Toolbook, and Dreamweaver), some better than others, but most have similar functionality. The bigger issue is not what tools to use, although that argument seems to never end as tools constantly fall in and out of favor. Rather, it is *who* should author and what constitutes *quality* that matters more. When thinking about authoring, keep in mind these seven points:

1. *The claim that* anyone *can author online training is false, to put it mildly.* First of all, no matter what a vendor claims, you can't go to a three- or five-day tool-based course and instantly become an online training or multimedia author. There is no magic button that can be pressed to automatically create high-quality online training. It takes experience, mentoring, and a lot more training in instructional design to do that, especially if the aim is highly interactive, innovative training. If a program promises that you can "build courses like the professionals," or that it will "totally automate the instructional design process for you," it's time to get very skeptical.

2. *Using SMEs as authors is a risky venture.* If this is a new role for the SME, consider the value of diverting his/her expertise in this way—it may be a waste of the SME's time and take the SME away from the primary function of being completely up-to-date on a particular field or discipline. Of course, there are many experts who are also great trainers and have a natural affinity for creating good learning programs. But the argument that *any* SME can quickly learn instructional design—or worse, use an authoring tool in lieu of that expertise—may not hold up. Authoring is an essential part of e-learning development, and many tools have gotten better. But they still have a long way to go (if ever) before they can replace the talent and expertise of a seasoned instructional designer. If the SME does not have adequate instructional design experience and/or is not motivated to develop learning materials, the resulting

rework, delays, and a less effective end product will more than negate any cost savings anticipated by having the SME do all the work. Consider an instructional designer/SME team approach as an alternative.

3. *No authoring tool is good at everything.* Expect a continuing analysis of learning requirements vs. functionality. You'll find that you will need multiple tools to do the job and that you'll be upgrading your software constantly to keep up. The most sophisticated development shops have built their own tools to meet their unique requirements—a significant investment.

4. *Standardizing on one tool may not be a good idea.* While it may keep costs down, it also may restrict functionality, flexibility, and innovation too much to be an acceptable trade-off.

5. *Templates can help.* It is possible to make authoring somewhat easier by using templates—either provided with the tools or custom developed—that allow less experienced people to "populate" the authoring tool with content without a full understanding of how the tool works (a performance supportlike approach). But again, there are limits to how far this technique can go, especially for more sophisticated programs. In addition, if you're not careful all of your online training will start to look the same (visually *and* instructionally). More important, different kinds of learning require different instructional or information strategies, so a "one size fits all" template could be very limiting.

6. *Much of the more complex interactions and simulations are often beyond the capabilities of authoring tools.* Often, programming in languages such as C++ and others is required. To make the e-learning solution capable of running on the Web, additional work in HTML, XML, Java, and other tools are needed. Generally most people find tools they are comfortable with. But those who start off with training authoring software will sooner or later need more advanced systems—and the skills that go with them—as their needs become more advanced.

7. *Authoring is just one aspect of building an e-learning solution.* Version control and revision tracking is another. Testing, debugging, maintenance, and upgrading of the e-learning

program also require specialized software—and more train-ing for the author. These costs could add up to more than the cost of the original authoring over the life cycle of the product (unless it's a "use once—throw away" product).

For these reasons, and others, many organizations are seeking to outsource e-learning development. Even large companies that have internal development groups are beginning to partner out-side to manage increased workloads and utilize more experienced talent when necessary.

Key Questions to Ask About an E-Learning Infrastructure and Tools

When assessing the readiness of your infrastructure to support e-learning, here are seven fundamental questions to ask:

1. *What is the level of Web access throughout the company?* Do people have access outside corporate offices? Do they need it? Because high-speed connections are less of a problem, be sure to determine the slowest speed that must be accom-modated. This will impact what can be developed and delivered.
2. *What is the relationship between the training and the IT com-munity?* A good, mutually beneficial relationship is essen-tial.
3. *How collaborative and coordinated around e-learning are all the training organizations in the company?* An environment where organizations are working at cross-purposes or for their own self-interest is extremely detrimental to a sustainable e-learning strategy.
4. *Is there a comprehensive e-learning portal strategy in place?* How well are the portals designed, and how easy is it for employees to find and use them? If there are no e-learning portals, what are the plans to deploy them?
5. *Does the organization have a core learning management system?* If not, is there a consensus about how to proceed in this area? A *single* good learning management system is very

important to systematic management of e-learning; multiple learning management systems can cause chaos and confusion across all the e-learning efforts of the firm.

6. *Does the organization have a position on interoperability?* If not, is there a consensus about how to proceed in this area?

7. *Does the organization have the right talent, positioned in the right roles, to make the best use of its learning infrastructure and tools?* Despite all the technology available, it is still people who make it all work. Be sure not to sacrifice a talented staff for the impossible expectation of a totally automated e-learning system.

"What we must remember is that this new information technology is only the pipeline and storage system for knowledge exchange. It does not create knowledge and cannot guarantee or even promote knowledge generation or knowledge sharing in a corporate culture that doesn't favor those activities."
Thomas Davenport and Laurence Prusak[16]

7

The Four C's of Success: Culture, Champions, Communication, and Change

"It's not the strongest of the species who survive, nor the most intelligent, but the ones most responsive to change."

Charles Darwin

ONE OF THE MOST IMPORTANT TENETS of e-learning is that it bridges work and learning. While the best classroom experiences bring work into the learning environment, the best e-learning experiences bring learning into the work environment. Whether it's online training or knowledge management, the premise of e-learning is that it can be accessed anytime and anywhere it's needed.

This is a fundamental shift from the time-honored practice of going to school (i.e., the training center). Now school comes to you—at work, at home, and on the road. As practical as it seems, there is often overt and covert resistance to e-learning on the job. Some of this resistance comes from the business's front line (difficulty equating learning with work); other resistance comes from the company's senior leaders (difficulty appreciating the value of e-learning). There can also be resistance within training organizations (difficulty accepting e-learning as a legitimate form of learning). In order for e-learning to prosper in a business—to be sustainable—a strong learning culture is required. It's not just a climate that supports classroom learning or e-learning, but one that embraces learning as a whole—as an important activity of everyone in the firm. Organizations that are truly "learning organizations" quickly move beyond the "where" and the "how" of learning, concentrating instead on ingraining it into the work culture. Bottom line—e-learning cannot thrive without careful attention to the "four C's": a *Culture* of learning, *Champions* who will lead e-learning efforts, *Communications* that position e-learning's value, and an integrated *Change* strategy to bring it all together.

Building a Learning Culture

The failure of e-learning to get any traction in a company is often related to the quality of the initiatives themselves. But even the best programs deployed with the best intentions often create little lasting impact. Although a particular e-learning initiative may prove a success from a learning and performance standpoint, it's often viewed as a unique occurrence, certainly not replicable throughout the organization, and most certainly not something to replace what's always been done! What we see over and over again is "reinventing the wheel"—organizations studying and restudying e-learning and trying yet again to break down the traditional walls of training, often by building "new and better" e-learning solutions rather than tackling the real culprit: the culture.

Too often companies invest in new technology only to find that the existing culture won't support it. For e-learning to be successful, the culture must get beyond lip service to recognize learning as a valued part of what people do—a productive activity and not a waste of time. Building a learning culture is hard work. You have to overcome the perceptions that learning and work are different (and that work is productive while learning isn't), that learning takes place only in the classroom, and that learning and training are one and the same. Clearly, eliminating resistance and changing these beliefs is essential to building a learning culture, but how do you do it?

Think about it this way. From the viewpoint of resistors, e-learning not only doesn't make sense, it constitutes a high risk and a certainty of short-term costs with a vague promise of long-term gain. They may integrate e-learning into their current practice in ways that make sense to them from their *current* perspective (such as seeing e-learning through the "eyes" of the classroom paradigm). But this is missing the point of the innovation or distorting it so badly that the resulting benefits are minimal—and their skepticism about the long-term benefit is confirmed. They have the best intentions, but kill the innovation anyway.

Culture-Building Strategies That Don't Work

In the past, organizations have tried several approaches to build enthusiasm and support for learning. Some create an air of success when, in fact, the efforts have foundered. This has been most notable when training organizations seek to expand their influence. In their efforts to create enthusiasm for training (not necessarily learning) they tried to:

Give customers what they want. Organizations that embarked on a "retail" philosophy have created a customer-supplier model for internal training. They believe that the customer (i.e., employee) knows best and that their responsibility is to do the very best job of meeting the wants or needs of these customers. Many training organizations see the students as the customer. While serving customers is well-meaning, for the most part, the students in the classroom are really not the customers. The customer is the person who pays for the training, and in most businesses that is usually the organizational leader who controls the training budget. Furthermore, giving customers what they want may not necessarily be giving them what they need. For example, a training organization continues to offer project management training when it is clear that the company has enough project managers. Why? Because it's in demand—perhaps some business unit declared project management training as a requirement for promotion. No one was interested in what the business will do with all those surplus project managers, least of all the training organization. Should they offer courses in other areas that are not business related? As one executive said to me: "Do you mean that if employees wanted a course in basket-weaving, we should provide it?" Incredibly, the response from one training organization: "If they're willing to pay, we'll do it."

Create and distribute a robust course catalog. If a little training is good, certainly more must be better. That's the philosophy of those who embrace the approach of having something for everyone. Catalogs get fatter and fatter. We take our five-day course and we break it down. You can take a shortened version of the training in three days or two days, and for executives, a one-day briefing if you want. This can result in numerous versions of the same training, only "sliced and diced" differently (a redundancy issue), or the offering of programs that have minimal worth but are in hot demand (a value issue). This is often designed to drive more business to the training center on the false assumption that if your classrooms are filled you might have a learning organization.

Think of training as just another product and sell it. A lot of training organizations are getting into the mode that they are an internal business and have to sell everything they do in order to generate the revenue to stay in business. Instead of hiring instructional designers, they hire salespeople. This is a direct result of telling the company: "Look, you don't need to fund us— we'll fund ourselves." At some of these training organizations you'll find half the employees in that organization are involved in some form of selling. Account management, receivables, billing— all kinds of activities that have nothing to do with the mission they're charted to do.

In each of these three scenarios the focus is in increasing training activity. Not only does this fail to create a learning culture in the organization, it is also very risky for the training group. First, all the measures are inwardly focused. How many students, how much tuition, etc.? These are not the cost, quality, service, and speed requirements to which businesses must adhere. Second, it disengages the training function from the workplace by emphasizing the business performance of the training organization in isolation from the rest of the company. No matter how much money an internal training organization makes, it's really money that's transferred from other parts of the company. Somewhere along the line it's not how much business the training department did, but how much value it provided to the firm that will be questioned. To their detriment, many training organizations get caught up in their own "results" and forget to whom they are really accountable. As expenditures are more closely scrutinized, some major training organizations in both large and mid-sized firms have been drastically downsized, or shut down completely when they failed to adequately answer the "value" question: Why should we invest, or continue investing, in e-learning—what benefits will it bring to the company? In the end, training activity, even lots of it, does very little to instill a learning culture in the organization if the value proposition (the response to the "Why" question) is weak.

Here are other attempts to build a learning culture that have been tried with little long-term success.

Make training "free." Instead of selling it, how about giving it away? The problem here is not so much the free access to training, but that it is usually accompanied by little in the way of direction on who takes what. In most of these situations, the training budget is exhausted before anyone realizes it. Some people may have taken the training that's right for them, while others may have wasted their time on unnecessary training. Still others may have missed their opportunity altogether. But when the money runs out, don't think for a moment that people will stop demanding their "free" training. Free training can work if it is managed well—through competency models (following), and strong linkage to business needs, career development, and training paths. This will control the "demand" side of the equation.

Build competency models...but don't actually use them.
Competency models are becoming important in the development of precision learning systems—the type of system that directs the precise information and instruction to each employee based on his/her competency requirements. The problem is that most competency models sit in big binders and never get implemented into the overall assessment system. And since competencies are driven by changing skill requirements and the changing knowledge base, they're always changing themselves. No sooner is a competency model for a job completed than it needs revisions. Saying you have a competency model is pretty worthless unless you are actually using it.

Call yourself a "corporate university." While there's a lot to be said for elevating the visibility of learning in the organization as a way to build the right learning culture, just changing your name and adding a more lofty mission statement is not enough. The best corporate universities are fundamentally different from the training organizations they replaced (which begs the question of whether the term "university" is even appropriate). So if selling seats in the training center remains the major driver of your business, calling yourself a corporate university will quickly ring very hollow.

Move everything to technology. Decide to end all classroom training. Just close the classrooms, put everything on the Web, declare victory, and move on. We know this is not appropriate, and organizations that believe the use of technology will bring some sort of learning utopia to the business are kidding themselves. It's not even close to being that easy. The classroom, when used appropriately within a comprehensive learning architecture, has a very important role in the learning culture of a company.

Mandate training. When everything else fails, organizations think about *requiring* people to attend training. Strategies based on expressions like, "If they won't come to training, if they won't take our training, we'll simply force them to and that will build a learning culture," do not work. Sometimes training should be mandated, as in the case of safety, sexual harassment, insider trading, etc. But simply using a mandate to force people into the classroom may create a resentful culture rather than a learning culture.

The problem with all of these efforts is that they are focused on the training function. There is little effort to shape the world outside of the training organization. There's lots of effort to push a message onto the company, but little effort in engaging the company in that effort.

Culture-Building Strategies That Do Work

There is an emerging set of strategies that can help create a climate for learning. Instead of a training organization "push," these approaches are designed to "pull" the company into a learning mode, and as such, require collaboration outside the training organization and across the firm.

Make the coach or the direct manager accountable for learning. We like to say that employees are accountable for their own development. That's fine, but it should not take the responsibility away from the direct manager. Managers have a major role equal to that of the employee. They can meet with people before and after key learning events, helping them integrate new skills, knowledge, and ideas into the workplace. And they can foster their own small learning organization by providing time for sharing and discussion of ways to improve everything from morale to productivity. Build requirements for people development directly into managers' job descriptions and appraisals, and provide training for them on how to make this work.

There is no one in the company more influential than frontline managers—they can make organizational change easy or kill it outright. Robert Brinkerhoff and Stephen Gill[1] point out the problems encountered when trainers and managers are at cross-purposes. The attitude of trainers that "I can teach but I can't make anyone use what is taught—that's the manager's job," and the manager's view that "training is irrelevant if it contradicts my way of doing things," points directly to a culture problem that needs to be addressed up front. Once managers are on board with support for learning, you've cleared a major hurdle.

Focus at the enterprise level.   Cultures can be modified when there's enough critical mass of people wanting the change to happen. Working culture issues group by group can be frustrating and failure-prone. If the training and development community within the company is fragmented, work first to bring unity to the function, otherwise there will not be enough clout to change much of anything.

Integrate learning directly into work.   Wherever possible, make e-learning (and other forms of learning) a part of everyone's daily work activities. Simply taking time out to share new insights or problems is a start. Encouraging all employees to spend some time each day accessing information from the Internet and intranet, and providing forums that enable everyone to participate in discussions, helps solidify the learning communities that are the essential building blocks of a learning culture. But more can be done. Institute a process of personal and managerial assessment of each employee—not for appraisal purposes, but for developmental purposes—and then ensure that the resources to close performance gaps are made available to all who need them. Reward knowledge sharing and penalize knowledge hoarding. People who willingly contribute their knowledge and expertise can be recognized through financial incentives. Organizations can also create an environment that allows contributors to be recognized as experts and to "own" the content. When others see that knowledge sharing is a rewarded behavior, more will participate. If the incentives are well-designed, knowledge hoarders will be left behind. Their expertise will be eclipsed by others and they will soon realize that the only way to be recognized as an expert or leveraging what they know is by sharing it with others. If your business has an appraisal or compensation system that doesn't bring out this distinction, you need to improve it so it does. Creating an atmosphere of learning builds a strong new culture that has the momentum to displace the old.

Design well and certify where appropriate.   Learning cultures are influenced by quality learning products. This is especially true for e-learning, as it represents something new and untested. So make sure the quality is there. If you have quality programs, based on valid and implemented competency models, certification becomes a possibility. Certification is a performance-based assessment, as opposed to knowledge testing or credit hour models—what you can do rather than what you know or how many classes you've taken—although there are many certification programs based solely on these weaker criteria. Some jobs can benefit from certification because it provides a sense of accomplishment for the learner and a barometer of the capacity of skills for the firm. If done right, certification can be a valid predictor of job performance. And when people see that certification is tightly linked to jobs, performance, pay, and other recognition, they'll take notice and become involved. Many high-tech companies, such as Microsoft, Cisco, Lucent, and Oracle, have developed extensive certification programs, increasingly administered on the Web. Being a Microsoft, Cisco, Lucent, or Oracle "certified" technician or engineer is becoming a general entry-level requirement in the communications, computing, and other technology industries. Certification is impossible if you don't know exactly *what* people are supposed to do and how *well* they are supposed to do it.

Pay for knowledge.   We often talk about pay for performance, with top performers earning more than poor performers. But why not pay for knowledge as well? This is not simply an incentive for learning *anything* an individual wants to learn; rather, it is motivation for people to learn in areas that the firm believes will be useful in the future. If people take the initiative to learn new skills that can be directly applied to improve performance in a demanding business environment, isn't that effort worth recognition, maybe even monetary recognition? This is where a good certification program can be useful in setting the standards for a pay-for-knowledge strategy. Perhaps the reverse is even more of an issue. If the firm sends a message that building your own intellectual capital—capabilities that can help the company succeed—is not important, the "learning organization" can shut down.

Everyone's a teacher. There may be no better way to create a learning culture than to create a teaching culture, where everyone has an obligation to teach others. Whether as a formal classroom instructor, a seminar presenter, an e-learning designer, a knowledge management contributor, or a mentor, the experience of creating and delivering information or instruction is not only rewarding, it can change an entire firm's perspective on learning. Think about it: When was the last time your CEO taught a course at your training center?

Get rid of the training noise. Stop using jargon that continues the confusion between learning and training, and between information and instruction. Emphasis on tuition, registration, courses, and objectives can interfere with people opening up to new e-learning approaches.

Eliminate the ability to pay as a gatekeeper. The ability to pay for learning can certainly be a roadblock on the way to building a learning culture. How often do we say: "The training is available; here's how much it costs." In many companies, business units that are doing very well have the money to send their people to training. So training becomes a perk for the parts of the company that actually have the most money and are doing well in the first place. The business units that are not doing well may not have the money to send their people to training. They're the people who need it most, yet they're also the people who can least afford it. A learning culture can be nurtured by eliminating ability to pay as a barrier. Instead, target a more equal share of training opportunities where the business is weak, even if that part of the business can't afford to pay for it. By radically lowering delivery and access costs, e-learning breaks down this barrier.

Make access as easy as possible. Enable people to get to e-learning resources easily. This means placing key e-learning access points on the intranet pages people visit most. Don't rely on people remembering a variety of URLs or having to use search engines to find the particular online training or knowledge management site they are interested in. Even more innovative—extend access to learning to the home. This may create concerns about cost and security, but the advantages are often worth it. Delta Airlines and Ford have given computers and Internet access to all of their employees. Besides the obvious employee-benefit aspects of this initiative, these companies now have instant access to everyone in the company for communications and learning—including those employees, such as assembly line workers or flight attendants, who do not regularly work with computers. Furthermore, this will help build a Web-savvy workforce that will be more accepting of change brought on by new technology.

People embrace learning when they see direct relevance and benefit for them and when they sense support from the firm. When you hear: "We can't get our people to take the computer-based training. They don't want to take it...They don't do it... They don't like it," you are hearing more than a simple rejection of an e-learning product. The same is true for comments like: "When we bring people to the training center, we take them far enough away from their boss/job so that they'll pay attention to the training. If we do it over the Web, this won't happen. Therefore we need to keep the training center/classroom model." Either way, you are hearing the culture tell you that e-learning, or any learning for that matter, is not important.

Signs Your Senior Leadership May Not Be Serious About E-Learning

Organizational cultures and their leaders are reflections of each other. Building a culture that will embrace e-learning means building senior management support for that culture. There may be lots of activity, in terms of programs launched and money spent. But without support from the top, these initiatives have no "legs"—they just aren't durable enough to build the momentum and critical mass that's necessary to transform the organization into one that accepts e-learning, and learning in general, as a natural part of the firm's everyday work life.

How can you tell whether senior management is truly behind e-learning? How do you know if they are willing to back these initiatives up so they can be sustainable? How will you know if those at the executive level are committed as *champions* of these initiatives? While many senior managers say they support e-learning, it would be unwise to invest your resources and completely change your direction based just upon a statement of support. There are many cases where executives say they support a new initiative (whether it's e-learning or some other initiative), but their actions tell a different story. The following are telltale signs that what senior management says about e-learning may not be what they believe.

Work is assigned to people already overloaded or who don't have a clue. Giving this work to people who, because of their current workload or lack of experience, cannot possibly accomplish the goals of the e-learning initiative can be devastating to any e-learning strategy. Whether the basis for the assignment is a lack of understanding of what it takes to do this work (from a time or expertise point of view) or a failure to prioritize and eliminate work that is no longer necessary (thus freeing up time), this behavior can be disastrous, even if the people assigned are enthusiastic about it. Of course, even if the work is assigned to the right person or group, if leaders don't convey the message that e-learning is everyone's responsibility, there's a chance that those not directly involved will ignore it.

Support or directives are given without any money. While e-learning is very cost-effective, the initial work to get it going requires a significant up-front investment. Without the financial resources necessary to get e-learning initiatives going, they often wither on the vine. It's important to determine if this is a true budget issue (i.e., there really isn't any money to spare) or if it's a priority issue (i.e., money is allocated to other projects that might be curtailed to free up funds). Management support for e-learning is questionable at best if they are unwilling to help find the money that's needed.

During budget cutting activities, the e-learning budget is always cut first. This is related to the overall issue of money availability. But if you hear something like, "I really do believe in this, but the needs of the business come first," you have a problem. And the problem is compounded if most of the training and development budget "sacrifice" comes from e-learning, especially if the cuts are coming from the leadership of the business, and the leaders of the training and development functions cannot or do not intercede.

Senior managers refuse to learn anything about e-learning. Sometimes, executives are too busy to devote a considerable amount of time to learning about e-learning, or they don't have a deep enough understanding of the broader perspectives of what e-learning is. Leadership in e-learning doesn't necessarily have to come with e-learning expertise. But if executive disinterest appears less like a time or education issue and more like an obvious signal of lack of real support, or even fear, you may have a problem. This concern is compounded if no one on the executive's staff is interested, or if you can't find *anyone* at the top who wants to learn about e-learning.

> **"Tech-based learning has been slow to move up the corporate ladder, in part because older managers are less comfortable with computers and the Net than younger ones."**
>
> **Business Week[2]**

Leaves it to the team to make *all* the decisions. Compounding a disinterest in e-learning is the abdication of all decision-making to subordinates. This is different from having specialists on staff for advice and decisions of a technical or implementation nature, while strategy decisions remain in the hands of the leader. Together, the refusal to learn about e-learning and the deference of *all* decisions to others often represents a complete and destructive disengagement from the process.

Refuses to tell his/her boss anything about it. When leaders express support for e-learning, but then display behaviors that seem to indicate that they don't want anyone to know about it, there's a problem. It's natural for people to be hesitant about fundamental change and the level of risk they've exposed themselves to. But refusal to communicate can mask a much higher level of insecurity about e-learning and a lack of confidence in those who are working on it. The key is to differentiate between cautiousness associated with a new venture and an extreme need for self-preservation should something go wrong.

Does not assign any deliverables or accountability. When no actual deliverables are assigned and no consequences are articulated relative to an e-learning initiative, the perception becomes one of a meaningless exercise or "flavor of the month." Saying you're serious without defining the expected results and the rewards and consequences associated with the assignment can lead to insurmountable disbelief, and a subsequent unwillingness of senior managers to see the transformation through.

Believes that going to training is either a perk or a sign of a performance problem. Sometimes the wrong signals about the role of training can impact an e-learning strategy. If business leaders believe that training programs are a reward for good performance (i.e., "best workers") or only for those who need remedial work (i.e., "worst workers"), they will be less likely to support corporatewide, all-employee initiatives—e-learning or otherwise.

Approves other learning strategies that undermine e-learning. Be wary if the leadership says one thing ("I support e-learning!") but does another (e.g., builds more classrooms or purchases a popular but unneeded training program in an effort to generate "student days"). Without a rationale that signifies a broad-based, strategic approach, it's more likely that the decision maker is being influenced by different advisers, factions, or political pressures, and that a coherent, agreed-upon e-learning strategy is not in place.

Suggests that employee use of the Web at work is disruptive. When business leaders say they want to restrict employees' Web access at work because they'll engage in unproductive, non-work activities (such as visiting sports or entertainment sites), they are putting up a smoke screen. In almost all situations, employees who are likely to spend time on the Web instead of working are the same employees who would find reasons to "goof off" even if the Web wasn't around. Labeling this as a technology issue masks a probable management or supervisory failure. Concentrate on increasing access to the Web, not restricting it.

Helping Senior Managers Become
True Champions of E-Learning

It we're not careful about these signs, we're likely to think we have management support when we don't. This could lead to questions a few months later by the same managers who now say they never authorized the expense or didn't really understand what you were telling them in the first place. This creates tremendous credibility problems for future endeavors.

But how do you get senior managers to support e-learning? That's probably the number one question on everyone's list of issues, and with good reason. Without support at the executive level, it is highly doubtful that an e-learning initiative will succeed. The challenge is to move from just words of support to true ownership of the initiative. That means senior management will have to put some "skin in the game." Besides simply supporting e-learning, managers can show ownership through their vigilance—they can personally get involved in helping to lead the initiative, to make sure it goes the way it should. They can involve themselves in the experience, becoming "e-learners" like everyone else. But most important, they can pay for the initiatives. As sponsors, they will put up much of the financial resources to get e-learning off the ground. Like any investor, when you put up some of your own money, you have a vested interest in seeing the investment pay off.

Wishing business leaders would free up funds and support e-learning is not the same as making it happen. Here are seven ways to engage executives so their support will be genuine and long lasting.

1. Build a sound business case.   Any good business case must justify the investment in e-learning in three ways. First, that e-learning does in fact meet specific business needs of responsiveness to fast-paced change (speed of deployment, updating), support for front-line workers (availability and access where and when needed), and performance improvement (increased competence). Second, that it is more economical than other forms of delivery. And third, that the company recognizes the need to manage knowledge as an asset, not just a cost (i.e., what is the value of the firm's intellectual property? If it has no value, why do companies try so hard to protect it?). All of these justifications are required.

2. Use success stories. Senior managers want evidence that e-learning works. If it represents a new way of thinking for them, they will probably want more evidence than might be thought necessary. This is why finding opportunities for small successes is a good move. Just finding that one manager or one business unit that is willing to try something new can make all the difference. Often, these opportunities are in areas of the business that are in trouble and willing to try some radical new ideas to improve their situation. Or you just might find a risk taker who wants first-mover advantage in e-learning (he/she wants to get there first to have more control over future direction). Work carefully but speedily to demonstrate the effectiveness of e-learning in this unique situation, and then, when the positive results are in, showcase your work to a larger audience (always sharing credit with your sponsor/client).

3. Educate executives. This doesn't mean sending executives to school; few learn that way (which calls into question the way we do so much management training). What it does mean is letting senior managers learn how other organizations and companies are succeeding with e-learning. Identify those leaders whom you feel are most likely to come around and support e-learning, and provide opportunities for them to visit with their peers in other parts of your own business or at other companies (or invite leaders of best practices in other firms to visit your company) to see what e-learning can do. Give them some short business-oriented e-learning publications that address their chief concerns. Provide benchmarking data that indicates the efficacy of e-learning. Recommend a business conference where they can talk to their peers and experts about e-learning. Have them hear positive stories from people who have experienced e-learning themselves.

4. Coach executives. This is a little different from education. Here you are an adviser, helping the leader develop policy or strategy around e-learning. Some of the assistance you can provide includes:

- helping reprioritize learning initiatives
- creating the proper messages about e-learning
- preparing recommendations for the discontinuance of training and other programs that are no longer needed (this

includes preparing the people associated with these programs for the change)
- developing motivational and incentive strategies that support the change
- helping with the business case

5. Overcome prior perceptions. If you're inside the training organization, chances are you're perceived as responsible for classroom training only. Repositioning yourself in an e-learning framework from an online training perspective is challenging enough, but convincing people that you can do knowledge management (and performance support) work is even tougher. Again, having a success story to showcase is a real boost. But you may also have to take people from where they are and help them understand where you're going. So if you get enthusiastic support from a business leader for traditional CBT, don't say no, or "We don't do this anymore" so quickly. You may not find such a solid supporter elsewhere. See if you can begin with CBT but move to a more advanced strategy, educating your executive client along the way. It's okay to take one step backward if this will enable you to take many steps forward in the future.

Another useful strategy is to come at the issue from the perspective of the benefits of learning and e-learning. Talk about productivity, lower costs, etc., and deemphasize technology if you feel your audience is not ready for it. You may find more receptivity to a business approach than one centered on learning.

6. Work the politics. If you know a leader who's been pleased with the results from e-learning, ask him/her to spread the word for you with his/her peers. If you are a chief learning or knowledge officer, or have access to him/her, use the power of that office to set the tone about e-learning throughout the business. Training directors can also play a critical role by being the link between the operational issues of training (what they do) and the learning and development strategy of the business (what they can become). The key is finding and leveraging an e-learning champion—someone who is at the level of the people you need to convince. Peer-to-peer conversations can be instrumental in opening up the doors you need to get e-learning started and keep it sustained.

7. Ignore the disbelievers. Don't waste time trying to sell e-learning to those who don't want it or, worse, are bent on destroying it. Their resistance could be based on good intentions, genuine strategic disagreements, or on personal issues such as fear of losing power. Many come around when they see the benefits. When senior management sees something that works and can be replicated, they'll be more likely to jump on board. However, there will always be some people whom you cannot convince of anything. If they are disruptive, you may have to deal with them, probably politically through your champions (although I have seen more direct approaches, such as asking hostile participants to leave a meeting, which almost always adds to the credibility of the meeting for those who remain). But if they simply ignore you, return the favor. There's plenty of work to be done with people who are willing to try something new.

Leadership and Communication

In the end it all comes down to leadership. Whether you're on the front line or in a support position, in the executive suite or in the training organization, you need to find opportunities for leadership to emerge: leaders who can make a compelling case for e-learning and who can convince some groups to give it a try, leaders who are knowledgeable in the e-learning field but who also place the needs of the business at the center. Finding the right leader, or champion, is a critical step. Leaders must be able to chart a course without seeming dictatorial, and help the organization develop a shared vision about e-learning. They must also have the resources necessary to fund the e-learning initiative *and* the organizational clout to get it applied. The only thing worse than not being able to build a desperately needed e-learning solution is to actually build one only to find the organization for which it is intended is unwilling to use it.

> **"There is nothing more difficult to take in hand, more perilous to conduct, or more uncertain in its success than to take the lead in the introduction of a new order of things."**
>
> **Machiavelli**

With a leader in place, you set about evaluating and carefully reworking the organizational climate to create an environment that will support your initiative. Developing an effective communications plan will be an important element in this effort. Here are nine steps to follow to ensure that your communications are well received.

1. Consolidate your strategy development. Multiple e-learning strategies within an organization can create confusion and convey a lack of mission. It's best if you can establish an enterprisewide strategy. If not, work to create a seamless linkage between the efforts of each business unit or organization. Communication suffers if your audience perceives that there are multiple groups vying for their attention with virtually the same message. It gives the appearance of chaos, which will not help your efforts to change the learning culture.

2. Trash old training communication vehicles. Start fresh. If you're going to focus on e-learning, especially in the broader sense of online training and knowledge management, don't rely solely on your traditional training communication strategies, such as quarterly schedules, catalogs, or your training registration Web site. You don't want to create the perception that this is still the old training organization in a new suit of clothes. Communicate more from a business and learning perspective, and less from a training and course perspective.

3. Use the Web to communicate. This would be a good time for a new Web site that focuses on the relationship between learning, community, and business performance, with e-learning as a way to get there. Print, video, and other formats may have a role to play in your communications strategy, but make the Web your *primary* medium and create a seamless link between your Web-based communications and your e-learning portal. Don't just use the Web as an elaborate advertisement—the days of the Web as just "brochureware" are over. Add content and tools that can add immediate performance and business value to the user. And don't forget to use online communities as a way to get your message out.

4. Avoid selling and focus on value. People should not equate your communications as a sales pitch, especially if you have previously used the same vehicles to sell training classes and registrations. Clearly articulate your value proposition and demonstrate its worthiness to your clients and stakeholders. But be careful not to confuse the features of e-learning, which describe facts and characteristics (e.g., the technology allows instant updating for greater accuracy) with its benefits, which describe how it meets specific needs (e.g., people will be able to make faster, better, and more informed decisions). When the value of embracing your strategy is clear, usage will follow.

5. Communicate value from the top down. Get your sponsors involved in your communications. After all, if you've built management ownership, getting them to communicate your message should be easy (and, if they don't participate, it may be another sign of their marginal support). Communication from the top also lends credibility to your efforts to institute a learning culture. When Dell Computer found that many of its employees didn't have adequate Web experience, it launched a "Know the Net" campaign, championed by Michael Dell himself.

6. Build support with coaches first. Create a separate communications strategy for front-line managers, as their support is critical for workplace learning. Begin your work with them early, before the deployment of your e-learning initiatives—it will take some time to win them over. Use knowledge management to build a manager community (which can be more universally beneficial than just supporting a learning culture), and use that community to create heightened awareness of their role in supporting learning.

7. Build and promote an initial win. Center your communications around best practices and examples of what e-learning can accomplish. Showcase what you have already done, even if it's a small win, along with endorsements and testimonials of benefits and impact (from senior managers and learners, if possible). It's fine to back this up with more theoretical or conceptual "white papers" about e-learning, but don't lead with them. An "ivory tower" image is not helpful when you are trying to demonstrate your business value.

8. Control external messages. This is very important. All the while you are trying to communicate your message, you can be sure that outside vendors and consultants are also communicating to your target audience. These groups will certainly have a role to play in your strategy (as we'll see in Chapter 10), but their sales messages must not create additional noise in your communications channel. Create a communications funnel through which all messages will be filtered before passing them through to your audience. You may not be able to stop vendors from sending literature and e-mail to your stakeholders and clients, but you can work with them to be sure that what is said is supportive of where you're headed as a business. This is not an easy task, but it is important for the effectiveness of your overall communications plan.

9. Encourage Web savvy. Create messages that tell employees that the Internet/intranet is just as much of a work tool as the telephone or the computer. The more people use a new technology, the more comfortable they become with it—and the more comfortable they'll be with online training and knowledge management. Remove barriers like charging for use or restricting access to only senior departmental managers. If the Web is abused, deal with it as a supervisory and performance issue, not as a technology or a learning issue. For most people, if they're motivated to work, the Internet shouldn't prove any more of a distraction that anything else in the workplace—the technology will become transparent.

Why a Successful E-Learning Strategy Needs an Effective Change Strategy

Preparing your business for a shift to e-learning requires that you build your learning culture, find and leverage your champions, and create sound, value-based communications. But these efforts cannot be accomplished haphazardly. The best way to approach these important issues is through a systematic change strategy, often referred to as "change management."

Change management focuses on ensuring that an organization and its people are committed and capable of executing a business plan. It involves establishing an environment for change, enabling high performance, and sustaining workforce commitment over the long haul. It is about moving an organization toward its goals by improving the performance, productivity, speed, flexibility, and motivation of the workforce, and about building the capabilities of business leaders to lead sustainable change.

From an e-learning perspective, many change management techniques have already been discussed within the culture, champions, and communications strategies presented. But in order to know precisely where to target your efforts, it's important to determine the readiness of the organization to accept e-learning.

The question of acceptance has three dimensions. First, there is the issue of motivation. Are people supportive of this change or are they inclined to create roadblocks? Before you introduce your first e-learning communication, and especially before the first e-learning solution is deployed, conduct a readiness assessment. Look at your stakeholders, from executives and front-line managers to your target audience. Listen carefully to what they say about a particular change. Assess their attitudes and willingness to try this new approach.

Understand why people are resistant to e-learning. Look not just at the outward symptoms (e.g., refusal to participate, demands for reinstatement of classroom training), but at the underlying causes as well (e.g., loss of attending training as a reward, fear of technology, supervisor distrust of learning on the job, fear or inability to learn without help). As stated previously, sometimes people appear resistant when in fact they are simply following a different path that seems better for them—you're not even on their radar screen. Use your champions and communications plan to help turn change avoiders into change acceptors. Target specific messages about your value proposition to the specific groups having problems making the transition. Provide extra help along the way, especially peer-to-peer support. Create the right incentives (monetary or otherwise) that will encourage participation. And finally, make the new way easier and more comfortable than the old.

> **"The problem is not how to get new thoughts into your mind, but how to get the old ones out."**
>
> **Nancy Austin, coauthor of**
> *A Passion for Excellence: The Leadership Difference*

Second is the issue of competence. Do people have the skills and knowledge to successfully engage in e-learning initiatives? We've suggested that the learning curve for the Web is pretty quick, but that doesn't mean people won't need some help. This is especially true if computers are new to the work. For example, when computer technology was first introduced into manufacturing, workers resisted because they didn't believe that technology could equal their artisanship. When this was overcome, most workers needed extensive training on how to use the new tools. Once they were comfortable with these new systems, learning additional systems was significantly easier. So don't simply plop computers down in the workplace where they haven't been before and expect everyone to rush to use them. Remember that you are radically changing the work environment as well as the learning environment. Plan for this and take some time. Keep in mind the importance of motivation—involve people in the change as much as possible.

The third issue is one of resources. If you are going to introduce e-learning into the workplace, be sure everyone has access and that the technology is adequate to make the experience worthwhile rather than painful. And be sure there is enough money and other resources to sustain the program over the long haul. You don't want to reorient people to e-learning only to have budgets cut, forcing everyone to go back to the way they used to learn. If this happens, your next try will be far more difficult.

Four Additional Rules of Change

In addition to culture, champions, and communications, if you're introducing e-learning into the organization, follow these four additional rules to ease the transition.

1. Don't put change management off until deployment. The longer you wait to implement effective change management in support of e-learning, the greater the likelihood that the e-learning initiative will fail. Graph A in Figure 7.1 shows what can happen if the change strategy is implemented simultaneously with an e-learning initiative. In this scenario, the introduction of e-learning causes work disruption, which is natural with any major change. But because the supporting change management

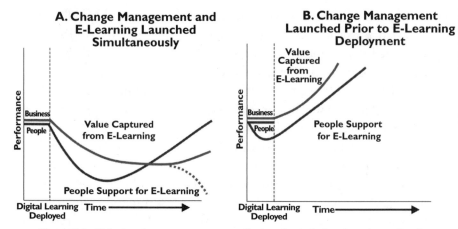

Figure 7.1 Delaying change management until e-learning is deployed can jeopardize the entire initiative, but launching a change management initiative prior to e-learning implementation can enhance its success.

intervention was not introduced until deployment, it can take a significant amount of time to turn things around. And, in some cases, a change strategy may be introduced so late in the game that the e-learning initiative will not recover. However, an early focus on the human dimensions of change assures employee readiness and ability, and the highest business impact.

Graph B in Figure 7.1 shows the beneficial impact of deploying a change strategy in advance of any e-learning initiative. In this scenario, the change strategy is deployed *in advance* of the e-learning intervention. People have the information and especially the time to get ready. There's still a dip in performance and other issues as e-learning is introduced, but it is far less severe. Recovery is quicker and acceptance over the long term is more assured.

2. One size doesn't fit all. Don't assume that everybody needs the same approach to helping them accept change. Senior executives will likely respond to a different strategy (perhaps observing best practices or benchmarking their peers in other companies) than rank-and-file workers (who may be more interested in what's in it for them). Front-line managers, who are key "change leaders," will also require special attention.

3. Focus on change from start to finish—and beyond.
Acceptance of change cannot be accomplished in one- or two-hour meetings scheduled the day before your e-learning solution is deployed. Not only is starting early important, but to prevent old behaviors from reemerging, the change strategy must be maintained long enough so this new way of learning becomes the *preferred* way of learning.

4. Be open and don't oversell. Don't hide critical information from employees or assume they can't be trusted. Don't white-wash the real reasons, probably economic and business related, why classroom training has been replaced with e-learning. Don't portray e-learning unrealistically or create unnecessary hype that employees will recognize as just propaganda. Tout benefits for the company and benefits for employees, and be honest about the increased responsibility e-learning makes on individuals.

How Dell Creates an E-Learning Culture

Dell Computer Corporation is a high-tech company, full of young, computer-savvy employees. Yet even in this environment, the classroom is still an icon of learning. To create a culture where people will accept e-learning, Dell Learning, the company's training organization, and Dell regional training organizations combine technology with some aspects of the "old school." When a new program or tool is released on the Web, it is sometimes introduced in a nonthreatening classroom situation to help people feel more comfortable with it. This results in higher levels of use on the job.

Dell did a thorough analysis of why many people prefer classroom training and turn away from Web-based CBT. One of the reasons cited most often is the need for, or lack of, feedback—from the instructor and from each other. So the company built a variety of feedback and coaching mechanisms into each e-learning component—both instructional and informational. From simple quizzes and practice exercises to role-playing and extensive simulations in a "safe" environment, getting people engaged is the key. In every product there are opportunities to check understanding. Even more static Web sites use some feedback to create a level of inter-activity and "stickiness" (i.e., getting learners to come back to the site as needed). People aren't forced to do exercises, but they can use them if they're concerned about their mastery of the content.

Meeting the requirements of senior management is not enough; often there is a wide chasm between what managers and users think is needed. Basing an e-learning solution on what people say should be done, rather than what is actually done often dooms the program because it is unauthentic. So Dell brings end-users into the development process in the beginning. By ensuring that both groups are intimately involved in development, the company ensures that each solution bridges any potential "divide" between the company's strategic initiatives and what individual contributors actually do on a daily basis.

Each Dell e-learning solution is prototyped and tested repeat-edly. Whereas most companies conduct alpha and beta tests, Dell goes further, putting the program out to the field for users to "try out" and comment on its usability and value. Targeted end-users can provide comments on the program during the user-acceptance testing (UAT) period. By the time the solution is put into produc-tion, many end-users have already had some experience with it.

Dell also has deployed a competency assessment system where employees can rate their skills (and be rated by their managers and peers). The results form the basis of an appropriate e-learning solution customized to the user and designed to address specific deficiencies. By linking personal development with e-learning, Dell has found that employees see a direct benefit of each pro-gram. Larger deployments are usually preceded by a communica-tions initiative to let people know what's coming. Finally, every effort has been made to help managers create an atmosphere where learning is a legitimate part of the workday. At Dell, many call center representatives, for example, have time set aside for learning—time when they don't have to be on the phones.

None of Dell's techniques for creating e-learning acceptance are a radical departure from its culture. Dell's tagline is to "Be Direct," and most e-learning solutions eliminate unnecessary instructors, processes, and other impediments in the process. Dell uses thorough implementation of good instructional design and user testing to create a quality product, and good communication to help everyone understand its benefits. The key is using these techniques systemically, rather than haphazardly, so that they are ingrained in the e-learning development process.

Knowledge Management as a Facilitator of Change at AT&T

Learning has always been a powerful tool in the facilitation of change, and e-learning can be especially useful in large change situations. Take one of the most disruptive changes that can befall a company—a merger or acquisition. For each partner in a merger, or for the acquirer and the acquired, the ability to handle change can mean the difference between success and failure.

One good example can be seen when AT&T acquired the cable company TCI. While AT&T was a huge, primarily centrally controlled global business, the local cable franchises were much more independent, having themselves been acquired over the years. And while AT&T faces significant competitive challenges, many of these franchises were, for a long time, sole providers in their geographic areas, having signed multiyear contracts with local governments. Each franchisee had its own way of doing business; it's own accounting and billing systems as well as divergent methods and procedures for operating its business.

So the task of building a unified, nationwide broadband communications network required the merging of two cultures. Each time a local cable market was "launched," it was critical that any problems experienced were not repeated in the next launch. In addition, it was also important to capitalize on the best practices that were uncovered. Valuable insight and information needed to be shared by subsequent markets. The company wanted a way to share learning so the team would get better and smarter. The result was a *Lessons Learned* knowledge management (KM) system.

While people were always encouraged to post on the intranet what they learned as they went through a conversion, it was mostly a lot of information provided by well-meaning individuals who had no format and no framing to guide them. This clearly wasn't working, as each posting was written differently and at a different level of detail.

The new knowledge management solution did two things. First, it allowed users to submit a lesson learned via a template/input tool that was easy to use and ensured that each contribution would be in the same format and depth. The tool also enabled the filtering of some invalid content, such as gripes and rumors. Each contribution was automatically sent to an SME for validation prior to publication on the site.

The other part of the KM system was a knowledge retrieval tool for searching the Lessons Learned repository to find information of direct value to the user. This helped reduce information overload and helped create a stronger sense of community among the teams moving from market to market.

The results of this project have been invaluable in reducing occurrences of "reinventing the wheel," and in providing everyone with access to best practices. But there were other findings from this work that have implications for any e-learning deployment. First, don't assume that everyone has access to the Internet. It's important to balance "e-enabling" with reality. In this case, field installers didn't have access on the job, nor did some of the technicians on the cable company side. So the KM system allows people to phone or fax in their contributions. Second, it's important to provide people with the incentives and time to use the system. Just because it's on the server doesn't mean anybody will use it—or value it. When workers are in crisis mode, learning in any form can take a back seat, if you're not careful. Third, identify the project's owner. In the early stages of this project, no one was held accountable for the project, so it was virtually ignored. Now that the project is part of the charter of the national rollout team, people are taking notice.

Like every other effort, this example of e-learning (knowledge management) being used to facilitate positive change could not be successful without the correct incentives, support, and access. But because these issues were identified and leveraged appropriately, the system works.

What About the Training Organization Itself?

This chapter has dealt primarily with introducing e-learning into an organization and the obstacles that can get in the way or kill it. But one of the major obstacles can be the misguided assumptions, confusion, reticence, or downright anti-e-learning position of the training department itself. We'll deal extensively with this issue in Chapter 9.

An E-Learning Journey
by Raymond L. Vigil, Lucent Technologies

Leading an Organization Through the Change to E-Learning

WHEN I CAME TO LUCENT IN 1998 to lead the group responsible for training a global sales and technician force, as well as our external customers, I found the Denver-based organization in pretty good shape, with a solid reputation for quality training. But I also knew that to succeed globally, and to remain competitive, we had to be more nimble, more responsive, and more flexible than ever before. In a nutshell, we had to get faster and get better while at the same time lowering our costs. So I knew that some significant changes were necessary. I think the staff knew it, too, although there was a lot of uncertainty as to how to get there.

With the long tradition of quality classroom training, the organization also had a lot of experience in technology-based learning, most notably in satellite delivery, as well as CD-ROM and traditional CBT. (We're currently using outbound satellite broadcasting to hundreds of downlinks worldwide, with an Internet-based connection back for interactivity; and we intend to move to the Web as broadband capabilities are deployed in our company.) This technology would enable us to be the connecting point for anyone in the business who wanted to reach a worldwide audience of employees, resellers, or customers. We needed to make our messages easy to understand and easy to access. If we were just going to do satellite-based training, the transition would have been easier. After all, we were already doing that—we just needed to do more and make it interactive. But I recognized that we also had an opportunity, and an obligation to use learning technology to deliver information—such as product announcements, competitive intelligence, technical briefings and manuals—in addition to training.

I began to talk about the power of moving beyond just training, of using technology to provide a wide range of informational services as well. While many folks on my team understood where we needed to go, others were confused. So were our stakeholders and clients. We not only had to deal with issues of reducing our classroom training offerings, we also had to explain this broader mission. Resistance surfaced and the natural "antibodies" began to form. If our mission was to succeed and if we were to survive, I had to deal with the technological and the people side of change simultaneously.

I took a strategic business approach, not an educational approach, to explain the road ahead. I talked less about training and training issues and more about the state of our business. I repeatedly asked everyone to see beyond their jobs, to understand how we impact the company and what the company expects of us. If there was confusion, we would clear it up. Nobody should be in the dark about the direction we're going, and we set out to address this on day one.

I had prior experience in organizational change (at U S WEST and IBM, among other companies), and that experience was invaluable. I worked to understand the culture that I came into. It was very powerful and I had to respect it. I never denigrated training or the training profession. I never led anyone to believe that it was a second tier job in the company. Once people realized that I was not here to destroy them, they opened up. I was bringing in a new perspective, but I was not just passing through to get my ticket punched. I was in the same profession as they were and I was going to stay around for a while. I began to ask questions like, "What could we become?" and, "How do we create our future?" In addition to being a practitioner in this field and having good business acumen, I think leaders need a change orientation and an open mind.

I worked to create the context and the frame of reference that would enable people to hear my message. I elevated professional development to an activity of high importance. I asked everyone to focus on the training marketplace as hard as they focused on the telecom marketplace.

We used force field analysis to identify opportunities for initial e-learning and "e-information" wins. We looked for people who wanted to do things differently and partnered with them; we didn't force ourselves on anyone. We'd take small victories if necessary— we knew that a couple of small wins were better than one big disaster. We turned bad news into opportunities. When companies issue the dreaded financial emergency-induced "travel ban," it normally sends waves of panic throughout training organizations. But what if we could respond quickly with e-learning solutions that negated the client's travel problems? We found a few partners that liked this idea, and we worked with them—quietly, until we had the successes we needed.

The results? We've gone from having to sell ourselves to worrying about being able to meet all the demand for our e-learning services. It's no longer a matter of me convincing anyone, it's now a matter of me keeping up with the growing requirements of our clients. Greater needs in shorter time frames. We have to deliver, and we do.

So in turning an organization around to e-learning and expanding its mission and value proposition, I recommend a strategy based on performance. Low-key it in the beginning, but move quickly. There is a window of opportunity between when a need is recognized and when a client will move past you to another solution. Create a sense of urgency and take some risks. There's not a whole lot of this around, but you cannot play it safe and make this transformation. Solutions create opportunities for more work and more solutions. You grow on your reputation. Then you cross the line between hanging by a thread and being invaluable. It's a great feeling and you'll know it when you get there.

As we become more invaluable every day, there are some lessons we've learned along the way. First, quality instructional design is paramount. No matter what technology or business pressures you have, you can't cheat on quality. Second, people want options and choices; there's no single answer. Create multiple opportunities to help end-users enhance their performance. Think about them having many needs. Third, think "no boundaries." From the classroom to being a part of the knowledge supply chain, you can't allow artificial barriers (between training and information) to get in your way. Fourth, develop your people. Seeding is an important tool. Bring in new people who think differently and who have different approaches. They can stimulate change. I think the fact that I was from outside the company was helpful here. Finally, focus on collaboration as a key responsibility of leadership.

When I interviewed for this position, I was told that Lucent had great managers in this business and that any number of them could manage the training function very well. But that wasn't what they were looking for. They wanted a new perspective and new ideas; someone who could help them understand how the resource could be used differently. When I came on board, I was perceived with fear. No one knew what my agenda was. I focused on leading the change effort as my initial and most important objective. I let my performance, and the performance of our organization, speak for itself, and people have changed their point of view. They've come around to a new way of thinking—an appreciation of the progress we've made together.

Raymond L. Vigil, Ph.D., is Vice President—Learning Architecture for Lucent Technologies and is charged with consolidating and transforming training operations in the company into a single, integrated global e-learning organization (rvigil@lucent.com).

Justifying E-Learning to Top Management . . . and to Yourself

"E-Learning is good, e-learning is great—so give us money."

Corporate trainer
describing typical e-learning justification
in his company, with little positive results so far

"Every organization is looking for ways to save money on training . . . When managers grasp the return on investment of computer simulations —their eyes grow large."

Roger Schank[1]

ONCE YOU GET E-LEARNING ON everyone's radar screen, you're likely to be called to task to build a business case that justifies it—not only in its initial phases but also as an ongoing requirement. At first you can expect to have to *over*-justify every e-learning decision, especially if it entails a large investment or replacement of the old, comfortable way of doing things. As you demonstrate the value of e-learning, you'll find that justification won't go away, but it will become more routine.

Success Criteria

There is a tendency to justify e-learning by just evaluating how well it improves the performance of learners. This is certainly important, but it is not sufficient. In their book *Reengineering the Corporation*, Hammer and Champy identified four major criteria for business performance: cost, quality, service, and speed.[2] The best way to ensure that you can completely justify e-learning is to base your efforts on these four measures. As seen in Table 8.1, these same criteria apply to learning.

Table 8.1 Key Business Measures Applied to Learning

Criteria	Implications for Business	Implications for Learning
Cost	What will it cost to operate the business successfully, and how can those costs be better managed? Savings here translate directly to the bottom line in higher profits, earnings per share, etc., and free up capital that can be reinvested in helping the business grow.	What will it cost to acquire or develop learning programs and deliver them to all who need them? How much will it cost to take employees out of productive roles and put them in a learning mode? These are typical budget questions that we've been dealing with for years. Only now, these costs are becoming more critical and visible, yet harder to justify. The pressure for cost control is more intense than ever.

Table 8.1   *(Continued)*

Criteria	Implications for Business	Implications for Learning
Quality	How are the company's offerings meeting customer expectations? Improvement in quality is also clearly related to bottom-line results through increased customer loyalty and market share growth, among other measures.	What is the quality of the learning programs? Is learning taking place and, more important, is this learning being translated into higher performance? These questions are requiring answers that go beyond "What did people learn?" to "What can they do?" and even more important, "Was it worth it?"
Service	How well does the business respond to customer needs? Customer satisfaction with and access to service can be a key differentiator in the marketplace.	With an increasingly dispersed, mobile, and diversified workforce, and a more global business operation, learning now must be available 24/7. With loosely coupled organizational structures and rapid change in the business environment driving decisions and innovation to lower levels of the company, learning will have to be more tailored to each individual, while at the same time allowing that individual to explore new areas that may be outside predictable patterns.
Speed	How fast the company can change its strategy to meet new challenges, how quickly the business can bring a new product to market, or how fast the firm can respond to customer needs are examples of key measurements of speed. The digital economy exacerbates the need for speed.	How fast can learning respond to changes in the business? If employees expect learning programs to reflect up-to-the-minute accuracy, relevance, and completeness, and if that information is constantly changing, how will learning providers respond? How can learning be effective, scalable, *and* responsive at "Internet speed"?

These are the criteria to evaluate learning, and the criteria for which e-learning will be justified. Today, no business can afford to have high-quality learning programs that take too long to deploy, aren't available at the moment of need, or cost so much to deliver that they become unaffordable. If learning is to have any value in a business, it must be successful along *all four* criteria. There is simply no way for this to happen unless technology—e-learning technology—is part of the mix, along with more traditional forms of learning.

> **"With the interactivity of the Internet, we get the equivalent of a one-to-one teacher-student ratio. The means are finally at hand to improve productivity in education."**
>
> Peter Drucker[3]

Justifying E-Learning Costs

The first question you must answer is: *Does/Will e-learning save money?* When you compare a quality e-learning alternative to a quality classroom program, most research has shown that the ability of people to learn is at least as good as the classroom program, if not better. In other words, if you assume there is no detriment to learning with an e-learning solution, then your goal should be to achieve this level of learning at less cost. How is this done?

Understanding how e-learning solutions can cost less than a comparable classroom alternative involves four basic principles.

1. E-Learning is more efficient. It can take anywhere from 25 to 60 percent less time to convey the same amount of instruction or information as in a classroom.[4] Saving time rather than money may be the defining factor in an e-learning business case. Graph A on Figure 8.1 shows the time compression for a typical five-day classroom course converted to e-learning.

Why is this so? First of all, no time is needed for housekeeping, class introductions, breaks, lunch, etc. Second, because of the individualized design of e-learning, "learners" can move at their own pace, often skipping material they already know (often the system itself makes a diagnosis and automatically skips unneces-

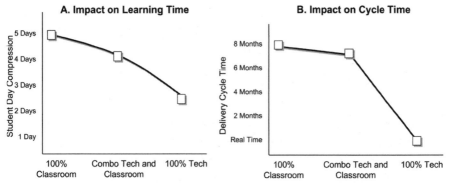

Figure 8.1 E-Learning's impact on learning and cycle times can be substantial.

sary material). Learners are not held up when "slower" students need more time, nor do they have to sit through instructor presentations targeted at the mid-level learner. Finally, because a quality e-learning solution has probably gone through a more rigorous instructional or information design process, it is likely to be inherently more efficient.

2. Delivery cycle time. As shown in Graph B in Figure 8.1, for a hypothetical requirement to train 1,000 people, placing about 30 at a time in a five-day classroom course with one instructor will take more than eight months for everyone to go through the program. In most cases, by the time even half the people are trained, the content will have changed so much that the first half will need retraining, or the company will have moved on to new priorities and the second half of the group may never be trained.

Even if you shorten the training by a day, the impact on cycle time is negligible. That's because the instructor still can only teach one group a week. Of course, you can add instructors, but in doing so you increase your costs substantially. You also open up the training program to the risk of different messages or different interpretations of the content being delivered by the different instructors (no matter how specific the instructor guide or how rigorous the train-the-trainer sessions). You can also increase the amount of students in the class. But how many can you add before you negatively impact the level of interactivity and personal attention that can be given to each learner? You can probably go to 35 or 40 students, maybe even 50, but you start hurting the effectiveness of your program if you go any higher. Even if you double the number of learners in each session, it will *only* take you *four* months to train everyone! Equally important, the instant scalability of e-learning allows delivery to many *more* learners without increasing development or delivery time.

3. The financial benefits of e-learning accrue to the client organization, not to the training organization, and these benefits are almost always on the delivery, not the development, side. These benefits are most apparent when viewed over the total life cycle of the learning product. This is probably the most important of the four principles, but it is a hard point for many trainers to swallow. The development costs for e-learning can be three times that of classroom learning, or more. This is money that the training organization will have to spend. But the savings on the delivery side are so significant that in many cases the initial investment in e-learning can often be recouped in the first year.

4. The largest chunk of money to be saved is not in instructor costs, or travel and living, as is the popular belief, but in "student" costs (i.e., lost opportunity costs). Let's assume that a typical employee in a company earns an $80,000 loaded salary (salary plus benefits) per year. If the typical work year is about 230 productive days (deducting weekends, holidays, vacation, etc.), the average pay per day is $348. In a five-day class, that's $1,740. And that's not counting any additional travel days. Now, while the employee is in training, someone else is doing that person's job, or worse, the work is not getting done. Sales calls aren't being made, repairs are delayed, calls aren't returned, customer wait times are just a little longer, etc. In fact, the productivity of a person in training is *zero!* At the very least, the productivity impact of each person in this five-day course is a *negative* $1,740.

If as a result of moving from a classroom to an e-learning mode, assume that this employee can complete the learning program in three days, and return to the job for two additional productive days. The new productivity impact is now only a negative $1,044, a *savings* of $696. Multiply this by the 1,000 people to be trained, and the productivity savings are over a half-million dollars ($696,000), certainly enough to pay for the e-learning solution.

More important, because all 1,000 people were trained all at once, the new knowledge was rolled out to everyone instantaneously and would most likely contribute more to overall productivity. The classroom format could result in delays in reaching everyone, which could represent serious business costs.

While productivity is the largest bucket of money that can be realized from e-learning, it is far from the only savings. Suppose we needed to train 1,000 people a year for three years. Table 8.2 shows a spreadsheet of savings (be sure to substitute your own company's numbers, as appropriate, when you do your own calculations). The cost curves for the classroom and e-learning approaches are shown in Graph A in Figure 8.2.

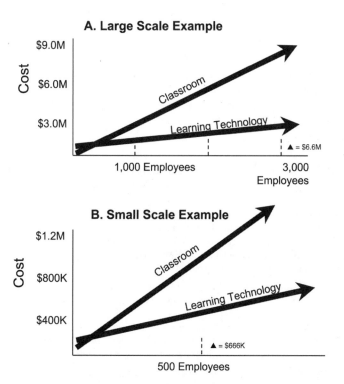

Figure 8.2 Because of savings in diverted labor, delivery, and travel, the business case for e-learning is easy to make in both large and small scale situations.

Table 8.2 Cost Calculations for Classroom and E-Learning

Data Point	Classroom	E-Learning
Number of people to train and duration of program	1,000 people a year for three years	1,000 people a year for three years
Length of program	5 days	3 days (40% more efficient)
Estimated development cost*	$100,000	$300,000
Estimated maintenance costs in years 2 and 3 (20–40% of development cost per year—30% used in this example)	$60,000	$180,000
Delivery costs over three years	$3,000,000 (based on an average of $200 per student day)[†]	$150,000 (administrative costs estimated at $50 per user)
Travel costs (estimated at an average of $1000 per trip where 50% of the learners will travel)	$1,500,000	$0 (assumes desktop, same building or home-based learning)
Diverted labor (loaded salaries of employees in a learning mode)[‡]	$5,220,000	$3,132,000
Additional diverted labor for travel days (assume one extra full day for round-trip travel)	$522,000	$0
Total cost (e-learning saves $6,640,000)	$10,402,000 ($160,000 for development and $10,242,000 for delivery)	$3,762,000 ($480,000 for development and $3,282,000 for delivery)

*The cost of the e-learning infrastructure, either classroom facilities or intranet costs, are not included because they are considered sunk costs paid for by the corporation and would be in place whether or not any specific e-learning initiative (online training or knowledge management) was undertaken.

[†]This average of $200 per day was computed by dividing training expenditures per employee ($770 to $1,616) by number of hours of training per employee per year (28.9 to 57.5). This result is then multiplied by an average 7.5 possible instructional hours per day (Source: American Society for Training and Development 2000 State of the Industry Report). It includes instructor and materials costs for that particular offering. This is only an estimate. Substitute your firm's own numbers when making these calculations.

[‡]Loaded salary *divided by* the number of annual workdays *times* the length of the equivalent classroom course *times* the total number of learners.

This cost analysis also works for small implementations. Instead of having to training 3,000 people over three years, assume you have to train 500 people in just one year (Table 8.3). The cost curves for the classroom and e-learning approaches in this smaller implementation are shown in Graph B in Figure 8.2.

This approach works equally well for synchronous delivery. In such cases, travel and living costs are reduced to zero for both

Table 8.3 Cost Calculations for Classroom and E-Learning for a Small Implementation

Data Point	Classroom	E-Learning
Number of people to train and duration of program	500 people, one time, within the same year	500 people, one time, within the same year
Length of program	3 days	2 days (33% more efficient)
Estimated development cost	$60,000	$180,000
Estimated maintenance costs (this is a short-term project)	$0	$0
Delivery costs	$300,000 (based on an average of $200 per student day)	$25,000 (administrative costs estimated at $50 per user)
Travel costs (estimated at an average $1,000 per trip where 50% of the learners will travel)	$250,000	$0 (assumes desktop, same building or home-based learning)
Diverted labor (loaded salaries of employees in a learning mode)	$522,000	$348,000
Additional diverted labor for travel days (assume one extra full day for round-trip travel)	$87,000	$0
Total cost (e-learning saves $666,000)	$1,219,000 ($60,000 for development and $1,159,000 for delivery)	$553,000 ($180,000 for development and $373,000 for delivery)

approaches. However, the overall delivery costs for the e-learning approach increases substantially. While a classroom is still not necessary, an instructor (and his/her accompanying resources) is required. The process also works if your primary solution is knowledge management with further savings on diverted labor but probably somewhat higher delivery costs (for the central KM system managers and staff as well as for a higher level of ongoing maintenance). In all of these scenarios, the savings derived from even a partial e-learning solution can free up enough money to support the continuing classroom components of your learning architecture.

> **"IBM estimates that for every 1,000,000 classroom days converted to e-learning, more than $400,000 can be saved. For 1999, the company expects 30% of its internal training materials will be delivered online, with anticipated savings of more than $120 million."**
>
> *Business Week*[5]

Demonstrating E-Learning *Quality*

The second measure of business performance is quality, and the question to be answered is: *Does/Will the e-learning solution result in an appropriate increase in knowledge and improvement in performance*, and *was it worth the investment?* This is the area where Donald Kirkpatrick's four levels of evaluation[6] are most appropriate, although we shouldn't be limited by them. But in e-learning situations, there are some important considerations to take into account.

Level 1: Reaction. The typical end-of-course evaluation, or rating sheet, is perhaps even more important for e-learning than in the classroom. With a classroom event, it is possible to observe students' reactions, and to interview the instructor for what she/he observed to gain additional insights into students' reaction to the program. But with e-learning—be it online training, knowledge management, or a combination—employee evaluation is essential because, generally speaking, there is no additional source of information. With increased importance comes the need for better, more insightful questions—questions that focus on a variety of experiences with the content, interface design, authenticity, value, etc. Building such a survey into the program will encourage people to respond, and showing them how their responses compare with the responses of their peers is even more motivating.

Level 2: Learning. This is the level that answers the typical question, *What did the employee learn as a result of the program?* Whether it's a testing situation following an online training course, or a more complex problem to solve as part of a business simulation, in an e-learning environment the emphasis is more valuable in providing feedback to learners and developers (to improve the program), not reporting results to some sort of corporate tally sheet. Unfortunately, in an effort to either justify the original decision to use an online solution, or simply to prove that people have actually accessed the program, there is an increasing use of level 2 evaluation simply as a tracking strategy. Even worse, some people try to incorporate testing in a knowledge management system. Bottom line—level 2 evaluation is primarily for providing feedback and not assessment. The rubber meets the road in level 3.

Level 3: Performance. It is here that efforts must be made to determine if the e-learning effort was effective. At this level the key question, *Can people perform better and faster?* goes to the heart of why the initiative was undertaken in the first place. Ask people who went through the online training program or who have used the knowledge management system. Watch them as they work and look at their outputs. Have they gotten better? Are there fewer mistakes? Are they working faster? Ask their supervisors and other stakeholders, including upper management, if they've noticed any changes. See what their customers or clients might have noticed in terms of knowledge gained, behavior change, or performance improvement. Don't just do it once or twice—do it constantly. Set up a system of continuous monitoring of the effectiveness of the people who use the e-learning systems you deploy, and create an ongoing report that equates your results back to business performance.

Level 4: Results. At this level, the question pertains to the contribution of e-learning to the effectiveness of business. When we were justifying costs, the emphasis was on *saving* money (reducing operational costs) by moving to e-learning. Here the emphasis is on *making* money—showing that e-learning results in more sales, fewer mistakes, higher productivity, etc. Both are important. Another question to answer pertains to the consequences of doing *nothing*. Can you show that a lack of instruction or information would have a detrimental impact on the business? For example, showing that a failure of the sales force to perform at a higher level may result in lost sales can bolster your argument for greater investment in a learning solution, and more specifically an e-learning solution. As important as the financial contribution of e-learning may be, don't limit your level 4 activities to financial aspects. Ask other simple but important questions such as: Are we a smarter, more insightful company as a result of this investment? How has learning impacted customers? or What effect has learning had on employee retention, morale, etc? The right questions and the linkages back to key business measures are best developed in collaboration with the client.

Requests for level 4 results are often couched in a demand to *prove* that e-learning works, and works better than the classroom program it might have replaced. But because there are so many variables that can account for some of the perceived improvement—such as a better recruiting program, an improved economy, new manufacturing processes, and so on—it is very difficult to accurately and completely account for the impact of the e-learning intervention in isolation. It is better to settle for *evidence* rather than proof. If you ask the plant manager and all the supervisors of an engine plant if a recently introduced e-learning solution has resulted in higher productivity, and all or most of them say yes, that's pretty good evidence that a correlation between the learning solution and the business metric exists. This evidence can be reinforced if you ask a variety of groups, including the same types of people you asked in level 3 evaluations. Coupled with extensive observations and product evaluations, it is possible to make some reasonable conclusions about the business impact of e-learning.

Beyond determining the financial benefits of the e-learning effort, there is an increasing awareness that intellectual capital—what the business as a whole knows—has value (even though most accountants don't see it that way). Sometimes a company may spend a great deal of money simply to improve the knowledge of its people with no immediate financial benefit—just the strong assumption that the new knowledge will be of value down the road. What is it worth for your company to have knowledge or expertise that your competitors don't have, and to have that expertise captured in a knowledge management system that can't resign, retire, or otherwise leave the business? Thus, the ability to grow the intellectual capital of the firm is another "result" that should be reported.

For example, while it is true that better leadership in the firm can reduce employee turnover, the investment in leadership training may be more compelling because of the company's conviction that better leaders are more open and forward-thinking about the impact of change on the company. Very hard to measure, but certainly a worthwhile goal—one that shouldn't be abandoned because a specific ROI could not be calculated. If this means that sometimes you invest money in learning, including e-learning, based on a strong belief or faith in its long-term value, so be it.

Thomas Stewart has identified some interesting ways to measure the human contributions to intellectual capital. One way is *innovation*—measure the gross margins on new innovative products, compared to the old ones they've replaced. Another is *employee attitudes*—employees who feel they are learning and valued tend to be more productive. Other measures include *tenure, turnover, experience,* and *learning*—each can give an indication of the firm's ability to retain and grow its talent base.[7]

Sometimes evaluation barriers are put in place to kill e-learning —you negotiate one evaluation hurdle only to find a higher hurdle thrown down in front of you. If this is the case, you have a political and culture problem, not an evaluation problem, and you need to deal with it in that context. Sometimes, government regulations or union agreements may compel you to measure learning in ways that you feel are inappropriate. This can be a huge barrier unless an equivalent model is put in place that is acceptable to you.

Evaluating E-Learning *Service*

Another important criterion area for e-learning is service. Programs that are cost-effective but hard to get aren't worth much. The question to answer here is: *How accessible is the e-learning program?* Essentially, you want to ensure that online training or knowledge management systems are available to all those who need them. That means easy accessibility. Saying that an employee can walk over to the next building is not the kind of accessibility that's desirable. Access at home may not be an issue. But if you have employees working from their homes who need access to a knowledge management system, for example, home accessibility becomes important.

Associated with accessibility is the quality of access. If equipment is out of date (e.g., low-speed modems) or your infrastructure is unreliable, people will question whether accessing the program is worth the trouble. This is why collaboration with the IT department is so important.

As implied above, access is both the ability of everyone who needs the program to be able to get it, and the ability of everyone to get it wherever they are. System availability cannot end at 5 p.m. on the East Coast of the United States. There are people in California and around the world who are still working who need access. Even if your business is located only in one place, some people are most productive late at night or very early in the morning. So along with anyone and anywhere, we add *any time* as key justification and evaluation criteria for any e-learning initiative.

Evaluating E-Learning *Speed*

The last of the four criteria is speed, and the question to be asked is: *How responsive is the system to the changing demands of the business and the changing requirements of its employees?* There are three major considerations here. First, how quickly can an e-learning initiative be up and running (the development question)? Second, how quickly can the e-learning initiative reach everyone who needs the content (the delivery question)? And third, how fast can the e-learning initiative be altered due to a change in the business, or the need to distribute new or revised information (the "turn-around" question)?

Of all the four major e-learning justification criteria, speed is the key. Without the need for speed, technology might not be necessary. Without a speed criteria, the Internet, or intranet, would be far less important. But in an age where overnight mail is often too slow, speed does matter. And the business case for e-learning must have a speed component to be complete.

The Two Questions Every Training Organization Asks ... but Perhaps Shouldn't

When a training organization wants to build a business case or set measurable e-learning goals for itself, its leaders almost invariably ask the same two questions (or variants of these questions):

1. How many hours of development time does it take to deliver one hour of e-learning? Doesn't *seem* like such a silly question. Isn't it a good idea to be able to predict development times and costs? Perhaps, except for the fact that this question is usually impossible to answer with anything more exacting than "it all depends." It depends on the:

- experience of developers
- availability of resources (talent and money)
- severity of project timelines, level of criticality for the company

- business risks of a poor implementation
- complexity of the proposed learning, amount of multimedia used
- nature of the content, sophistication of the programming
- quality of management and the degree of general resistance to new ideas

In other words, every project is different—the best you can do is make reasonable assumptions based on prior work *and* the specific learning problem you are trying to solve, assuming that none of the criteria have changed (which is unlikely). It is far better to map out a specific schedule and project plan for each initiative based on all the criteria. Over time you'll get a feel for development times in your own shop, but because of all the variability, specific models or predictions, as well as their transferability, are not likely to hold up. Vendors with significant experience can usually provide ballpark estimates based on cost trade-offs for any level of production value, programming, and instructional design, but again, these estimates will only apply to *their* work. Do not think that a ratio provided by one vendor can be automatically applied to others, or to your internal people.

2. What percentage of all our training should be technology-based? It's one thing to set goals for the transition to e-learning, but quite another to set an arbitrary number. That's why setting a percentage of training that should be converted may not be useful. Assume that an organization selects 40 percent as the amount of courses to be "technologized." Here's a way to do it overnight: Count the number of classroom courses currently on the books. Let's say you have 100 instructor-led courses. Now, simply sign a contract with a training vendor for 66 online courses, giving you a total of 166 training courses, and presto—your 40 percent goal is reached! And who's to say the number should be 40 percent—why not 50 percent or 30 percent? These goals are almost always arbitrary and usually set far too high to be realistic. They make great press but mean little.

No matter how often the preceding two questions are posed, they can be as meaningless as the first time they were asked. They focus on internal "accounting" measures and not organizational impact. They do little to reflect the cost to the business, actual quality, level of service, or development/delivery cycle times. Better measures include the level of corporate or organizational investment in e-learning or the value of the programs. (If 10 percent of your courses are on the Web, but are by far the most impactful, wouldn't this be a better goal?) Reduced operational costs or contribution to competitive advantage (increase in flexibility, responsiveness, and adaptiveness to change) are other goals to consider.

The E-Learning Value Proposition

So instead of concentrating on how long it takes to do something or how much of it ought to be done, the focus should be on delivering value to the business. And the value of e-learning is the *sum* of its ability to save money, generate benefit to the business (enhance skill and knowledge, improve job performance, and impact results), be available to anyone—at any place and at any time—and do all of this at the speed of business. Eliminate any one of the criteria—cost, quality, service, or speed—and e-learning's value falls precipitously. Thus the value proposition for e-learning is:

E-Learning **Cost Efficiency** +
E-Learning **Quality** +
E-Learning **Service** +
E-Learning **Speed** =
E-Learning **Value**

Now, with an effective infrastructure in place, a solid change management/culture-building strategy under way, and a well-laid-out business case to justify e-learning, the next step is to look inward at the training department to answer the question, "Can dinosaurs learn to dance?"

An E-Learning Journey

by John P. McMorrow, AT&T and Talent Alliance

From Blissful Ignorance to Semi-Techno-Wonk: A Five Year Plus Odyssey

My BEGINNINGS WITH LEARNING technology was as Vice President of Education and Training for AT&T. In 1995, I chartered an interdivisional team to determine how to get better value for the company's annual investment in training. Among their recommendations was the establishment of a robust e-learning capability in the education and training organization by year 2000. This was supported by a tightly reasoned thesis, built on the growing availability of desktop access, the low retention of content from classroom training, cost reductions based on smaller faculty size, less student time away from the job and less travel, and the benefits of access to learning when and where needed. I set about selling this to AT&T's leaders.

Most memorable was distributing, at an executive committee meeting, a CD-ROM that we had developed to demonstrate some of the capabilities of using technology for learning. The reactions fell into three groups. A few said they would pop it into their computer and take a look at it, a few jokingly said they would ask their children or grandchildren to help them look at it, and a few said nothing—but later in the week I got calls from their assistants who had been directed to brief their bosses on the content. Fortunately, we were able to get executive support by stressing cost savings, emphasizing the importance to our business of leadership in using our own technologies, and stressing that this was a five year plan—we'd start slowly.

Learning: Fellow executives range widely in their comfort and experience level with technology (including learning technology). Many who are uncomfortable with it may be hesitant to say so in public.

Also challenging was the selection of the technology to use. After a detailed analysis of alternatives, we decided to begin with CD-ROMs, believing that the Internet would not be a viable vehicle over the next few years. A mistake. But since we started small, we were able to transition to Internet products, although I'm sure there are CDs accumulating dust in some storeroom.

Learning: Don't underestimate the speed of change in technology. Recognize you may make some wrong choices, but be flexible to adapting to new options as they become available.

While I learned much about the use of technology, I was not using it myself. As typical in a large company, I had assistants who retrieved and sent e-mails for me, prepared visual aids for my presentations, and searched the Internet for information, preparing reports and analyses.

When I was 58 years old, I decided to take advantage of a retirement incentive. But I was asked to stay on for a while to lead the transition of the HR department to a new organizational structure. All of a sudden I became a one-person show, with no administrative support.

I was forced to begin to use e-mail myself, prepare status reports, do travel and meeting arrangements, and to make visuals for presentations. After a few weeks of ponderous two-fingered pecking at the keyboard, I decided that I had to learn to type and found a number of typing software packages to use. My favorite allowed me to shoot down descending letters with scoring and sound effects, just like a video game. I was fortunate during this time that near my small temporary office were technically literate people who were willing to answer my never-ending questions and help me through impasses with the technology. However, when I was under time pressure, I had to steel myself to not rush to my former staff to do work for me, but to endure and slowly produce the work myself.

Learning: Most of us will only learn to use technology if we have a need to use it personally, not just because it seems the right thing to do.

Learning: People will help, generously and repeatedly. Having technology literate people nearby to answer your questions and help with problems on the spot speeds the learning process immensely.

Learning: Patience. Computers are not user friendly to the first-timer. Also, once you set out on the learning road, you have to be willing to put up with the frustrations of mistakes and impasses and not give in to the temptation of letting others do the work for you.

When I finally did retire, I started to do some consulting. This forced me to take the next step in my technology-for-learning process, learning to use the PC on the road, preparing reports on the go, using e-mail from hotels and airports, and learning all the nuances of connections and servers. It meant lugging a laptop around the country (not as light as claimed), trying to work on airlines in the middle seat of coach, and squatting on the floor in airport terminals to access a power outlet.

Learning: You can access the Net from almost anywhere, but at times you must put your dignity aside.

The final step in the odyssey was a surprising opportunity to be President and CEO of Talent Alliance, a nonprofit consortium of companies using the Internet for employee development. I was attracted by the idea of companies working together to support employees' career opportunities and using the Internet to do so.

As a start-up high-tech organization, we have been a prototype of a virtual organization, with people working from their home locations. Marketing was in Florida, our Service Center was in Georgia, and our Web design group was in California. We have used experts at universities across the country, and a small staff in our borrowed New Jersey headquarters (but even they often worked from home; a necessity if we were to attract skilled staff for what we could afford to pay). I divided my time between my Montana home, member and prospect locations, and our small headquarters office.

Talent Alliance also opened my eyes to the wealth of information available from the Web; on member companies, prospective members, and competitors. We made extensive use of financial Web sites, company home pages, and other business sites when preparing for sales calls, member interactions, and even site content decisions. I often had the feeling that I knew as much about a company's direction, products, and finances as the individuals with whom I was meeting, an invaluable asset in building a relationship.

Learning: With both Talent Alliance and AT&T, I have been selling the benefits of cooperation across organizations. At AT&T that meant cooperation across divisions by training leaders in establishing learning technology targets and sharing some development costs. With Talent Alliance it was membership by different companies and sharing Internet development costs for providing employee development and career support tools. In both cases, persuading top leaders was relatively easy, but middle managers presented an almost insurmountable barrier. Possible reasons—negative impact on their staff size and budgets, their own discomfort with technology, and the realization that cooperation does not provide the same opportunity for recognition of their accomplishment as doing it themselves. This is an issue for leaders to address.

Final Learning: The future of technology for learning is bright. The range of information and learning content added daily to the

Web continues to amaze me—as does the continually improving processes for organizing and allowing efficient access to it. Industries are being changed by it. Consider the changes under way in those industries dependent historically on controlling customers' access to information—for example, financial markets, insurance, consumer durables, even higher education. These transitions will continue and no doubt expand to other industries. Through Talent Alliance, I have visited with many companies who say they are not ready to use technology for learning. They are accurate in one sense—that they may not be prepared to deliver much formal training via technology. But in another sense they are inaccurate—that most of them are providing essential customer and product information at the desktop to their customer support units and others, while all through their company individuals are accessing the Web for information they use in their day-to-day decision making. And with broadband access coming soon, allowing real motion video and instantaneous dialogue, a wealth of formal leaning should move from classroom to wherever it is needed.

And with it I hope to continue my odyssey from invincible ignorance to semi-techno-wonk.

John McMorrow is now a consultant in change management and high performance organization development, with particular emphasis on improving Human Resources systems and processes.

9

Reinventing the Training Organization

"When the rate of change outside exceeds the rate of change inside, the end is in sight."

Jack Welch,
Chairman and CEO, General Electric

"Faced with the choice between changing one's mind and proving that there is no need to change . . . almost everyone gets busy on the proof."

John Kenneth Galbraith

A FTER ALL IS SAID AND DONE, the e-learning revolution stalls out and dies if those directly responsible for leading the charge fail to do so. Even with senior management support and a great learning culture, the ability of an organization's training department(s) to deploy their systems and resources in support of e-learning is still essential.

Signs the Training Department May Not Be Truly Interested in E-Learning

Many training organizations and their leaders say they're moving into e-learning, but often their actions tell a different story. Too often, you'll hear the following position statements in corporate training groups:

- *We're studying e-learning to determine its viability.* In some cases, *study* is a code word for stalling. Some organizations that show this behavior either are waiting for e-learning to go away or are dangerously uneducated about it. The first is a cultural issue that may require a reexamination of who is leading the effort. The second may be a learning issue that can be overcome (learning about e-learning will be discussed later in this chapter).
- *Nobody's asking for it, so we're not doing it.* Of course, no one was asking for online bookstores or online auctions either, but that didn't stop Amazon.com or eBay. This is the classic distinction between being market-focused—meeting *current* demand—and being future focused—creating *future* demand. Like the best businesses, the best training organizations are those that can look ahead, see what the critical needs will be, and be ready with an offer that meets those needs.
- *Of course we have an e-learning strategy . . . you should see our Web site.* This is a classic statement of confusion between artifacts of e-learning and an e-learning strategy. Web sites, online catalogs, and registration systems are certainly part of an overall e-learning deployment, but they are not sufficient. It matters more about the direction the e-learning effort is taking rather than all the "activities" it generates. For example, having Web sites that are essentially online advertising

for online courseware represents a far less sophisticated view of e-learning than having Web sites that are an integral part of an organizational knowledge management system, or providing guidance to employees about what learning experiences are most appropriate for them.

- *We've got a couple of pilot projects going right now.* This could be good news—the training organization is trying out e-learning. But sometimes pilot projects go on for years. The technology or the people change and things start over, or the organization can't seem to get beyond a trial to full commitment—so *everything's* a pilot! Successful pilot projects are best followed with larger, full-blown initiatives. If you have lots of pilots but can't seem to get out of the "trial phase," the level of commitment may not be as strong as you think it is.
- *We're waiting for senior management approval.* What if approval never comes? Some training leaders may be hoping precisely for this. "Well, if the boss doesn't say she/he wants this, why should we do it?" is the refrain. However, it's far more likely that the boss is waiting for a demonstration of the value of e-learning. It is incumbent on the training and learning professionals in an organization to proactively help senior managers see the benefit of e-learning for the business, not wait for the CEO to have an epiphany about it and come down from the mountaintop to proclaim, "It shall be done."
- *We're waiting for the technology to improve.* While there are certainly baseline technological requirements for e-learning (such as broad access) that must be met before it can be successful, saying that the technology is not quite ready can lead to paralysis. The key is to get involved now, use what's available, develop momentum in the organization, and constantly improve as the technology improves.
- *We're not really sure if this is here to stay.* In 1977, Ken Olsen, former CEO of Digital Equipment Corporation (DEC) said that he didn't see any reason why anyone would want a computer in his or her home. At the time, experimental personal

computers were being built in garages and not yet available in the marketplace. Olson had a huge mainframe-type business to protect, and this failure to see and embrace the coming change eventually contributed to the downfall of DEC. Like the personal computer, the Internet and e-learning are not going away—to think otherwise is foolhardy.

- *It will hurt our classroom business.* In the 1930s the railroads refused to get into the business of flying people from city to city for fear that it would hurt train travel. They saw themselves in the railroad business, which precluded airlines, not the transportation business, which included them. The rest is history. The same is true for training organizations. If they see themselves in the classroom training business, not the learning (and performance) business, their influence will be substantially reduced.

- *Let's see who else is doing this before we jump in.* Today, most companies have already jumped in. The International Data Corporation (IDC) notes that corporate spending on e-learning will rise from $1.5 billion in 1999 to more than $9 billion in 2002.[1] And this does not include knowledge management, which IDC estimates will grow 40 percent annually.[2] All of these organizations recognize the power of the Internet (and their intranets) to improve business performance, and are now working to get the maximum benefit for e-learning. Furthermore, if training organizations don't get involved, there is an increasing likelihood that their clients will employ e-learning solutions anyway—purchased from the outside.

- *Our instructors are against it.* Much of the resistance to e-learning can come from the instructor corps, who feel a loss of prestige and perhaps their jobs if e-learning "takes over." Unfortunately, "taking over" is precisely how e-learning is often portrayed inside a business. But it doesn't have to be this way. First of all, it should be apparent by now that the classroom will continue to have a significant role to play and that instructors can continue to teach those courses that are deemed integral to the overall learning architecture.

Second, this is a great opportunity for instructors to retrain themselves as e-learning developers or learning/performance consultants with their client groups. When done right, and when effective change management and reskilling opportunities are made available, trainer resistance can be significantly reduced.

- *Our students don't want it.* We often hear that it's the student/customer who doesn't want to learn via computer. However, in many cases this may be more the perception of the training leadership than the actual views of the potential learners. A study of training executives by the OmniTech Consulting Group[3] indicates that this is precisely the case. Some interesting findings from this study include:

  ♦ While more than 90 percent of trainers in the study believed learners need to be instructionally guided through all learning events, only about 50 percent of learners held this view; the other 50 percent expressed more interest in learning how to find information for themselves.

  ♦ More trainers (66 percent) favored group learning over individualized learning, but more learners (56 percent) favored the individualized learning mode.

  ♦ Three-quarters of all trainers surveyed stated a preference for learning events taking place away from the work location. Only one-quarter of the learners actually held this view, with three-quarters favoring learning at the work site.

At Microsoft, Chairman Bill Gates reports that in 1999, online training usage increased five times faster than classroom training and that twice as much online training is offered than classroom training. Gates notes that while people want to improve their skills, the value of time is clearly influencing the way they choose to learn.[4]

The results of these studies indicate a growing and disconcerting split between what trainers think is in the best interests of learners and what the learners actually believe is in their best interest. It's very important to determine if this trend is evident in your organization, and if it is, to reconcile these beliefs quickly and effectively.

- *You can't learn at the worksite—that's what the training center is for.* A belief that learning takes place only in specialized facilities would indicate not just a possible hidden agenda to protect the bricks and mortar of training, but a fundamental denial of what organizational learning is or can be; so be sure to explore the underlying causes of the resistance. The argument that learning can't take place in the office because of interruptions is a problem for employees and their managers to solve, not an education problem. Besides, what classroom course today is not interrupted by pagers and cell phones going off, by people coming back late after a break because they were on the phone, or by people leaving early to deal with a work-related crisis (and you can't put the class on "Save" like you can with e-learning)?

- *We can't afford it.* More likely, you can't afford not to do it. As discussed in Chapter 8, the business case for e-learning is easily made. Saying you can't afford it may be a reflection primarily of the resource constraints of the training organization—an internal and narrow view. If you include the economic benefits for your clients and the firm, e-learning can free up a significant amount of money.

Can Training Organizations Change?

Whether your training organization displays any or all of these signs, or even if you are on the right road to e-learning, it's important to deal with four realities of change inside the organization. First, there is a long and reasonably successful tradition of classroom learning. This has been reinforced by our own personal experiences when we went to school. Whether a company has a modern, residential state-of-the-art training center, or just a small training room down the hall, there is a mystique about coming to training, a "specialness" that is enticing and satisfying for many people. Second, there is a legitimate ego-building quality about teaching—the sense of expertise and control that can be intrinsically rewarding for many instructors. Third, the instructor corps and the training facilities represent a major investment, one that must be continually used and justified. There is a fear that e-learning will empty out the classrooms and upset the whole economic balance of the training department. And fourth, there is the perception that if employees didn't want classroom training, they wouldn't come. And as long as they do come, everything's okay.

These barriers deserve additional discussion. There is no denying that classroom learning is a unique event—different from work and special in its own right. And nothing can or should change this. In fact, in a total learning architecture the attitude people have about going to a great classroom program can be very advantageous in reinforcing the entire learning program. The same is true for the feeling instructors enjoy when they are successful in front of a class. It's a highly motivating experience that should not be lost.

But the last two realities, which focus on the economics of sustaining the training organization, are the most troublesome. For training organizations that have developed a *retail* economic model for what they do, the change can be traumatic. In the retail model, the training organization charges internal clients for training—both development and delivery. In other words, it supports itself through tuition revenue. If the organization believes that its purpose is to provide product (i.e., training) for customers to buy, then the emphasis will always be on filling seats. If training leaders are not careful, the decisions they make can be motivated by their own economic survival (sometimes despite their intentions). So, training that's critical for a few people might not be offered, in favor of courseware that's marginal but can attract a high number of enrollees. Courses can be placed into learning plans simply to generate "enrollments." Marketing professionals, not training professionals, could have more say in what is offered. Giveaways, discounts, two-for-one deals, training in exotic locations, better food, and other marketing trappings creep into the learning decision-making process in order to generate additional training business.

As simple and attractive as it seems, this model for internal training can be a house of cards. If the training organization is funded solely by tuition, then efforts will flow toward tried-and-true activities (both development and delivery) that generate the greatest revenue. The statement that the organization is self-funding is untrue since its money comes from the other parts of the business.[5] With the realization that so much money is being transferred to the training department, cries for justification arise. And focusing on tuition revenue and student days just won't cut it. If the value isn't there, the organization can almost certainly expect to be cut severely.

The implications for e-learning can be catastrophic. In most organizations, e-learning is usually a small part of the budget, at least initially. These operations tend to have the youngest and least senior people. They are struggling to build a capability and redefine learning, but have probably not created the type of "demand" (or reached an existing, untapped demand) that a retail training organization requires. So when the budget is cut, guess who usually goes first?

The fact is, when training is in a survival mode, it sometimes eats its young. Like the desert creosote bush, which kills off nearby vegetation before it can become established and challenge the main bush for scarce groundwater, the fledgling e-learning effort is sacrificed to protect the cash cow of classroom learning. Over time, no new initiatives ever get started for fear that at the first sign of trouble, they'll be the first to go. Without new initiatives, the training organization becomes paralyzed and begins a downward spiral of survival cost cutting that often ends in the eventual elimination of the function altogether.

And many training organizations never see this coming. They suffer from what author Clay Christensen calls the "innovator's dilemma."[6] In a sense, Christensen suggests that many organizations, even highly successful ones, are unable to alter their present business practices and beliefs in order to better create their future. It's why U.S. car makers never saw the Japanese automobile as a threat until it was too late. It's why traditional brokerage firms were blindsided by Schwab and E*Trade, and why no bookstore anywhere saw Amazon.com as anything more than a joke—although they're not laughing now.

> **"As long as trainees are happy and do not complain, trainers feel comfortable, relaxed, and secure."**
> **Donald L. Kirkpatrick[7]**

It's a classic case of "If it ain't broke, don't fix it." Training organizations look at full classrooms and bulging revenue receipts and ask themselves, "Why change?" It's also a classic case of failure to see a shifting paradigm. Again, it's why the railroads never went into the airline business.

So while it's likely that most companies will eventually embrace a robust e-learning strategy, the likelihood that this will happen fast enough to allow the training organization to thrive in the future is probably questionable at many firms. Because while all this debate about change is raging within the training organization, front-line clients are going elsewhere. Even if training organizations recognize the need to deploy e-learning and begin some important initiatives in this area, their paradigms may be limiting the amount of change or risk they're willing to accept, slowing them down and decreasing their survivability.

For training to be viable in the future, simply embracing e-learning is not enough—the training organization must reinvent itself. This involves new business and governance models, a reexamination of facilities, outsourcing, an increased emphasis on professional development and talent recruitment, and, above all—thinking digitally.

A New Business and Governance Model for the Training Organization

For the training organization to successfully deploy an effective e-learning strategy, several assumptions and approaches to the running of the function will have to change. Some of the most fundamental changes are outlined in Table 9.1.

Table 9.1 Converting to a New E-Learning Business and Governance Model

Traditional View	New E-Learning Business Model
Training department *staff* are transferred into the e-learning group. This staff is in flux as people move in and out from the main training organization, depending on needs, assignments, and availability. The leadership of e-learning is within the training department.	E-Learning group recruits its own leaderhsip and staff, perhaps from the training department, but also from other parts of the business and even new hires. These people are permanently assigned to the e-learning venture. They have a clear mission and focus.
E-Learning *budget* is a line item in the annual training budget.	E-Learning budget is a multiyear, separate investment controlled by the e-learning group's leadership and outside governance (see below).
Economic model based on cost recovery, either through tuition or allocation across the business.	Economic model based on investment in programs and solutions deemed important for the business. In most cases, distribution should be part of the investment, but if a charge is necessary, it is *only* to recover distribution costs.
Funding requests are made and balanced in conjunction with the needs of the rest of the training organization.	Funding requests are made and balanced only with the needs and objectives of the e-learning plan.
E-Learning *reports* up to the head of the training organization.	E-Learning reports to a separate governance board on which the head of training may have a seat but does not singularly control. This governance board is comprised of key stakeholders and clients.
E-Learning is held to the same "accounting" *measures* as the rest of the training department, including tuition revenue and student days, if they are counted. This is usually annualized.	E-Learning is held to new measures of performance, including cost, quality, service, and speed (see Chapter 8). In addition, the measures are set against the timeline of the strategy, which may have multiyear milestones.
E-Learning is focused on developing *solutions* for current needs and uses.	E-Learning is focused on developing solutions that reflect both current and anticipated needs and uses.

Table 9.1 *(Continued)*

Traditional View	New E-Learning Business Model
E-Learning is considered part of the whole training organization not only for funds allocation, but for *budget cuts* as well.	E-Learning is considered separately for funding and budget cuts. Protections are in place to ensure that it is not sacrificed just to protect other operations.
Training operations are mostly *centralized* in one large organization (e.g., corporate university) or mostly *decentralized* by business unit, product, or region.	E-Learning requires centralization of several key functions, some of which include technology standards, development/management of instructional and information design processes and tools, vendor management, portal deployment and functionality, knowledge management system administration, professional development and strategy. However, content (informational and instructional) for both traditional learning and e-learning can be distributed to wherever the expertise is located.

Here's an example of how these two models differ, based on a composite of actual experiences at a number of corporate training centers. In one case, the company's "corporate university" was chartered with the bulk of the training responsibility for the firm. The leadership of the CU convinced management that their programs were so good that people would be willing to pay for them. Thus, the CU did not receive any direct budget from the company; instead it relied on tuition (a retail model) to stay in business. To generate business, the CU relied on a number of strategies, including increased marketing of courses and the inclusion of some of the most visible programs into everyone's development plans, and the deployment of a "something for everyone" catalog, focusing exclusively on courses. It saw its primary customers as the students in the classroom—they would let the training organization know how it was doing. This worked fine for quite a while, until a number of things happened. First, the firm had a series of bad business quarters and training money was frozen at the business unit level. Second, the mainstay courseware was generating too many people with unneeded expertise (think about programmer training in a company with too many programmers). When the organization switched to e-learning to cut costs, it still had to charge tuition for the programs. In this particular case, an all-company orientation program required a "paid subscription" so each employee would receive program access and information through e-mail. When local managers didn't have the money to pay for the subscriptions, the program—important though it was—died. For this organization there was no argument that the learning programs were of high quality. The issue was the use of a flawed business model that could not sustain either the organization itself or its new e-learning initiatives. The organization's viability has been under attack ever since, and the scope of the e-learning initiatives has been frozen with the rest of the organization's efforts.

The second company saw things differently. The training organization in this firm did not use a retail model. It would not develop or deploy any training program unless there was sponsorship at the top, an approved business case, and money made available for development. It saw its customers as the people who *pay* for the programs—the higher up, the better. The company didn't always have to supply all the funding—any business unit could contribute. The training organization reasoned, correctly, that if the company were directly paying for the development of a program, there would be more support for it. Although the number of offerings were far fewer than at the first company, the strategic impact of the total training program was more significant. And, even though the primary focus was on training, decisions were made at the architecture level, allowing for knowledge management and other approaches to be used where appropriate. The training organization also insisted that any product developed for one part of the business would be made available to any other part of the business—once the investment was made, it seemed wasteful not to leverage it. For classroom training, charges were only levied for the actual cost of delivering the program, and these charges were levied at the business unit level, not at the individual level. Finally, after some initial trials, the training organization determined that delivery of e-learning solutions on the intranet was so cost efficient that it no longer made sense to collect any fees. This immediately eliminated costs for billing, tracking, and collecting tuition. This company set up a separate e-learning organization and did not require it to recover its own costs (that's where the investment part came in). If budgets were cut, the e-learning funding would be judged on its own merits and not subject to the needs of the more traditional training program. Because of this investment approach, the impact of e-learning was more powerful than it was at the first company.

Reexamining Facilities as E-Learning Takes Root

As e-learning becomes more prevalent, are companies holding on too hard to their training facilities? This is a tough question. The most successful learning centers are those where the programs are very specific and corporate in nature. Other characteristics of successful centers are those where senior executives can play some sort of a teaching role and where the overall focus of the facility is on the future of the company (as in leadership development). In addition, programs that require very expensive laboratories and simulators are often appropriate for centralized training facilities. The best centers are linked to the corporate intranet in every classroom and every sleeping room (if a residential facility), and make it easy for anyone to "plug in" anywhere in the facility. Finally, many of these strategic learning centers are used not only to teach content, but to influence the company's culture, build teamwork, and provide opportunities for collaborative problem solving as well. Merrill Lynch and General Electric are just two examples of companies whose training centers meet many of these criteria. In each case, the central training center does *not* deliver any program that could be better delivered through e-learning. They've moved from a "bricks and mortar" strategy to an integrated "bricks and clicks" strategy.

When a facility is used just to deliver any type of training, including programs redundant with e-learning, it is probably in jeopardy. When people begin to accept e-learning, they will stop going to the training center. The training organization, if it's desperate to fill seats and preserve the viability of its most expensive physical asset, may continuously replace these programs with newer ones to keep attendance up. Even with the best of intentions, if the training organization manages e-learning based on the best practices for managing *classroom* learning, the new initiatives may not survive.

Some organizations are shutting down all classroom facilities and moving everything to the Web. When a classroom is needed, it will be rented—perhaps from a hotel or another firm. But although the inventory of classrooms may shrink, getting rid of all of them is risky. Outside resources are not as easily controlled or scheduled, are difficult for technology-centered programs (such as programmer training), and cannot create the right corporate atmosphere that's often needed for the best learning environment. A better strategy would be to share internal resources with other groups that need space (spreading the cost and increasing the capacity), and use external facilities for overload periods.

Specialized training facilities still do have an important role to play in corporate learning, especially when they are tied into the total learning strategy of the business. They are complements to e-learning, not alternatives or replacements. For a central training facility to be successful in the digital learning age, it must use its physical space in ways that cannot be duplicated through e-learning. If it tries to compete with e-learning, it will eventually lose. This is another reason why planning learning at the *architecture* level is so important.

Outsourcing and E-Learning

There is an increasing emphasis on the value of outsourcing a variety of e-learning services. Indeed, there is a lot of merit to a well-managed outsourcing program, but there's danger in a poorly managed one.

The first and most important rule of e-learning outsourcing is to be sure you have enough in-house expertise to effectively manage the outsourced suppliers. This is not just vendor management.

It is also the e-learning expertise to be able to judge quality and effectiveness. While the vast majority of vendors are reputable, it is still sometimes a "buyer beware" world (see Chapter 10).

Expertise that should be retained in-house include: project management, needs assessment/task analysis (or at least management of this process—you still have to provide the SME), priority setting, approval of the design of the learning solution, providing a test bed and learners for usability testing, pilots and field trials, evaluation strategy, and communications and change management. E-Learning services that can be outsourced include: conducting the needs assessment, preliminary design, authoring and programming, media development, program assembly, and implementation of evaluation initiatives. In addition, you need to formulate a plan for ongoing maintenance of the product, either completely in-house, outsourced to one or two full-service prime contractors, or a combination of approaches.

The technical components are particularly good candidates for outsourced services. Unless you are prepared to spend a great deal of money on highly technical staff—who need constant upgrading of the hardware and software they use—it's better to leave this service to a vendor for whom this is their core business. This does not mean you should not have any technical staff inside. It is essential to maintain at least a few experts in the field, not only to do maintenance on e-learning products, but to develop and maintain product and platform standards, and to act as effective contractor interfaces. Additional responsibilities include maintaining the growing learning objects library, working with internal IT support, software upgrades, etc. Even though you are outsourcing your authoring, programming, and media production, the contractors should never perceive that you are abdicating your knowledge or control of their work. One company recently outsourced all of their e-learning work to several vendors and, after several downsizings, found they had little expertise left on the inside to manage the vendors. The result has been delays, inconsistencies, and lower quality.

Other good candidates for outsourcing are those content areas that are not proprietary or competitive in nature and are readily available in the public e-learning marketplace. The general rule is: Outsource commodity training content, and insource organizational intelligence and competitive advantage. For example, there are dozens of leadership programs available for purchase from a variety of vendors. Does it make sense to reinvent the wheel? Even if the best vendor only matches 90 percent of your needs, should that program be rejected so you can achieve 100 percent alignment by spending a lot of money on your own solution? This is the classic "build or buy" dilemma. In most cases, buying, even with some customization, may be the better route to take. This frees up your resources to build those solutions that are truly proprietary, mission critical, and/or unique to your business. Whether you build these solutions or contract the project out depends on your overall staffing and outsourcing strategy. Here are some key criteria for determining which way to go:

- If you already have a well-honed production staff that can do this kind of work, and they have the capacity to do it, then you may be able to build internally. This will be made easier if you have begun the process of building learning objects and have a library from which to draw.
- If you do not have an internal production staff, it would likely not make sense to create one just for a couple of projects, no matter how important they are. So in this case you're probably better off building externally.
- If your internal team is capable but is operating at or over capacity, this is a good opportunity to find a compatible partner to handle the overload.
- If you have no internal resources and no proven external partners, and you are charged with building a high-profile, company-specific program, this is a good time to begin the process of finding the right long-term partner (see below, and Chapter 10).

The way to get started with outsourcing is to first select one function or one product to hand over to well-researched and highly capable vendors. If this works well, additional functions and projects can be outsourced, thereby increasing the scope of the contractor's work. Finally, a specific function can be completely outsourced with only internal management and quality control (i.e., supply chain management) left to employees.

Eventually, the training organization could consider exiting one or more e-learning curricula or content areas, turning over the program in its entirety to one or more contractors. The internal organization then serves more of a brokering role, matching internal needs with approved, external suppliers. As the scope of the outsourcing becomes greater, the need for internal vendor management expertise also becomes greater. As more work is done on the outside, it's a good idea to reduce suppliers to just a handful of proven "partners" in order to ensure maintainability, portfolio management, reusability, and economies of scale. Your long-term relationship will cover multiple generations of the products you get from them. It is a far superior model than the "per-project, fixed price, low-bid" contracting approach so often taken.

> **"The training industry is benefiting from the outsourcing megatrend, with corporations increasingly relying on the expertise of third-party specialists to provide the training and education necessary to prepare their employees."**
> **Michael Moe, Merrill Lynch[8]**

The benefits of outsourcing for e-learning are clear. You reduce (but do not eliminate) the need for large internal expenditures in development and delivery technology and talent. You move more of your expenses to variable costs that can be managed up or down as the business requires, without massive disruptions to your internal operations and staff. You can refocus your attention and resources to more strategic issues. And you avail yourself of the latest innovations, best practices, and new thinking by constantly reviewing the e-learning marketplace for the best service providers.

Professional Development and Recruitment

As training organizations change, the skills and capabilities of their staffs must change as well. There's a great deal of pressure to be "up" on the technology—HTML, XML, Java, authoring tools, etc. In a recent survey, leading experts (practitioners, consultants, and academics) were asked what skills were most important for e-learning and how prepared they felt the field was to successfully apply them. The results are shown in Figure 9.1.

Instructional design, evaluation, information design, performance consulting, and human factors were deemed far more important to the successful launch of e-learning than were skills in areas like Web programming, HTML, and authoring. But for all of the areas, the opinion of the experts is that the field is not well prepared to undertake this change. What can be done?

First of all, more money must be put into reskilling the current training workforce. There are many ways to do this. First, find people who are willing and interested in acquiring these new skills. There's little sense in retraining people who will fight it all the way. Public and in-house seminars and attendance at specific conferences are ways to expose these people to the fundamentals. But it may be appropriate to remove some promising employees from their work assignments and immerse them in a longer, more in-depth training experience, perhaps in conjunction with an accelerated university degree program. This may be expensive, but these will be the key individuals—the "seed corn"—of

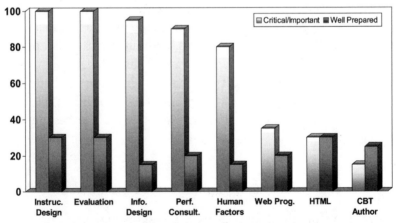

Figure 9.1 Experts find that traditional instructional and information design skills are more critical for e-learning than technological skills, but that the field as a whole is not as prepared as it should be in any of these areas.

the emerging e-learning operation. They can serve as role models and coaches for the bulk of the workforce that is making the transition.

But training of any kind will not be enough. Experience is just as important. Work to assign people to e-learning projects, even if it's in a support role. Get people comfortable with new processes and techniques. Don't try to make a graphic artist out of someone who can't draw, or a scriptwriter out of someone who can't write, or an instructional designer out of someone who can't think analytically. Try to match interests and capabilities to new functions that have transferable skills, like instructional design. Over time, people will find their niche and begin to develop the new skills they need to move into e-learning. Once they're established, move quickly to have these people work in teams so that expertise is shared.

Having made the investment in these people, you'll need to keep them current in their technical skills and keep them happy in their dual roll as corporate people and technical specialists. Providing continuous learning, so they're at the "cutting edge" of their technical field, is as important as compensation. Perhaps your prime contractor can transfer expertise to your internal staff. Whether or not this happens, it's important that professional development happen—it pays off in higher retention rates.

Overall, make reskilling a key activity of the organization, and do it in a way that reflects the legitimate professionalism of the field, complete with its own set of skills, research, and discipline. Create incentives for people to learn new things in this field. And for those who don't want to make the transition, perhaps they can remain serving the classroom component. But if there is no fit in the new organization, they need to be counseled out. It's not that e-learning reduces jobs for people, but it changes the mix and types of jobs. With proper planning and a good internal change-management program, job loss can be minimized.

Recruitment is the other side of the professional development coin. If e-learning is going to make it, the organization can ill-afford to bring in unqualified people. Certainly some people with potential can join the group and participate in professional development, but resist a wholesale dumping of new people from other parts of the business who have neither the qualifications nor interest to work in e-learning, or little likelihood of developing any new skills to the level you require. Organizations often resort to this approach when the work is outstripping the ability of the staff to handle it. But having a larger staff of unqualified people can only make matters worse.

For the most part, if outside hiring is in the plan, hire the best talent you can find and afford. Focus on finding a few great people who fit in nicely with the organization, rather than a legion of new hires that are "just okay." If there is a large internal staff, the need for outside hires may be minimized if those who are brought in play a coaching role not unlike the internal people who received in-depth retraining. Hiring seed corn is a good supplement to building the crop from within. With a more professionalized staff, the organization will be in a better position to get the most benefit from its e-learning outsourced partners.

Professional development and recruitment activities can provide telltale signs of corporate support for e-learning—you must determine if it's a reflection of the company's commitment to e-learning. If reasonable activities in these areas are not supported, it may be that e-learning is not being given the priority it needs (or that the e-learning *people* believe they have).

Reinventing Training at Cisco Systems: A Case Study

When Tom Kelly came to Cisco Systems two and a half years ago, the training function was similar to most other companies—predominately offering classroom-based courses with some isolated e-learning efforts under way. As Vice President for Worldwide Training, Tom was asked to rapidly move the organization forward into e-learning for Cisco's sales force, its "ecosystem" of partners and resellers, and for its customers. The company knew that these groups needed a new approach to help them keep up with the pace of technology and product innovation that poured out of Cisco each year, and that current training methods weren't scaling to meet the rapid growth and change in the marketplace.

As technology changes at a frenzied pace, e-learning is not an advantage, it's an element of corporate survival.

Learning from initial efforts to bring e-learning capabilities into the business was fixed on delivery without a strong emphasis on content. Cisco created a new model that involved teaming product engineers, product marketing, and salespeople in the training development process. These coalitions (subject matter experts, learning specialists, sales leaders, etc.) identified specific learning needs and requirements.

With learning requirements in hand, SMEs became actively involved in the building of learning products—not necessarily courses, but a variety of content—white papers, videos, audio files, presentations, screen cam demos, etc. At Cisco the differentiated forms of learning products (education, training, information, etc.) were replaced by logically sequenced content arranged by specific job and function-related *learning maps*. These maps are structured plans that integrate the needed content with a sound instructional framework. But in order to increase the efficiency of the process, most of the instructional design requirements are embedded into sophisticated tools, with a small core of design specialists available for consulting, coaching, and support. Additionally, rapid application and design processes (including rapid prototyping) became a mainstay of the work. These technology-enabled process changes helped reduce development cycle times which were four to nine months, to a much more efficient one to four months. The learning development process became more like that of any product development cycle, and increasingly less like the traditional linear-training development methodologies.

For Cisco sales force training, quality control is managed through a centralized e-learning portal. To "publish" on this portal, learning products have to meet specific content guidelines and infrastructure criteria. When learners enter the portal, they can easily identify the learning map for their job or role and access the specific content module that they need. They can also access pre- and postassessments that measure knowledge and competence associated with the modular content. In the technologically enabled world, Cisco no longer requires completion of any particular learning component—it simply requires that employees demonstrate competence. So even if a learner doesn't use any module from a learning map, as long as she/he completes the assessment successfully, that's what matters. In this way, the company deemphasizes the question *Did they go to class?* in favor of the question *What can they do?* And assessment works both ways. Learners hold the authors accountable for what they create by rating the quality of the content and the media choice. Thus, programs that don't support successful assessment or that are poorly received by users are redesigned.

Even more sophisticated labs are now online—employees around the world can now remotely practice experiences in real time. In addition, Cisco is implementing new learning tools to simulate a variety of complex network problems and design appplications.

Today, the vast majority of field sales training is on the Web, and more e-learning is being deployed for partners and customers. Yet some classroom programs will remain, especially for customers. While e-learning technology has moved aggressively to enable "telling" and "doing"-type learning on the Web, the industry has done less to address the valuable unstructured, interactive parts of the classroom experience—team building, collaboration, and Q&A activities. This is the cultural part of learning that also must be addressed by blending learning strategies and human interaction to create a *total* learning solution or architecture.

In reinventing training at Cisco, a big problem was the misunderstanding of trainers that their jobs would become obsolete. Cisco's experience shows that this is not the case. Trainers are becoming more strategic, transitioning to new roles like online mentoring and coaching, refocusing their attention toward ensuring a high level of "teachability" in the e-learning products that are produced. Another problem was overcoming the doubt that people had of the validity and effectiveness of e-learning—it just wasn't comfortable at first. But the company's internal research has shown that quality e-learning can improve competence, do it faster, and result in higher levels of learner satisfaction than with similar classroom programs.

An enterprisewide learning council and a special four-person e-learning core team govern all of this transition at Cisco. Composed of Tom Kelly, representing worldwide training and representatives from HR's employee development group, corporate IT, and the customer advocacy group, this group guides Cisco's continuing e-learning revolution and garners the executive-level support and ownership to get it done.

The future calls for a convergence of training with knowledge management and performance management. Access to learning will evolve from portals based on communities and job roles to learner-centric access. Dynamic portals will enable users to customize their individual learning portals based on their role, developmental needs, current business initiatives, and career aspirations. The individual portal will offer learning based on those needs, and on individual user preferences (learning style, for example). This will continue Cisco's move from an emphasis on managing its human resources (it's not how many people you have) to managing its intellectual capital (it's what they know).

What Can E-Learning Organizations Learn From E-Business?

While some organizations, like Cisco, have been successful in deploying a robust e-learning strategy, many others have been stymied, often repeatedly, in their efforts. For them, another approach may be a little more radical but in the end more successful: to treat e-learning as a new venture inside the corporation. In many ways e-learning is like e-commerce, and there is a great deal that can be learned by looking at these new business models. In their book, *Unleashing the Killer App: Digital Strategies for Market Dominance*,[9] Larry Downes and Chunka Mui identify 12 principles of killer app design that are just as important for e-learning as they are for e-business (Table 9.2).

Table 9.2 Twelve Principles for Killer App Design and Their Implications for E-Learning Organizations

Killer App Design Principles	Implications for E-Learning Organizations
1. *Outsource to the customer.* Build interfaces to your information sources and give customers the tools to navigate and customize them.	Many companies have already transferred training registration to learners by allowing them to use the Web to sign up. Now, some organizations are placing diagnostic tools on the Web to allow users to determine for themselves what learning programs are best for their needs. Ultimately, people will be able to construct their own learning programs without the assistance of the training group. Decision-making passes to learners, giving them more control and adding value to the e-learning interface.
2. *Cannibalize your markets.* Allow the new e-business to take the market away from the traditional business— or someone else will. This will force a reexamination of what parts of the traditional business are worth saving, and what parts are not.	Many training organizations "allow" e-learning to exist within the company—as long as the programs don't threaten the classroom cash (sacred?) cow. This often unspoken policy inhibits the growth of e-learning, while artificially supporting a less efficient approach. According to Mohanbir Sawhney, Northwestern University's professor of e-commerce, "A siege mentality that tries to build a fortress around current practices is not only doomed, it's also dumb."[10] While it may be necessary to replace classroom learning with e-learning, this should also be an opportunity to restructure the role of the classroom so the two are complementary. By viewing this problem from a learning architecture perspective, those training organizations that might have seen e-learning as a threat to be fought, might now view it more positively—as an expansion of the organization's role and influence.

Table 9.2   *(Continued)*

Killer App Design Principles	Implications for E-Learning Organizations
3. *Treat each customer as a market segment of one.* Technology allows e-businesses the ability to create customer offerings that are unique— every time (mass customization).	New instructional and information design techniques and technologies allow for each individual's learning to be treated uniquely, from personalized portals and assessment of competency and learning needs, to the "on-the-fly" building of a custom set of learning experiences. This adds additional value for the training organization, as well as for the learner. The challenge for the organization is to shift the management emphasis from groups of learners (i.e., the class) to individual employees.
4. *Create communities of value.* Provide opportunities for customers to interact with each other, not just with the e-business.	This is where the knowledge management comes in. Building knowledge or learning communities and engaging members before, during, and after a training or other formal learning event creates a greater bond between them and the training organization, making it less likely that they would leave for an alternative service. In addition, fostering communication among participants enhances the efficacy of the learning program and teaches people the power of learning from each other. Training organizations that believe their responsibility to learners begins on the first day of class and ends on the last may be "shortsighting" themselves into irrelevance.
5. *Replace rude interfaces with learning interfaces.* Build "cyber-intimacy" with customers and make their experience meaningful, easy, and pain-free.	For all the effort that is put into e-learning, if learners perceive that this approach is more work, or more painful than what it replaced, they will not participate again. This calls for much more consideration of ease of access, intuitive navigation, reduced bureaucracy (as in having to supply identifying information *every* time you log in), the ability to reuse and perhaps restructure the program, etc. Of course, content is important, but if it's too difficult to use, it will be abandoned.

(Continued)

Table 9.2 Twelve Principles for Killer App Design and Their Implications for E-Learning Organizations *(Continued)*

Killer App Design Principles	Implications for E-Learning Organizations
6. *Ensure continuity for the customer, not yourself.* Do what is necessary to protect customers from a bad experience as they move to e-business. If there are to be disruptions, let them be with the e-business, not with its customers.	Here's where training organizations must do everything possible to create a smooth transition for learners to an e-learning mode. Adequate preparation of participants, effective communications, and great user interfaces (see point 5) are just some of the areas that must be considered. Also, be sure that the first exposure to e-learning is an extremely positive one. Again, one bad experience and the learners won't come back. If this is done well, users will more quickly become more comfortable with e-learning.
7. *Give away as much information as you can.* Create value for customers by allowing them access to information that will form the basis for a broader e-business relationship.	There is a tendency for training organizations to restrict access to content or programs unless learners are registered and, in some cases, have paid for the program in advance. Many of these organizations also display an incredible (and often unjustified) need to track *everything* that the learner does. This undoubtedly will create some barriers to the free flow of content, which inhibits a learning organization. We've already discussed why tuition for e-learning makes little sense. Requiring too much registration effort or tracking too many activities can also cause problems. If users have to go through too many hoops in order to get to the content they need, they may not try. A better solution is to reduce registration and tracking to a bare minimum and focus more on providing extremely easy access to high-value content.

Table 9.2 *(Continued)*

Killer App Design Principles	Implications for E-Learning Organizations
8. *Structure every transaction as a joint venture.* The e-business of the future will be networked with partners.	This is directly related to outsourcing a variety of e-learning services. No training organization in any company can do it all—and none should try. The costs are too great. Finding high-quality partners that are easy to work with can be a great benefit to the training organization, as has been previously discussed in the outsourcing section. In addition, stronger collaboration across internal training organizations can be very beneficial for the company as resources and expertise are leveraged across the enterprise, and employee confusion is minimized.
9. *Treat your assets as liabilities.* In the e-business world, physical assets may have less value than information assets.	Training facilities, staff, equipment, etc., have for years been the pride and joy of training organizations. Bigger and better classrooms, the latest technology (albeit short-lived), and the largest staff have all been part of an historical training-centric ego that pervades many training organizations. This must change. These assets have costs—costs that cannot be maintained in an e-learning environment. This is not a call to blow up everything; rather, it's a strong recommendation that every physical asset be looked at carefully to see if it's truly needed.
10. *Destroy your value chain.* If the old ways of working are inappropriate for e-business, move quickly to new ones.	Training organizations have developed extensive processes for running their businesses. From registration services and the reproduction and distribution center, to the food served at lunch and "account management," there are often as many people supporting the delivery of a training program as there are teaching one. And this was all done in the name of "customer service." In the e-learning world, none of these services will be as important. Perhaps the best time to reinvent your value chain is before the old one completely breaks down.

(Continued)

Table 9.2 Twelve Principles for Killer App Design and Their Implications for E-Learning Organizations *(Continued)*

Killer App Design Principles	Implications for E-Learning Organizations
11. *Manage innovation as a portfolio of options.* E-businesses invest in multiple scenarios, getting out of those that fizzle and moving quickly to those that have greater potential. This helps avoid sinking too much money into any one track and then being in too deep to get out if it doesn't show promise.	Don't pour all your resources into a single grand e-learning project. And don't initially invest all your outsourcing requirements to one vendor. Work on a number of smaller projects and distribute work to a number of qualified contractors. Hedge your bets and go with the programs, strategies, suppliers, and technologies that appear to be winners for you. As those winners emerge, you are better able to jettison what doesn't work and transfer your assets to those that do. This same philosophy can apply to selecting outsourcing partners and moving to one or two prime contractors.
12. *Hire the children.* Bring in young digital savvy people who have the talent and the drive to take the e-business to the future.	While it's often true that younger, up-and-coming e-learning professionals tend to be more savvy than the current generation, this is not a recommendation to simply go out and hire a lot of kids. But it is a recognition that the next generation of e-learning specialists will add a great deal to the value of your efforts, and, over time, that's where at least some of your recruiting effort should be placed. This is also a reminder to look for open-mindedness with respect to e-learning—at any age.

Some of these principles can seem pretty radical for a training organization, but they may be necessary if e-learning is to grow and be sustainable in the business. These principles are not merely trends—they are the essential elements that successful companies are using to win in the highly competitive world of e-business. It seems that they may also be essential for the increasingly competitive world of e-learning.

Is It Too Late?

Reinventing training for the digital age is not moving boxes around an organizational chart or giving people "e-*sounding*" titles—that won't do at all. To succeed in the digital world, training organizations must become digital. They must think digital and they must act digital. As corporations expand their use of Internet technologies to run their business and embrace new e-commerce business models, the training organization cannot fall behind.

> **"Even if you're on the right track, you'll get run over if you just sit there."**
>
> **Will Rogers**

The prevailing wisdom in the e-commerce world was that old-line companies were dinosaurs—they weren't fast enough or innovative enough to respond to the new world of e-businesses. But the death knell for these companies is clearly premature. Many are using their vast resources, along with a new vision, to remake themselves into businesses that can succeed in a traditional way and online. Corporate training can do the same—embrace e-learning without giving up on other forms of learning. It is not yet too late. To make this work, however, training organizations must also change and adapt to the new world. In a few short years those that don't may be gone.

An E-Learning Journey

by John Coné, Dell Computer Corporation

On the Way to Technology-Enabled Learning

IT'S FAIR TO SAY THAT Dell Computer Corporation has a leg up when it comes to implementation of technology-enabled learning. We don't have the hardware issues that many large companies face—we make the stuff. More important, we use it. Dell sells over \$35 million worth of computer equipment and solutions over the Internet—each day. We get the Internet. We get technology in the workplace. Our leadership not only supports the use of technology—they demand it. An annual growth rate of 50 percent, coupled with the plethora of new products and service offerings, made the necessity of e-learning overwhelming. But despite our head start (and it is a big one), we probably share a lot of issues with everyone else.

My most fundamental learning on this journey is that *why* you choose to go digital will dramatically affect *how* you do it. I worry at the number of organizations pursuing digital learning seemingly because it is "the next thing." I've learned that it is vitally important to know why you are trying to move in this new direction. Of those who have thought it through, a primary motivator seems to be cost. Another is the need to support what has often been referred to as "distance learning." And for others the motivation seems to be that if people are spending more time on the Net, maybe that's where their training needs to be.

All of these are legitimate reasons for technology-enabled learning, and all of them are factors in our journey at Dell. But for us there's a more fundamental reason to move to digital learning: **learner control.** If there were a way to put learners in control of their learning without using technology, we'd probably do it. But we can't. It's technology that makes learning available 24/7.

Using technology, learners can control a variety of factors associated with the learning process. They can access the learning whenever it's most useful, access just the pertinent pieces, and navigate through the learning in a nonlinear fashion if desired. If adequate feedback and assessments are provided, they can bypass unnecessary or redundant knowledge or skills. Access can be almost immediate. And, when done well, most technology-enabled learning can double as performance support tools, embedded in workplaces and work flows.

There are three mental models we had to *unlearn* in order to gain real velocity around digital learning. The first was the **trainer control model**. For more than two decades folks in the training world have talked about *learner-centered* training. We talk a lot about it, but we've tended to continue operating in a trainer-control model. The training function still organized curricula, designed seminars and programs, selected faculty, and scheduled learning events. Only when someone showed up for class did we concede a little control.

Today, I see many organizations still doing what we attempted to do in the early going: apply that model to technology. We want to create online curricula, to "put online" entire courses, to be the virtual faculty, and in some cases to try to control the logistics of use. We need to move beyond this.

The second model we had to abandon is the **building for the ages model**. I can remember the good old days when you designed a workshop and ran it for years. We talked about course maintenance and debated how often it should happen. The digital world doesn't work that way. Today at Dell we assume that nothing we put online will last a year. In fact, we "freshness" date our learning interventions. A couple of weeks before the freshness date, an e-mail message is sent to the owner of the intervention. If they don't act to refresh or replace the learning solution, it disappears.

The last model we had to take down was the **university model** itself. That's the model that compels us to think of our role as collecting and organizing what must be learned. If we succumb, then we pursue a virtual faculty, a virtual science building, a virtual management building. In short, we try to bring the knowledge together in one place, codify it, and distribute it. Although there are probably some metaphorical limitations to it, we use the national parks model at Dell. Parks are where they are. You can't move them, collect them, or combine them. What you can do is to make sure people know where the parks are, what they will find when they get to them, and that they are easy to get to and get around in. So the job of the education function becomes one of finding out where knowledge resides and creating awareness and access.

These new models radically change how we operate. We make different investment decisions when we think of all learning solutions as disposable after a short shelf life. Learner control drives us to reduce learning to its smallest useful increment and to try to find ways of embedding it in the workplace. And this awareness/access model changes how we approach administrative systems.

We learned that if we attempted to figure out in advance the entire technology architecture for digital learning, we'd be in a state of continual analysis. The first fundamental we had to work out was with our IT organization. Simply stated, we had to know what would work easily with our existing infrastructure, what would tax it, and what would crash it. Maybe that goes without saying.

In our experience so far, the transition of learning solutions to technology-enabled formats has been positive on many fronts. Increased learner control has made training more focused, flexible, and scalable. But an important concern during this transition must be the willingness of all learners to embrace the change. This is not happening in all cases. Some people do not recognize digital learning as genuine training. Other potential users find it difficult, or at least uncomfortable, to access learning in unfamiliar ways. In the extreme, some see the move to technology-enabled learning as a strategy to encroach on their personal time, with the company eliminating the training they are used to receiving.

We've discovered at least three areas where improvements can be made to support the immediate and long-term success of technology-enabled learning. First, we must continue to improve the quality of the learning solutions themselves. Second, we must put systems in place to properly record and track the use of these solutions. And third, we must continue to lobby for active and visible management support for these solutions. But as we enhance our efforts in all of these areas, there are issues peculiar to this time of transition which are demanding our attention. A key to our success will be implementing strategies that ease users into the use of technology by making that use as similar to traditional learning as possible. Here are some initial lessons:

1. *Evaluating Learning Options.* When people decide they need to learn, they are used to being able to evaluate options. They feel qualified to do so, since they've been to many traditional classes. They can ask others who have been to the class, or get a recommendation from someone in the HR or training organization. But with technology-enabled learning, most people do not feel able to evaluate options. Few if any people they know have experience and can make recommendations. And, sadly, even the HR and training folks cannot make informed recommendations. If we are to address this transition issue, we must create a way for people to be comfortable about their selections. Among the items that have to be covered are:

- How can I judge the *source qualifications?* With traditional training, the user may know the provider and/or the instructor. They are familiar with methodology from past experience. *How can we make them comfortable selecting from technology options?*
- Where does it fit in a curriculum? Much traditional training has long been incorporated into categories and curricula. We know where it fits, and have a sense (if not a clear delineation) of prerequisites. We can be pretty sure if we are ready to take the class. With technology, we're not as

sure, largely because the program may require technical as well as subject matter expertise. (We all know how to go to a class.) *How can we help people feel comfortable with their own readiness?*

- How easy is it to understand the basics: cost and length. With traditional training, I know just how long I'll spend in class and how much I'll spend to get it. *How can we create that much certainty around tech-based learning?*

2. *Getting Permission to Go.* We are used to having a set time and place for training, and getting permission to be there. But the most important benefit of technology-enabled learning is the ability of the individual to learn anytime and anywhere. Simply stated, since it is unrealistic and impractical in the existing paradigm to get permission to learn anytime and anywhere, it can feel like we don't have permission any time at all. *How can we give people the sense that they have permission to take time to learn?*

3. *Getting Signed Up.* From the earliest days of our learning lives, we've been comfortable registering for school. It happens at a specific place, on specific days, and at specific times. We are registering for an event. When we register, we create a sense of obligation in ourselves. We have committed, and others are aware of our commitment. Asynchronous online learning means that we don't have to register until we show up for school. There is no implied commitment, no plan to act. And registration results in a schedule. We know exactly when and where we intend to learn. *How can we create this sense of commitment to specific learning solutions online? Is schedule still important? If it is, how do we create an online learning schedule?*

4. *Getting My School Supplies.* When we go to traditional training, we can almost always count on having all of the needed materials supplied. Even if *we* forget something, someone will be there to replace it. When we contemplate going online, we have no such assurances. Suddenly, the planning we should always have done—but wasn't important—now is. And perhaps daunting. What if we don't have the right software or enough memory on our machine? What if there are other materials we are expected to have as we start? *How can we make learners comfortable that technology-enabled learning comes complete?*

5. *Going to Class.* When we go to traditional training, there are things we just naturally expect will be part of the experience:

- *We get away from the usual workspace.* We are able to get away from the everyday distractions and pace of work, and pause to reflect. *How do we replicate that online?*
- *We get to meet the teacher.* We'll be able to make judgments about the learning based on how capable we think the instructor is. We will connect with a resource that can take us beyond what is in the materials. *How can we let online learners have a "teacher"?*
- *We get to meet other students.* We can all recite the list of valuable things that comes from being able to connect with other students. *How can we let them meet and interact with other students online?*
- *We get to take breaks.* And when we come back, class picks up where it left off. With technology, we're not so sure we can stop once we start. If we do, will everything be lost? Will we have to start over at the beginning? *How can we create breaks in the learning?*
- *We can affect the direction of the class.* By our questions, our level of interaction, even by our answers, we can take the class in directions that are most helpful to each of us. We can get the group or the teacher to spend more time in areas important to us (and maybe skim over things that are not.). With technology, we may assume we're stuck in the "program." *How can we let people influence the learning event?*

6. *Completion and Graduation.* When we finish traditional training, we can get feedback on how we did. We can ask questions that help us understand the feedback and what we might do next. We can ask for more help, to be delivered right away or later. And we often get a certificate—something that proves we succeeded (or at least attended). We even get used to grades. We got a sense of closure and that someone, somewhere, was aware of our success. In fact, our success is shared with others in the class. *How can we create this same sense of official completion, shared success (and acknowledgment) online?*

And finally: *How can we ensure that successful completion of online training is perceived to have the same value to our careers (our résumés) as traditional classes?*

We're well on the way to digital learning at Dell Computer Corporation. There are clearly technology issues, but there are other issues that have much more to do with people's feelings than their skills. For us, the biggest learning has been that if the scenery on the journey looks familiar, you're on the wrong path.

My most sincere advice for any considering the journey was given early in this piece: Know why you are doing it. Understand the models you are using. This effort is moving so fast that if you are just a few degrees off course when you set out, you will quickly find yourself somewhere you did not intend to go.

John Coné is *Vice President, Dell Learning, and serves as Dell's Chief Learning Officer.*

Navigating the Vendor Marketplace

"Glitz and hype. I was really offended by the helium heads trying sincerely to tell me about the virtues of interactivity as if I was from Mars and not them. The market seems to be perfectly content to buy junk by the curriculum load. The good stuff is out there, but comparatively rare. Reflective of a trend to hype over substance that pervades our culture: give 'em bread and circuses."

Training manager at a recent
e-learning trade show

"The marketplace has really matured over the last few years. Vendors are more sophisticated and in tune with my company's business. There's more product out there for me to choose from. I appreciate dealing with real salespeople and real companies that know what I need and can deliver, rather than the 'mom 'n' pop' shops of the past. I have a much better business relationship with them now."

Another training manager
at the same trade show

WHICH OF THE ABOVE TWO COMMENTS is more realistic? How do you and your organization see the vendor marketplace? Like it or not, outside vendor companies and professional services firms will play a growing role in e-learning strategy and implementation. Why will outsourcing continue to be a major business strategy for e-learning?

First, for most corporations, learning is a necessity but it is not a line of business. Since the investment in learning is fundamentally for the improvement of workforce performance, the level of investment, however adequate or inadequate, is limited. With the rapid changes in technology, it is prohibitively expensive for most companies to maintain a complete state-of-the-art e-learning capacity over a long period of time. So off-loading some of the work to vendors and consultants transfers some of the volatile capital and personnel investment to a firm where such expenditures are *their* business.

Related to the issue of investment is competency. If you're in the automotive, telecommunications, hospitality, or retail business, to name a few, it is likely that learning—especially e-learning—is not a "core competency" of the business. Certainly, most companies will have some competent learning and e-learning professionals, even entire departments, but it is not what differentiates the corporation in the marketplace. For example, while it may be nice for Motorola to gain recognition for its internal learning capabilities, it is much more focused on gaining recognition—and revenue—from its semiconductor and cellular technologies.

The third issue is capacity. Because of the general variability of business, internal training organizations will most certainly have their ups and downs. As the demands for learning solutions, including e-learning, increase or decrease with business cycles and other events or disruptions, having a variable workforce is a smart approach. With an internal corps of very good people, the use of qualified vendors and consultants enables the company to expand its capacity when there's lots of work to do and reduce its costs when business pressures constrain resources.

So outside contractors—vendors and consultants—will continue to play an important role in e-learning. The key to making this work is to develop a finely tuned approach to finding, securing, and managing the right service providers for your particular business situation.

E-Learning Vendors Can Be Relentless—How to Manage Them

Most people involved in any sort of e-learning decision making are inundated with messages from vendors and consultants: telephone calls, sales presentations, brochures, Web sites, etc. Many people think negatively about the relentless vendor selling. However, it's likely that your own firm also sells aggressively to its customers. The issue is more properly focused on professionalism. While most vendors take their role seriously, some questionable practices can emerge (often as much the fault of the buyer as the vendor).

Sometimes vendors will sell the same products, such as online training courseware or tools, to multiple parts of your business. So several business units buy the *same* training from the same vendor. If you say no to a vendor, chances are there's another part of the business they'll be speaking to the next day.

Some vendors will often resell the same products to the same organization over a period of years, as they know too well that groups that experience a large turnover of personnel often "forget" what they purchased two years ago and buy it again.

Another problem is that different business units will buy products, such as online courseware on the same subject, from different vendors. So business unit A buys a management training course from vendor A, and business unit B buys an essentially similar program from vendor B. Because of this the company never gains any economy of scale or curricula consistency.

Those who place these problems entirely on the shoulders of vendors or consultants should look around their own company. Chances are there are few safeguards against any of this happening. This is especially true when training organizations are disjointed across the business, and each group is doing "its own thing." Whether or not this is the case, there are a number of ways to better manage vendor access to your company (Table 10.1):

Table 10.1   Managing Vendor Access to Your Business

Coordinate efforts	If possible, work across business units to coordinate responses to outside marketing and sales. Establish a cross-company board that reviews all vendor and consultant offers and determines appropriate responses.
Set up a vendor management capability	Beyond coordination, establish a person or group responsible for vendor management. Let this group develop the relationships and expertise to deal with e-learning vendors. Be sure that e-learning expertise is well represented here.
Develop an internal e-learning "consumer reports"	Through a coordination and vendor management capability, periodic quantitative and qualitative ratings of vendors and their products can be developed and posted on the intranet. Include postmortems to document what went right or wrong, and what can be learned from the experience. This is easiest to do for off-the-shelf course titles, but it can also be done for learning management systems, KM systems, and especially for the vendors themselves. Insight into working

Table 10.1 (*Continued*)

	relationships, work quality, expertise, overall value, etc., can be collected from a variety of sources (including sources in the public domain) and published through your *knowledge management* system.
Work with the purchasing department	Enlist the help of vendor management specialists. Help them understand the importance of moving from a lot of vendors and a request-for-proposal (RFP) process to a long-term relationship with one or two prime contractors. Although they probably lack any expertise in e-learning or knowledge of the e-learning marketplace, the purchasing department can assist on the contractual and business side of vendor management.
Establish consequences for inappropriate vendor behavior	By letting vendors know what the rules and the consequences are, you are not only being fair, but you set a standard for vendors to meet—you begin to take control of the game. Of course, there should be consequences for inappropriate behavior on your part as well!
Reward appropriate behavior	Demonstrate that vendors and consultants who play by the rules have greater opportunities to sell you their products and services.

Generally speaking, most vendors and consultants respond positively to effective vendor management efforts. If they don't, the quality of their products and services would not compensate for their poor business practices. Vendor management not only helps to ensure that the best service providers are chosen, but that all potential vendors have an opportunity to be heard.

Finding Good Vendors

The vendor marketplace is growing by leaps and bounds, although the industry churn (new failures and new start-ups) is significant. Trade shows are getting larger, and individual booths are getting bigger as well. There are niche, custom vendors who do one thing, hopefully well. And there are larger e-learning companies who seek to be full-service providers. Both can be valuable. Here are nine approaches to finding the right service providers for you.

1. Know what you're looking for.   Do you want consultative advice or extra hands to help you get work done—or both? Do you want help in building a customer online training course, or are you looking to buy an entire package of solutions? Are you looking for someone to work with you and your team, your entire organization, or perhaps your senior management? Maybe you're looking for a firm to completely take over your internal operation. Often, the best firm for one type of service may be the worst firm for another. Large-scale e-learning development firms can cost less and may deliver more products in a faster time frame. But smaller, custom shops may have more flexibility, and you may have better access to their best people.

2. Know how you want to deal with the provider.   Small firms may allow you greater access to the business owner or a specific person you want to work with, while with a larger firm you may have to deal with a salesperson or an "account manager." Be careful that you don't fall into the trap of meeting the key experts at the firm during the sales phase but get nothing but junior people once the contract is signed and you're into the project.

3. Research the company.   Obviously, competence—in instructional design and e-learning, their reputation, and the quality of their service offerings—is essential. But don't stop there. Conduct a thorough review of the provider's business history. How long have they been around? Are they using the latest technology? Are they making any money? Are they well funded? Do employees turn over a lot? (You don't want rotating project managers on your project!) What about the leadership—do they turn over? Does it look like they're about to be acquired? (Not necessarily a bad thing—just run this analysis on the acquiring company as well.) What are their business practices, warrantees, contractual requirements, etc? Finally, do they have the "heft"—the capacity to service your needs? (Many e-learning companies still are not big enough to provide a complete service offering to the largest corporations.) These and other business questions, along with questions about quality and performance, will give you a well-rounded picture of the viability of the firm to deliver what you need.

4. Understand the industry as a whole. Again, this is a growing and unstable industry, full of mergers and acquisitions and a large influx of capital. W.R. Hembrecht & Co. suggests that corporate e-learning is "one of the fastest growing and most promising markets in the education industry." They expect the online training market to double in size every year through 2003, reaching approximately $11.3 billion by that time.[1] Read the major trade publications regularly and review vendor Web sites and brochures (with one "skeptical" eye) to understand what each firm is saying about itself. Remember, however, those glossy brochures and fancy Web sites do not necessarily equate with quality work.

5. See the vendors for yourself. Related to the item above, it's important to get out and meet vendors in places where you can talk with them and size them up. Certainly you can visit their headquarters, but it's probably best to make first contact on neutral ground. Fortunately, there are a number of trade shows (see Appendix B) where you can visit with many of the major firms at one time (smaller firms are less likely to be at these shows, but they're probably local companies for you). To make the best use of your time, develop a set of key questions you want answered and walk away from any vendor who can't, or won't, answer them. Britton Manasco, speaking in the online newsletter VELOCITY, suggests that trade shows can be a great learning experience, but don't be seduced by sexy "demos" into buying something that you don't need or is not right for your business.

> **"Software companies naturally adore their own tools
> (interfaces, features, and functions)—much as a new
> parent adores a baby. Most prospects, however, could care
> less. They want to know if the software firm's sweet little
> precious tool will address the critical business issues—the
> pain, the agony, the fear—that they confront every day."**
> **Britton Manasco [2]**

6. Road test. Try the solutions for yourself and have key people in your organization check out the solution as well.

Whether it's an authoring tool, a curriculum of online training courses, a learning management system, a knowledge management solution, or a performance support tool, insist on spending as much time with the product as you need. It's surprising how many companies buy entire curricula of online training without ever reviewing the products for accuracy, relevance, authenticity, or instructional design. Even fewer ask for evaluation data. If the vendor restricts access time or insists that only *they* demo the product for you—especially if you've already been through the sales pitch and have already seen the sales demo, be suspicious again. You want to be alone with the product, to have significant time to try it out and evaluate it free of vendor participation.

7. Develop a qualifying checklist. As you narrow your choices, develop a checklist and rating scale that addresses at least these key criteria:

- Reputation, both inside and outside your company. Look at business practices as well as the quality of the work. This is important for both product vendors and consultants. It's much more important than the size of a vendor—sometimes smaller companies can do a better job than larger ones.
- Resources that would be available for your work (not necessarily the same as total resources of the vendor). You don't want a vendor that has lots of people, just no one with the right skills to spare for *your* project. Be sure you understand whether the vendor will be outsourcing any of your work to a third party. Also, check for any indications of unusually high turnover of expertise—how will the vendor compensate you if key project people leave in the middle?
- Location and accessibility of their key people.
- Cost range—can you afford them? Beware of low-priced bidders who have little experience or who are way below the rest of the proposals. Also beware of vendors who are non-committal about maintenance and upgrade costs, which can be expensive—you want these issues clear up front.
- Knowledge of your company and its business (or, at least a demonstrated willingness to learn about what you do).

- Willingness to put their people "on the ground" in your operation when necessary, and the ability to work virtually, if appropriate.
- Subject matter expertise.
- E-Learning expertise and experience.
- Presentation skills (can they communicate well with your boss's boss?).
- Willingness to transfer skills to your organization, if appropriate.

8. If the vendors are new, invite them in for a face-to-face meeting.   Ask them to show similar work to what you are looking for. Ask them to talk about what they've done for other clients (obviously observing confidentiality). Ask to see work samples (if they say *everything's* proprietary so they can't show you *anything*, be suspicious).

9. Limit the numbers and lengthen the bond.   Your goal is to find long-term partners, not create an ongoing competitive marketplace for people seeking your business. You can start out with lots of vendor and consultant options, but in the end, strive to end up with just a few firms that you feel very comfortable with—companies and people you'll want to work with for a long time. This doesn't mean you won't ever change providers or consultants. But it does mean you're going to work for lasting relationships, not "here today, gone tomorrow" arrangements. Work toward consultative relationships that focus on collaboration, rather than just hiring a "pair of hands" to alleviate the workload, or an "expert" (doctor-patient-type relationship) who simply tells you what to do.

The E-Learning Request for Proposal (RFP)

Surprising as it may seem, your ultimate goal is to *not* issue RFPs. When you find a few vendors with whom you feel comfortable and who meet your needs, you will hopefully settle into a longer-term relationship. However, if you're just starting out, or moving in a new direction where you don't have a preferred vendor/consultant list, the RFP route is helpful.

Essentially, the RFP process is a prescreening device, designed to filter out vendors who are unqualified, uninterested, too expensive, etc. It augments the approaches for finding the right vendor, just noted, but it does not replace any action on that list.

The first step in any RFP process is to generate a reasonable list of vendors or consultants who appear to have the skills and the capabilities you are looking for. Recommendations from colleagues, literature from trade shows, Web sites, professional associations, and universities are just some of the sources for the preliminary list.

The RFP is usually composed of several parts. One part is likely your company's boilerplate material outlining legal, security, financial, proprietary, and other issues (seek assistance from your purchasing and/or legal department for the boilerplate language). Generally, this is a pretty standard document that is rarely altered for a particular RFP. If it's not in the boilerplate materials, be sure to add a statement that the RFP is not a contract and that it is a copyright document of your company—not to be republished or distributed beyond what is necessary for a quality response.

Another part of the document is the statement of work. This details what you are looking for. Some of the information you should provide includes, but is not limited to:

- An executive summary (one page) that overviews the entire project.
- A detailed description of your need or problem. This should include a description of the business and performance problems you are addressing and the parts of the business that are impacted. There should be enough information for a vendor to respond appropriately, but not enough to compromise corporate confidentiality or competitiveness. Cover technical, HR, and other requirements of the work.
- A profile of who will use the e-learning solution (target audience).
- The duration of the project or engagement.
- The resources you are prepared to commit to the project.
- Preliminary project schedule (unless this is to be developed as part of the project).
- The overall goals or objectives of the project or engagement.

- Success/evaluation criteria (unless such criteria is to be developed as part of the project).
- What parts of the deliverables can be retained by the vendor for reuse. This can be a great incentive for some vendors who might be willing to work on something that has more risk. Also, be sure you are clear on what *you* will own after the project, including the content, source code, resale rights, etc.
- Expectations about who will do maintenance, system upgrades, user support, etc.
- Expected deliverables.

A third component of an RFP are the procedures for submitting a proposal and the process you will go through to select the "winner." This section includes, but is not limited to:

- The specific steps the vendor must go through to be considered for the work. This may include demonstrations, face-to-face meetings, and other activities, in addition to the actual proposal document (which should follow prescribed format and length guidelines that you specify).
- The criteria on which each proposal will be judged. It is appropriate to tell the vendors how you will rate them.
- How you will respond to inquiries related to the proposal. You may allow them in one format only (e.g., e-mail) or during a specified time (e.g., only during the first two weeks). You can also say whether you will publish each vendor's questions and your responses for all vendors to consider. Finally, if you can, state what you will *not* provide or do (e.g., allowing a single vendor to visit you).
- Whether a prototype or sample of work is required as part of the proposal or shortly thereafter (be specific).
- The due date(s) for submissions, as well as dates when decisions will be made.
- Pricing information. Be sure you are specific, so you can compare "apples to apples." If necessary, ask for pricing by deliverable, time frame, or project phase. Ask the vendor to disclose all pricing information, including prices of services not specified in the RFP but that may be needed later.

- Information on any subcontractors the vendor may use.
- Where to deliver the proposal and how many copies are required.
- A specific person to contact for questions, etc.
- What constitutes a submission, and what doesn't, i.e., what you *won't* accept. You don't want a vendor sending you a truckload of everything they've ever done in a effort to impress you. This is where you will ask the vendor to provide supplemental information, such as:
  - references
  - bios of those who will work on the project
  - detail of the processes and technology that will be used (be wary of proprietary technology owned exclusively by the vendor—you don't want to create an unnecessary dependency)
  - history of this vendor's work with your company
  - the vendor's company history
  - a list of clients (most, but not all vendors will release this)
  - statements of warrantees
  - sample work if requested (be specific).

Finally, attach a cover letter to the RFP that reviews the major aspects of the work and highlights the key activities you require for proposal submission. Be sure to include the proposal due date and a contact person in your firm.

In checking the vendor or consultant's references, be sure to ask about the work that was done, to determine if there's a match with your work. Ask the references about quality and how easy the vendor was to work with. Check to see how well the vendor kept to the budget and schedule. Finally, be sure to check the vendor or consultant's flexibility, presentation skills, and trustworthiness. When you bring a vendor or consultant in for a face-to-face meeting, you'll need to balance the vendor's effectiveness in selling with your perception of their capability. Remember, great sales pitches don't always reflect a great capability, so you'll have to do your "due diligence." After all, you're going to be working with these people for a while, and your career may depend on the results!

The Vendor's Perspective

While it is often easy to talk about the abuses that characterize some vendors, it's also helpful to understand some inappropriate behaviors on the buyer's side as well. Treating vendors decently and fairly is one part of a good relationship. Here are a few of the most flagrant problems vendors face when dealing with some customers—avoiding these behaviors is a key to a solid, long-term partnership.

No intention to follow through. The buyer asks for proposals simply for their education or interest. They have neither the money nor the approval to actually begin any work, and may be using the proposals to generate internal interest. Vendors do not expect to win every proposal they make, but they do have a legitimate expectation that the RFP represents a serious intent on the part of the buyer to move forward with the project.

Vendor already chosen. Sometimes a vendor is already chosen and the buyer is simply issuing an RFP to satisfy some purchasing or legal requirements. Vendors who suspect that the job is "wired" will be less likely to participate the next time when the process is truly open. If this happens again and again, the vendor community will avoid doing business with you.

Something for nothing. Buyers may require a great deal of intellectual property and other work products as part of the RFP simply for their own education or as input for work with another vendor. All respondents to an RFP know that they have to give away some intellectual capital, but they hope for something in return—a contract for work. If vendors perceive that they are simply educating the buyer, they'll be less forthcoming with important information.

Add ons. Sometimes vendors respond to RFPs and get a contract, and *then* find out about additional work that is expected of them, with no increase in the price of the job. If this is the case, they'll be less likely to ever work with that buyer again (and they may be far less enthused about their current contract). Remember that vendors are in business to make money, just like you.

Failure of customers/clients to do their part. When vendors are constantly frustrated by their clients' failure to complete timely reviews of their work, provide access to SMEs, stick to their decisions about their needs, etc., the cost and frustration level on all sides will go up and the result will be far less than a satisfactory conclusion.

Maintaining a Good Ongoing Relationship

Once you've decided on your vendor or consultant partner, the job is not over. Some companies hire an outside e-learning vendor to develop an online training curriculum and don't expect to see them again until the products are ready. Others want to be involved in every aspect of the project. For most businesses, the best relationship is probably somewhere in between. You'll need specific milestones and review points along the way to assure that the project is on track and there are no surprises. But you hired this firm to do a specific job, and too much "micromanaging" of the project can hurt the efficiency and effectiveness of the contractor, and perhaps lead to mistrust. As you work through a first project, sit down with your "partner" and talk about how it's going. Make adjustments as you both see fit.

When hiring a consultant, primarily for strategy or assessment work, facilitation, advice, and recommendations, the relationship is a little different. In this case, the consultant is there because of a certain expertise or capability that you either don't have or don't have the time to pursue. There may be times when the consultant will speak for you with stakeholders and senior management. Early on it's important to work out how your outside expert will be presented and perceived in your firm.

Finally, whether you are buying "off-the-shelf" online courseware, customized learning packages, e-learning infrastructure components, or high-end advice, one goal should be to learn from the experience. That is precisely why you should work to build a consultative, collaborative relationship with vendors. Expect that some of the skills and knowledge of your vendor or consultant will transfer to you and that you'll be able to take over some of the vendor's roles and responsibilities. The contractor should be open to this because as soon as one skill is transferred, new skills will be needed and there will be more work for all. This is not to say that a vendor or consultant should transfer all their intellectual capital to their clients, but it certainly implies that outside contractors of all sorts should seek to improve the client's capability to carry on in the future without creating an intractable dependence on the vendor. After all, a relationship with an outside supplier or service provider ought to be a two-way learning experience—not just a good business deal.

11

E-Learning on a Shoestring

"Any business can become a knowledge business."

Stan Davis and Jim Botkin[1]

"Empty pockets never held anyone back. Only empty heads and empty hearts can do that."

Norman Vincent Peale

THERE IS A COMMON BELIEF that e-learning is only for large companies. Small and mid-sized firms are going to be left behind. This is untrue. There are many opportunities for smaller businesses—companies without an intranet, or a training department for that matter, to participate in the e-learning revolution. This chapter looks at many of the concepts and capabilities raised in this book so far and suggests ways to apply them in the small business world.

When You Don't Have an Intranet

Obviously, not all companies have an intranet. Very small companies, located in one or just a few locations, may not even need one. In these firms, personal communication may still be the best and most cost-effective way to learn. Using the phone and visiting with other people in the business are still and will continue to be important for learning. In small companies where it's relatively easy to know "who knows what," this may be enough. In slightly larger firms, e-mail can be a decent replacement for a knowledge management system, especially if those involved establish some basic protocols of how content will be shared through the e-mail system (products like Microsoft Outlook and Lotus Notes are adding features to support content sharing).

Small companies without an intranet can still reap the more sophisticated benefits of e-learning. Today, it's possible to use the public Internet to get training in almost any subject area. Many of the e-learning portals discussed in this book are positioned to do this. Any firm can subscribe to a variety of online learning services, delivered via the public Internet, and have their people take online training and be tracked in their progress by the e-learning service provider. Many of these portals can customize some of the look and feel of the site so that, from the employee's perspective, the online training will appear as if it's coming from inside rather than outside the company.

Pricing can be based on an annual subscription fee (usually based on the number of users and/or the number of products to be made available) or on a usage sensitive basis. Billing can be individual, credit card based (requiring the learner to "voucher" the expense), or it can be direct-billed back to the company, depending on the policies of each particular provider.

Buy as Much as You Can...Build Only When Necessary

Small firms should never try to establish their own e-learning development groups. First of all, the expense—people and technology—is far too large for most small companies. If the content is generic, such as sales, management, leadership, technology, etc., there are literally thousands of online training courses that can be subscribed to, purchased, or leased. If the content is very specific or proprietary to your small company, you may have to hire someone to build it for you, assuming, of course, that simply gathering everyone around and talking with them won't work. But be careful—one massive online learning project can be very expensive, especially for a small firm. You may need to build a solution, but with partnerships, you may not have to build it alone.

Use Partnerships

Partnerships between companies, often referred to as *consortia,* allow similar businesses to pool resources for common, noncompetitive endeavors, achieving great economies of scale. Small building contracting firms, for example, may get together, perhaps in cooperation with building trade unions, to develop or buy online training on new construction techniques or new government regulations. Local merchants can have access to better online learning by combining their resources, sometimes in cooperation with a Chamber of Commerce. A local medical practice can get online training through the American Medical Association; almost every other trade group can do likewise with their professional association. Franchise owners are finding that e-learning is one of the services that the franchise company provides. In the automotive industry, companies like Ford, General Motors, and Lexus are installing e-learning at their dealerships. Groups like these and many others can also work to form online communities, starting with e-mail and chat room dialogue and then moving on to elements of knowledge management.

Great partnerships can often be struck between small businesses and the local school district, community college, or other academic institution. These organizations, especially the more entrepreneurial community colleges, not only have the technology and infrastructure in place, but increasingly seek out opportunities to work with small to mid-sized companies in their service area. E-Learning is a very good way to build this relationship.

Needed: One Good Professional

For the smallest firms, e-learning advice and direction probably comes from consortia, professional associations, and other partnerships, vendors, and government agencies. For companies that are too small for a massive internal e-learning capability but have a small training organization, it can be very beneficial to have one person take responsibility for e-learning, even part-time. Some of the functions this person could take on include:

- Determining the priority learning needs of the company that might be met through e-learning.
- Reviewing e-learning companies to determine which one(s) to do business with.
- Reviewing online training products, before purchase, for content and instructional design quality (or finding the right SME to do so).
- Managing e-learning vendors and consultants.
- Managing the e-learning budget.
- Working with the technical staff (either internal or outsourced) to ensure that e-learning is accessible (even in a small business, this can be a problem).
- Constantly learning more about e-learning and sharing it with the rest of the business.
- Being the company "advocate" for e-learning.

For a small business, outsourcing a lot of e-learning makes sense. But like any company, keeping control of the prioritization process (based on needs), vendor management, and the continuing development of the company's e-learning strategy should remain inside.

Don't Do E-Learning When It's Not Necessary, but Be Ready When It Is

For some organizations, e-learning may never make a lot of sense. The company is just too small or everyone is located in the same place—so don't force it. Keep to more informal learning and use outside classroom-based programs as needed. But reassess the situation at least yearly. Keep an eye on the e-learning marketplace for new products and systems that may make sense for you. And keep that one professional looking at the e-learning industry—

you may never know when it will be time to make the leap to e-learning, but when that time does come, you'll need to be ready.

E-Learning on a shoestring is meant for businesses that are too small to ever leverage the investment in the technology and people necessary to deploy a comprehensive e-learning strategy, or too small to ever take advantage of it if they did. It is *not* meant for larger companies with the appropriate resources who simply don't want to do it, or don't want to spend any money on it. For those firms, e-learning remains an essential tool in keeping up with the speed of business. The consequences of ignoring it can put their competitiveness in jeopardy.

12

Creating Your E-Learning Strategy

"Flawless execution cannot compensate for implementing the wrong solution."

Daryl Conner, Change Consultant

"Sell the future benefit of what you do."

Daniel Burrus, *Techno Trends*

F ROM E-LEARNING "TALK" to e-learning "action" requires a strategy—a detailed plan to get your e-learning operation up and running, and to make it durable over the long term. Building a strategy requires two fundamental things: enough knowledge about what you want to accomplish, and a willingness to articulate your plan in a way that is meaningful to all your stakeholders.

If you've spent enough time looking at the learning needs of your company and understanding the capabilities and impact that e-learning can have, you are most likely at a key decision point—whether or not to move forward and develop an e-learning strategy. Assume that you've decided to move forward. What now?

Who Should Participate?

Before any work can begin, identify the key stakeholders who should participate in strategy development. Sometimes the work requires input from a broad cross section of the training organization (training managers, developers, instructors, administrators), its clients (students, organizations, sponsors), and other stakeholders, especially senior managers and the IT organization (in some cases customers and outside suppliers may also play a role). These larger groups are best used to generate ideas and suggestions, as well as identify key issues, problems, or needs. Often this work is done in a concentrated all-day meeting, likely off-site so as to keep the focus on the strategy work, not office work. It's also helpful to have a professional facilitator (someone who is neutral and not a member of any stakeholder community) to help the group work through any controversial or confrontational issues.

Other times, a small task force should be used. The task force, possibly with the aid of additional expertise in e-learning, can first do an environmental scan to best understand the business and learning needs that must be addressed. It can then create prototypes or frameworks around the strategic issues, which are then fed back to the larger group for feedback. Finally, an even smaller group of senior managers can convene, with experts if necessary, to make final decisions and to sell the strategy even higher in the organization.

Analyze Your Current Situation

The first step is to fully analyze the current situation as it pertains to the ability to launch and sustain e-learning. Take a look at the current state of your overall learning and development efforts and the state of your e-learning initiatives. Determine how well you are aligned with the goals and direction of your business. For example, if your company is basing its future customer relationships on the speed of its responsiveness to their needs, you may want to determine how fast you can retrain the people who will have to carry out this objective. This is derived from a broad assessment of your overall costs, effectiveness, flexibility, etc., plus the value perceptions of all your stakeholders. Here are ten key questions to ask.

1. How is your business direction changing and what are the causes of this change (technology, competition, financial, regulatory, etc.)? How have these changes impacted the requirement that the business has for learning?

2. How is learning and development viewed in your business, in terms of:

   - perception of what learning is
   - support/ownership by senior management
   - learning as an integral component of work
   - support from front-line managers
   - perceptions by the people in the training and other related departments
   - flexibility and responsiveness to changing business requirements

3. What is the current state of e-learning in your business, in terms of:

   - usage throughout the organization
   - value perception by key stakeholders (including prospective students and the training organization itself)
   - sophistication of both the technology and approach (e.g., broad or narrow focus; instruction vs. information)
   - perceived or actual level of success or failure with previous projects, including reactions from users/learners
   - vendor management
   - outsourcing
   - consistency of policies and implementation across the enterprise

4. What is the current state of the technology (Inter/intranet) infrastructure in your business? Who owns this infrastructure, how well is it run, and what is the state of your relationship with this group? What is the level of Web access for employees in your business?

5. What is the current level of funding for e-learning? Is it adequate or inadequate? How is e-learning accounted for and how sensitive is it to budget cuts?
6. How are learning efforts evaluated in the business?
7. What is the current state of your internal e-learning talent?
8. How coordinated are your e-learning efforts? Is there redundancy or process gaps? Are you "reinventing the wheel"?
9. How is e-learning currently accessed in your business? Is there a common access and management strategy or multiple divergent strategies?
10. Are e-learning initiatives, expertise, and funding evenly distributed across your organization or concentrated in a few places?

Describe Your Desired Situation

Now, create a detailed description of where you want your learning and development efforts (including e-learning) to be. This is derived from the goals and mission of your business and an assessment of its future needs, plus input from all stakeholders, especially senior leaders. In detailing your desired situation, here are ten key questions to ask (for each, try to answer with the perspective of a two- and five-year forward view).

1. What is the mission and what are the goals of your business? Where is your business going?
2. What should be the role for learning and development in your business?
3. What are your competitors doing in the areas of learning and development, and e-learning?
4. What are the best practices in learning and development, and e-learning, that are appropriate for your business situation?
5. What should be your e-learning value proposition?
6. What is the business rationale for e-learning?
7. What is your vision for how you want to be viewed and valued in the future (two and five years)?

8. What is the mission for learning and development (and for e-learning specifically) in your business? How does e-learning play into that mission? (Building a vision and mission will be discussed next.)
9. What principles[1] are most important to you in guiding how you will implement your mission and realize your vision?
10. How will your mission, vision, and guiding principles manifest themselves in:

- your position in the business
- how learning and e-learning are defined
- your organizational structure
- the support you receive from the top
- the stability of funding
- vendor management
- outsourcing
- your ability to recruit or develop the right talent
- the level of coordination across all learning activities (including e-learning) in your business
- how you and the business define learning and e-learning

Set Your Vision

Part of describing the desired situation is to see into the future. What will you and your organization look like if your e-learning strategy is successful? How will you be different? How will you be the same? What will people say about you and the services you provide? What will be your value proposition? How will stakeholders (learners, managers, executives, customers, etc.) react to you?

A vision statement describes a future state as if it were the present. In other words, don't say "We will be." Rather, say "We are." The vision statement describes accomplishments, not performance—what you have achieved, not what you do. It is not about how many online courses you'll have or what technology you'll be using. It's more about how you'll be recognized and valued internally, and through the eyes of your clients and customers. Table 12.1 presents two examples of e-learning vision statements.

Table 12.1 Sample Vision Statements

Vision Statement #1: A high-tech computer software company (hypothetical)	"We don't exist—at least not in the minds of our users. Our learning products are so embedded into what they do that they don't know if they're working or learning—it's all the same. We are the facilitators of knowledge sharing. We build and support the ability for everyone in the company to share information with everyone else—instantly and electronically. Our classroom experiences are so tied into our e-learning activities that people view them as an important adjunct to online learning, not the other way around."
Vision Statement #2: A department store chain (hypothetical)	"Salespeople on the floor learn on the floor. Every store has an e-learning center right off the sales floor where all associates have opportunities not only to take online training related to their career development, but to access the chain's knowledge management system to better understand our industry, our company, and our customers. Every associate has a learning plan, approved by their department manager and store director, and is given up to two hours every week to participate in an e-learning experience. And that learning is tied into all that they experience as an employee of our company—from compensation and promotion to a higher quality of work life."

Vision statements are usually developed through some sort of consensus-building activity, followed by refinements by senior managers. They reflect a future, ideal state.

> **"The very essence of leadership is you have to have a vision. It's got to be a vision you articulate clearly and forcefully on every occasion. You can't blow an uncertain trumpet."**
> **Theodore Hesburgh**

State Your Mission

Once you have an agreed-upon vision, develop a mission statement that encapsulates your purpose, i.e., what you will do to achieve your vision. Unlike a vision statement, the mission is much more succinct, specific, and powerful. In as few words as possible you need to tell everyone where you are headed—your mission. Table 12.2 shows two example mission statements (one with problems), derived from the visions shown in Table 12.1.

Mission statements are usually developed by senior managers and then tested/refined with stakeholders (who should be solicited for their initial ideas first). They reflect the direction the organization must go in order to realize its vision. With a vision and mission in hand, you are ready to build your e-learning strategy. But bear in mind that as you build your strategy, your vision and mission may change, based on the data you uncover and the various forces (people, technology, business, financial, etc.) that are working in support of *and* against your efforts.

Gap Analysis

Create detailed specifications of the key disparities between the current and desired situation, along with associated descriptions of root causes (not symptoms).[2] Consider a large corporation that is com-

Table 12.2 Sample Mission Statements

Mission #1: *A high-tech computer* *software company* *(hypothetical)*	"To create an online training and knowledge management environment that is so totally aligned with the work of our people that learning becomes an integral part of what they, and our company, do."
Mission #2: *A department store chain* *(hypothetical)*	To improve the performance of our front-line teams through the highest quality education, training, and career development programs."
	This is a reasonable mission statement (albeit a little too vague), but it doesn't align with the associated vision. To do that, it should address e-learning more specifically:
	"To improve the performance of our front-line teams by bringing the benefits of e-learning directly to the sales floor of every store and seamlessly integrating it with the career development of our salespeople."

Table 12.3 Sample Gap Analysis Summary for Senior Management Support

Area	Current	Desired	Gap Statement	Root Cause(s)
Senior Management Support	• Support varies by business unit. • Lots of discussion but little consequences for nonaction.	• Consistent support across the business. • Ownership by President. • Consequences for nonaction.	• E-Learning does not appear to be a high priority for senior management, resulting in inconsistent implementation.	• No single champion. • Senior leaders unaware of value proposition. • Support not tied to compensation.

posed of a number of semiautonomous business units. The goal is to build an enterprisewide e-learning capability that will bring huge economies of scale for the overall corporate learning function. Corporate HR, where you are located, sees the benefits that this can bring but is hesitant to mandate cooperation across the company. You're told that if you can get senior managers to endorse this idea, the president of the company will provide the resources to make it happen. Your gap analysis is shown in Table 12.3.[3]

Conduct Force-Field and SWOT Analyses

There are two good analytical techniques that can be used for looking more closely at strategy issues and decisions. The first is a force-field analysis that can be conducted for each gap statement. For each statement, identify factors that appear to be inhibiting the closing of the gap (i.e., inhibiting the elimination of the root cause) and factors that might aid in closing the gap. Verify your gap analysis with stakeholders.

Continuing our hypothetical scenario, as you work to find ways to gain senior management support for e-learning, you conduct a force-field analysis of the problem to uncover areas where problems may occur, as well as factors that may open opportunities for you to influence them. Table 12.4 prsents a high-level view of how a force-field analysis might look.

Table 12.4   Sample Force-Field Analysis for Senior Management Support

(Gap: E-Learning does not appear to be a high priority for senior managers)	
Inhibiting Factors	**Aiding Factors**
• Senior managers are too busy.	• Business is adopting an e-commerce strategy that senior leaders endorse.
• Senior managers delegate this responsibility down.	• Tight labor market making recruiting difficult; need more internal redevelopment.
• Senior managers are unaware of the value of e-learning.	• Corporate intranet has proven to increase productivity.
• Training department weak in justifying its value.	• Most employees have access to intranet.
• Perceived history of e-learning failure.	• Chief Knowledge Officer recently appointed.
• Senior managers come from a classroom culture.	• Performance appraisal process currently undergoing review—good opportunity.

A force-field analysis clearly points out key leverage points that enable organizations to surmount factors that are blocking its progress. This is an excellent technique to identify "low hanging fruit," opportunities for making quick inroads in areas that must be overcome in order for an e-learning strategy to succeed.

A SWOT analysis looks at the entire organization to determine its strengths, weaknesses, opportunities, and threats, either at the moment or at some future point in time.

> *Strengths* signify what you're good at, reflecting a high level of competence and support. It also looks at the surrounding environment (e.g., the business) to identify how the strengths of the company support the training or learning effort.

> *Weaknesses* also look inward, at areas that are underperforming or nonexistent that pose a risk to the organization. Characteristics of the business as a whole (culture, leadership, finances, etc.) that convey weakness are also noted.

Opportunities highlight the key areas where progress could be made if the strengths are accentuated and the weaknesses diminished. This represents some quick victories and/or the biggest impact that can be attained in the time frame examined.

Threats highlight the consequences if the opportunities are not realized or if the organization's weaknesses overwhelm its strengths. Threats also detail what might happen if nothing is done.

Essentially, the goal of a SWOT analysis is to surface issues relating to each of these four areas and devise strategies to accentuate and build on strengths and opportunities, while, at the same time, reducing weaknesses and neutralizing threats. One of the best areas to conduct a SWOT analysis is on your training organization's readiness to implement e-learning. Table 12.5 shows what part of this SWOT analysis might look like. (Most SWOT exercises are much more detailed.)

A SWOT analysis can be an eye-opener. It helps the organization see itself more clearly. By doing so, it will be in a better position to marshal its resources to proactively overcome weaknesses and neutralize threats. And it will have a much better perspective

Table 12.5 Sample SWOT Analysis for a Training Organization

Strengths	Weaknesses	Opportunities	Threats
• High-tech company with lots of tech savvy. • Long tradition of training gives us lots of experience. • Established intranet.	• Long tradition of training may lock us in old paradigms. • Everybody doing their own thing. • Business not doing well at this time.	• Easy to leverage our technical expertise. • By showcasing e-learning as more efficient and cost-effective, may get support.	• Failure to move quickly will lose window of opportunity—facing downsizing of critical talent and budget cuts. • Business units will buy from outside sources.

on what it does well, which is often hard to find, especially in times of crisis or change. Together with a force-field analysis, the organization can develop a very clear picture of what it must do not just to build an e-learning strategy, but to successfully deploy it. These become the key strategy recommendations.

Strategy Recommendations

Based on all the work you've done to this point, you can now make specific strategic recommendations to close the gaps, implement the mission, and achieve the vision. Table 12.6 is a recommendations example, again around senior management support.

Table 12.6 Recommendations Summary for Senior Management Support

Area	Gap Statement (Findings)	Strategic Recommendations
Senior Management Support	E-Learning does not appear to be a high priority for senior management, resulting in inconsistent implementation and a suboptimization of resources across the business.	• Identify one champion who will take up the cause at the senior level. • Develop one e-learning solution, perhaps sponsored by that champion (that addresses a business problem), as a showcase product. • Build an e-learning business plan focused on the issues senior managers believe are important (even if some of them are not your issues).

Build an Action Plan

Implement your e-learning strategy recommendations through a comprehensive action plan. This is where the specific tactics are described in enough detail so everyone knows what needs to be done. Following are eight basic steps for developing your e-learning action plan.

1. *Begin with strategic findings (from your research) followed by specific recommendations.* Prioritize recommendations. Start with the most important issues, which may be the most difficult. Eliminate challenges that you can't overcome immediately, but note which of these are true inhibiting factors (e.g., lack of access to the Web). If there are too many of these, your initiative may have to stop while you work to overcome them. That's okay—it's better than climbing up a mountain without the right gear, leaving you no hope of reaching the top. In building a set of e-learning implementation recommendations, be sure to address issues of leadership, culture, support, justification, and organizational realignment in addition to those of technology, learning design, and infrastructure.

2. *Specify tactics to operationalize your recommendations.* Get into some detail about how you will make the strategy real, answering the typical questions: who, what, when, where, why, and how.

3. *Identify critical success factors.* Determine what constitutes success. Seek out the input of all stakeholders—including senior leaders, front-line managers, the IT organization, learners, customers (if appropriate), and the training staff itself. Blend measures of learning success with measures of business success (cost, quality, service, and speed). Align them specifically with your strategy, by detailing at least one specific metric in each area and then linking that metric directly to stated business goals.

4. *Set and stick to timelines and milestones.* Get agreement from everyone about deliverables and accountabilities. Be sure all involved understand their assignments, who they need to work with, when results are due, how to deal with problems, etc.

5. *Provide adequate funding for implementation.* Be sure there's enough money to implement the strategy. "If you build it,

they *may* come"—but they may not stay if you can't *sustain* the quality and value that drove people to your initiative in the first place. Building a strategy that can't be deployed or maintained due to lack of funds or other resources can be an exercise in futility, and, if this has happened before, your credibility is at stake.

6. *Write it down.* Some people are satisfied when everyone comes out of a strategy discussion in agreement. Others simply want a few charts with bullet points. However, to assure that everyone understands what was just agreed to, where everyone is going together, and what the benefits and consequences of the journey are, write up a strategy document. This is an important test. If you can't articulate your strategy, recommendations, and action plan in writing, how can you articulate it to your people? This should not be an elaborate "white paper." Rather, it should be a practical, business-centered document that details your e-learning strategy so rank-and-file employees, senior executives, and stockholders (if warranted) will understand it. Besides, it gives everyone a common base from which to make improvements.

7. *Define and implement a change management plan.* Don't wait to begin helping the organization adopt the changes your e-learning strategy will bring about. Begin as soon as possible to identify barriers to the implementation of your e-learning strategy, and develop appropriate change management initiatives to reduce resistance.

8. *Define and implement a communications plan.* Commensurate with your change management initiative, develop and implement communications designed to both inform everyone about the new e-learning strategy and help people overcome their own doubts and resistance to this new approach. For both change management and communications, waiting until deployment of your e-learning initiative can be devastating. So start as soon as you can.

Be Wary

Developing an e-learning strategy is essential in setting a direction for the organization and sticking to it. But to accomplish this, it's important to be on guard for issues and behaviors that will surface. Some people who see e-learning as threatening will challenge the strategy as unworkable or not in the best interests of the client. Issues of turf and responsibility will emerge. After all, someone will have to take responsibility for e-learning. If it's centralized, some people will set it up as a target if the strategy doesn't work. If it's distributed throughout the organization, some people will seek to bury it in other work. But even if people are supportive, if they approach e-learning from a more familiar frame of reference—if they don't see it as fundamentally different from what they have been doing—they could kill the initiative without even wanting to.

If the work on e-learning is in response to a budget or other crisis, there may be a lot of words said, but survival will be at the top of everyone's agenda. And if e-learning is perceived as a diversion from surviving, it will not be supported no matter how dedicated people seem to be during the strategy development process. This is straight from Maslow's Hierarchy of Needs: People need a sense of survivability before they can truly set their minds, and their hearts, to inventing their future.

The bottom line, and the main premise of this book, is that an effective and durable e-learning strategy is not just about technology or instruction/information design. It must also be about the culture, the leadership, and the business justification that just doesn't surround the strategy—but is part of it. So after setting a sound direction, take aim at *the most* critical success factor: maintaining a razor-sharp focus on all of the organizational factors that will either make or break any e-learning strategy in any business.

13

The Future of
E-Learning

*"One day, training for every job on earth will be available
on the Internet. Are you ready?"*

Cisco Systems ad slogan[1]

*"I skate to where the puck is going to be, not to where it
has been."*

Wayne Gretzky

I T WOULD BE EASY TO dismiss e-learning as just
another in a string of technological "flavors of the month" that
will soon pass by, making way for the next great thing. But it
would also be foolish. This time, perhaps, things are different.
Against a background of more than 30 years of effort, with not
much to show for it, there are signs that e-learning is no longer to
be taken so lightly.

We have an opportunity to capitalize on the virtual institutionalization of the Internet into our businesses and our lives. E-mail is as ubiquitous as our street address, and almost all businesses now have some presence on the Web. The technology that we will use for e-learning is as commonplace as the telephone, and almost as easy to use. For the first time, the transition to e-learning will not require people to buy and learn a special-purpose and complex piece of equipment. In the near future most learners will know how to use the tools of their new learning environment before they need to use them. Although deployment of the Web trails in some industries and in some developing parts of the world, the challenge of an easy-to-use, universally available technology platform has essentially been met. However, there are other, equally important nontechnological challenges that lie ahead.

The Challenges Ahead

Challenge: Getting to the decision makers. With corporations moving more business operations to the Web, more business leaders are more familiar with the Internet than with any previous technology. And with cost and competitive pressures greater than they've ever been, they are more open to new ideas on how to be more efficient and productive. It may be on the coattails of the rush to e-business, but e-learning is opening a door more than ever before to the executive office, and to the decision-making table. Whether we can open it even further, move inside, and *stay there* is a key challenge before us.

Challenge: Leveraging a growing and vibrant e-learning industry. The e-learning industry is maturing rapidly, replete with mergers, acquisitions, roll-ups, and other forms of consolidation. At the same time, new e-learning ventures are launched every day. The American higher education system, long viewed as a bastion of tradition, is moving faster into e-learning than some companies. The result is more choice, lower costs, and more consumer power (individual and corporate). How that power is effectively used is another important challenge.

Challenge: Reasserting instructional and information design. Amid the hype and glitz of the Web, instructional and information design is reasserting itself. There is a greater realization that effectiveness really does matter, and, without a live instructor or coach, the system must work to perfection. So we are again worried about interactivity, authenticity, and learning beyond the regurgitation of facts. The challenge here is to maintain an elevated set of professional standards that work well on both sides of the track—learning and business. In many situations, current methodologies may be too labor intensive and specialized to meet the resource, cycle time, and unique needs of diverse business people. There continue to be attempts to automate parts of the process, but for the foreseeable future there's still a lot of "art" embedded with the "science" that will make total automation difficult, not to mention capturing critical experience, creativity, and innovation. So expect a combination of new technology and new thinking about design to help it keep pace with the demands of business.

Challenge: Breaking the bonds of "the course." Courseware will remain an essential component of a total learning architecture, but knowledge management and performance support are as important, and sometimes more important. Thinking more strategically about learning means embracing a wider variety of e-learning and other solutions that can be used to solve a performance problem, many of which are not *instructional* at all. The challenge is to expand our paradigms of what learning, and e-learning, is.

Challenge: Speed. If all we were asked to do was develop lower cost, higher quality, and more responsive learning programs, we might be able to do it without technology. But doing these things at the speed of business demands a technological solution for a significant part of what we do. Waiting is not a luxury. Deploying critical content to widely dispersed people immediately and simultaneously requires a well-honed e-learning capability. The challenge is the alignment of e-learning technology, processes, resources, and organizations to make this happen.

Challenge: People. With all the movement to technology-based learning, human interaction and sharing could be at risk. If e-learning does not have a human element—if people do not have opportunities to meet each other and work with each other, face-to-face or online—we may not like what we'll get. With any new revolution the challenge is always not to throw out "the baby with the bathwater." In a technological world, we must continue to preserve the people-centric nature of learning.

Challenge: Reinventing training. While every training organization says it's all for e-learning, there is all too often a "but" at the end of those statements. Call it "hedging their bets," "avoiding risk," or "protecting their self-interest"—many training organizations have resisted e-learning as much as they've said they support it. The bottom line is that training organizations need to reinvent themselves—this split personality cannot continue. They need to rethink their economic and value propositions, and reengineer their processes to make e-learning as second nature to what they are all about as the classroom. The challenge is to complete this transformation before it's too late and e-learning opportunities go elsewhere.

> **"The future arrives so quickly that the designers of
> Disney's Tomorrowland have given up."**
> **Larry Downes and Chunka Mui[2]**

As we work to build an e-learning strategy where these challenges are met, it's important to fully understand some major trends in this field. As hard as it is to keep up with the future, there are some changes we can expect to see not too far down the road.

First, we'll see a convergence of e-learning (online training and knowledge management) and e-business. Informania (www. informania.com) has been working in this area and defines the combined world as *knowledge commerce*—the ability to leverage an organization's intellectual assets to improve its competitive advantage. We'll see more e-learning companies recasting themselves as business-to-business (B2B) or business-to-consumer (B2C) firms, with e-learning as a service offering rather than the defining characteristic of the business.

with e-learning as a service offering rather than the defining characteristic of the business.

This is no longer a small, insignificant industry, but it is not a fully matured one either. Despite the growing pains, the e-learning industry is attracting increasing attention from Wall Street and will draw in more investment capital. Many e-learning companies are launching IPOs, with some firms doing better than others. The e-learning industry may rise and fall with the fortunes of the stock market, but these are rough spots, not insurmountable barriers. E-Learning is here to stay.

> **"The Internet's next big thing just might be going to school."**
>
> *Newsweek*[3]

Speaking of universities, the combined public and higher education e-learning market will explode and could easily equal or surpass the corporate e-learning market. And as the ways kids and college students learn change with the times, so will their expectations for how they will learn on the job.

Content providers will proliferate on the Web. E-Learning companies will provide turnkey services that merge content with learning management and sell that service in a variety of ways, including individual and corporate subscriptions. They will offer complete learning solutions to companies—offers that some businesses will find very compelling.

Electronics retailer Circuit City is an example of what's to come. In mid-2000 the company began installing 600 Web-based learning and information systems in its stores so employees could get up-to-the-minute product and sales information and training instead of relying on outdated flyers or waiting for regional classes to be scheduled. What's more, it didn't do this by itself or through an internal training department. Instead, it is partnering with an outside e-learning business (DigitalThink) for both content and infrastructure. This type of arrangement is proliferating. While there is great benefit to having instant and consistent access to a wide array of appropriate learning solutions, if all you

Business to Employee (B2E) and Employee to Employee (E2E) Web models are joining the Internet lexicon, placing e-learning center stage as efforts are ramped up to create more collaborative, knowledge-sharing work environments.

We'll also see a tremendous growth in knowledge management, as intellectual and human capital become more definable, and therefore more valuable, assets of a business. With this will come increased incentives for contributing and sharing knowledge in the context of everyday work experiences rather than simply in classrooms. This means a probable decline in classroom usage, and, for those classroom programs remaining, a redefinition of their important role.

The economics of e-learning will also change. Performance certification will become as important as academic degrees (or perhaps more so), and the range of providers for certifiable learning will increase. The valuation of intellectual property will require more investment into its creation, utilization, expansion, and protection—a growth area for future training organizations.

There will be a tremendous growth and adoption of all forms of mobile, wireless devices. From cell phones to handheld computers, more people will be receiving more information on the go than we could have possibly imagined. Technological breakthroughs in miniaturization, broadband and the advent of third generation wireless technology will make this possible. What does this mean for e-learning? First, we'll likely be more focused on mobilizing knowledge management and delivering learning in very small chunks. Second, we'll be pushed even further into personalized learning as people will demand e-learning in ways not only designed for their needs, but also for the device they're using at any particular time.

> **"For a growing number of companies, the use of e-learning within e-commerce is proving effective in generating increased customer loyalty and value."**
> **Joel Krauss, Partner, DiamondCluster International**

E-Learning will also focus more intensely on servicing customers in cyberspace. Companies will recognize that helping people learn about products (including easing their transition from an old product to a new one) in the same online environment where they may have also purchased the product, will build a tighter bond with customers. For example, Nokia provides a web site to demonstrate the many functions of all their wireless phone products (www.nokiahowto.com). This site not only teaches users about their new phones, but it is far easier and faster to update than the user's manual, and it can also reduce demand and costs of the company's customer service call center. Expect learning communities to form around products and services sold on the Web and through other channels. The best e-learning capabilities can help distinguish an e-commerce site from an increasingly indistinguishable crowd. E-commerce represents an increasingly important growth area for e-learning, as many firms are using it as a tool to enhance the value of their online and traditional businesses, not only for customers, but for suppliers as well.

With the rapidly increasing number of e-learning providers, we will see a new type of training organization begin to form— one that *finds*, *brokers*, and *manages* an increasing number of learning options rather than building solutions itself. Some training organizations or corporate universities will be profoundly impacted as their mission and business models change. Some may not survive. Those that do will make these changes a strength, not a liability. And when the mission of the training organization is no longer just "training," what will we call it?

The End of "e"

E-Learning, like e-business, will soon become commonplace. There will no longer be a need to differentiate "e" from "non-e," A new generation of computer-savvy workers will see to that. But although the "e" may be gone (and e-learning will be transparent), learning will still be as important as ever. Today, the convenience and availability of e-learning is what attracts people. Eventually they will be as discriminating about quality as well. Thus, the ultimate challenge is *not* taking our eyes off the ball. Learning and performance improvement is what's important as far into the future as anyone can see.

An E-Learning Journey

by Gloria Gery

The Long View

INTERACTIVE LEARNING HAS always been in favor. From the time of Socrates, who perfected dialogues that stimulated students with constant questioning, answers, and reflection, we've sought activity and engagement in our learning. In simpler times people who actually knew what they were doing sat next to or were easily accessible to people who needed to learn. They could simply say, "Tell me about," "Why?" "How do I?" or "What will happen if," and the informed support, as represented by the master, presented itself.

Of course, things have become more complex, and knowledge is more fragmented and dissipated due to far-flung organizations, uneven expertise, and unprecedented time urgency. Learning in a work context, while still possible, is more difficult and uncontrolled. Without immediately available and knowledgeable coaches, motivated performers use trial and error, observation and modeling. If learners can make associations, observe patterns, derive rules, and differentiate between good and bad models, this works. But during periods of high growth and rapid change, when goals are unclear or, due to labor market conditions, people are hired without requisite skills, intellect, or experience, performance becomes increasingly uneven.

It's in this current, complex, and dynamic learning and performance environment that the computer, Internet, and knowledge management alternatives become increasingly important. These strategic interventions permit us to institutionalize best work practices and provide on-demand access to learning resources. The business of learning has burst out of the training center and into the business mainstream where it belongs. Since learning and performance are so tied to business results, the development and management of a learning architecture cannot be delegated or outsourced to vendors who are just selling tools or courses. The long view must be taken. Business leaders and human resource executives must truly understand the alternatives, trade-offs, and consequences of decisions, as well as the resources required to truly establish and maintain a learning and performance context that uses technology as a critical component.

Moving Learning Out of Context—Expecting More With Less

Over time, we've gone from learning while doing, to learning in a classroom with experts teaching, to learning in a classroom with instructors teaching courses from materials developed by others. We built huge curricula with the hope of creating individual employee competency. These curricula were anchored in the university model—and we decomposed complex tasks into subjects. In fact, it's difficult if not impossible to create synthesized skills and knowledge by learning the individual pieces. The whole is different than the sum of the parts, and without teaching in integrated and applied ways, we filled people up with content that was out of context and left integration and application to learners on their own. We then applied technology to this model in the hopes that the efficiency of the medium, and the ability to distribute it quickly and universally, would help. But knowing "subjects" does not performance make.

Looking Back

It's important to look back before we look forward to what must be done. I have been working to understand and implement various forms of e-learning environments since 1976. When I was at Aetna Life & Casualty, I began experimenting with computer-based training. The idea was to use the computer to teach nontechnical employees how to use software applications. Technologies were primitive, development tools were limited, developers were inexperienced, and learning requirements surpassed our ability to quickly develop, implement, and maintain sufficient (albeit not thrilling) courseware. Between then and now there was short-lived use of interim technologies such as interactive videodiscs and cameras that could record learners interacting with computer-driven role-plays. Developers experimented with all kinds of media, and a few got pretty good at developing interactive programs with sophisticated graphics, video, and animation. Accessible CD-ROMs and rich PC environments permitted excellent development. But demand outstripped skilled developer supply. One result was development tools increasingly touted "easy to use" which degraded the end product into rote tutorials that could be quickly populated and distributed. The trade-offs between power, simplicity, productivity, and creativity continues.

We have been struggling with the near impossibility of building simulation-based interactive learning programs that *do* generate performance under time and cost pressures that require developers to "get something out there quickly." We're expecting developers to produce more and better with less—and expecting employees and customers to learn more and better in less time. The equation doesn't work. We must explore what alternatives will be successful before we continue our "rush to the Internet." We have huge options for information storage and distribution, and overlapping organizational units working on various forms of e-learning—but not an integrated strategy. We haven't clearly differentiated between what must be learned and what is better referenced or directly supported with tools. We still develop software as if the applications are still used exclusively for processing accounting and operational transactions.

We have almost entirely failed to incorporate what we know about learning and performance into software design, even as we develop or implement strategic business software that is so integrated with work. So much of our software presumes that people know their jobs—and they don't. So much of our software requires extraordinary training and support to be used effectively. And as people use many software applications, huge efforts must go into teaching people how to interact with all of these products. More important and difficult, efforts also go into teaching them the relationship between their work tasks, the data in the various systems, and what part of which system to use when to accomplish the work successfully. There is much expense and little strategic business value in requiring thousands of performers to understand the organization's system and data models. And that knowledge never helps them perform at their major tasks of analysis, sales, customer service, etc.

What Needs to Happen

There are several things that need to happen to support learning within current and expected business environments.

1. Knee-jerk reactions to new technological alternatives must be avoided. Technologies, distribution systems, design alternatives, etc., must be adopted only when they match the organizational learning needs, architecture, culture, and business methods.

2. Business leaders and training professionals must determine whether it's desirable, or even possible, to attempt to develop competence for *all* tasks, or whether there are alternatives to supporting work through technology. In other words, the very model of training, with the goal of independent action by performers without adjunct technical support, must be questioned in a time of complexity, change, and new alternatives. While learning will always be a goal, the question of whether knowledge must precede performance—or whether it is better for it to occur collaterally with doing work—must now be asked.

3. Once goals and realities are articulated, the following questions must be asked and answered, and strategies and tactics necessary to achieve them must be developed.

- What should be learned and what should be available to reference at the time of need?
- What is the relationship between traditional training activities, documentation development, knowledge management, and systems development?
- What learning architecture should be designed to meet strategic objectives and business needs? Combinations of e-learning alternatives with technology-based programs—including online training, distance learning through satellite/networks, traditional instruction, and access to knowledge databases—must be developed. A one-size-fits-all approach is inappropriate and will be expensive and ineffective. The design and delivery media must match the nature of the learning and the culture.
- Can direct support for best practice performance be built into application software, and can related knowledge be linked to work in a way that models learning that is most natural to people? In other words, rebuild the natural doing/learning environment using the Socratic model discussed earlier.
- How do we ensure that the new forms of media-based knowledge representation are used appropriately and not gratuitously? The more we learn about value-added graphics and voice, the more we know that it must be judiciously used to be both effective and not tax technology infrastructures unnecessarily. Remember, the *Law of Diminishing Astonishment* prevails. A little bit goes a long way. Function and power are more important than sex appeal.

- As more and more work and human interaction becomes computer-mediated, should organizational experts on learning be more actively involved in, if not increasingly responsible for, the development of software interfaces, rather than compensating for badly designed software with training programs and help desk support? Software interfaces should directly support work and learning. Information Technology professionals should be masking task complexity rather than adding to it. This requires a strategy that brings together training, documentation, knowledge management, business management, and expert performers in designing software collaboratively with IT.
- What measurements should be applied to new learning architectures and kinds of learning events? Old models for "counting" participation and completions must come into question as granular learning experiences increasingly replace formal, lengthy, structured training courses. Outcomes and impact on performance are much better methods, and we must resist the temptation of saying, "Learning can't be measured"—certainly performance can.

It's clear that e-learning strategy must precede jumping on the technology bandwagon for its own sake. Strategy must also be continuously monitored as both new alternatives and results dictate. There is much power ahead of us. Taking the long and strategic view will make all the difference to those who seek to exploit e-learning in support of knowledge building, performance, and business success.

Gloria Gery is an independent consultant and pioneer in the field of e-learning and performance support systems (ggery@attglobal.net).

The E-Learning "Top 20"

20 Key Strategic Questions You Must Answer About the Sustainability of Your E-Learning Efforts

E-LEARNING PRESENTS great opportunities and great challenges. How ready are you? Answer these 20 key questions about building a durable e-learning strategy. Then, determine for yourself how ready you, your organization, and your company are to bring learning into the digital age.

The E-Learning "Top 20" is grouped into seven areas of understanding: (1) your business readiness; (2) the changing nature of learning and e-learning; (3) value of instructional and information design; (4) change management; (5) reinventing the training organization; (6) the e-learning industry; and (7) your personal commitment.

Your Business Readiness

1. *How well is your company using (Internet and intranet) technology to run its business?*
   Your e-learning choices are significantly impacted by the ways your firm uses the Web for its business. The more ingrained the Web is in the mainstream business, the easier it will be to use it for learning.

2. *How prepared (skills, knowledge, motivation) is your workforce to compete and win in the high-tech, new economy?*
   Understanding the readiness of your workforce to meet future business challenges will be a major driver of the type and sophistication of your e-learning initiatives. The more comfortable people are with technology, the more comfortable they will be with e-learning.

The Changing Nature of Learning and E-Learning

3. *How does your organization define "e-learning?"*
   E-Learning is much more than online training or CBT, encompassing knowledge management and electronic performance support. How you define e-learning says a lot about your e-learning direction.

4. *How will your organization overcome any bad prior experiences you and others have had with technology-based learning?*
   It's important to understand the history (good or bad) of your efforts with technology-based learning. You cannot know where to go, or how to proceed successfully, unless you know where you've been.

5. *How much access do people have to the Web (anyone, anytime, anywhere)?*
   Without access to the Internet, or intranet, there can be no e-learning. Creating access—in the office, on the road, and at home, if appropriate—is your first priority.

6. *Do you differentiate between instructional needs (training) and informational needs (knowledge management), and do you make the right decisions about when to use each?*
   Information is not the same as instruction, but it is just as important. A key value of learning professionals will be to help the organization make the right choices.

The Value of Instruction and Information

7. *What is the level of your organization's expertise in instructional and informational design?*
   Building high-quality e-learning is both science and art, requiring significant training and experience. Even if you're outsourcing parts of the process, it's still important to invest in the right level of talent and expertise.

8. *Is your organization ready to move beyond a predominant reliance on classroom training to a more balanced approach with e-learning?*
   The classroom will continue to have an important role to play, but it may be a different role. Integrating classroom and e-learning will be critical to success.

The Role of Change Management in Building a Durable E-Learning Strategy

9. *Does senior management support e-learning?*
   Leaders often say they support e-learning when they don't. But e-learning cannot succeed without them. Consider how you will get senior managers to "own" e-learning.

10. *Does your organization have a change management plan for introducing e-learning in your company?*
    The movement to e-learning is a major paradigm shift for most people, including the training organization and your clients. You must pay attention to the struggle people will have as they go through this change.

11. *Can your organization demonstrate the business benefits of e-learning?*
Learning effectiveness alone is not an adequate reason for deploying e-learning. Your value proposition must include cost savings, responsiveness, and speed in addition to effectiveness.

How Training Organizations Must Reinvent Themselves to Support E-Learning

12. *Does your organization have a plan to help the training function reinvent itself for the digital age?*
Training organizations can be the most e-learning resistant group in the company (sometimes without even knowing it). Reinventing the training organization will take a special and focused effort.

13. *Is your training organization's economic model predominately dependent on selling seats in the classroom?*
The retail model for internal training organizations can be a disaster waiting to happen and is incompatible with e-learning. Moving from tuition to investment will be very helpful to your e-learning strategy.

14. *What is the climate in your organization to learning in alternative locations, especially the work site?*
The barriers between doing work and learning are fading. You need to vigorously support workplace learning and help managers and employees successfully learn where they work.

15. *Is your organization willing to allow e-learning to thrive, perhaps at the expense of some of the more traditional parts of the training organization?*
The failure of training organizations to adopt an e-learning strategy will not necessarily kill these initiatives, but it may kill the training organization if it is not prepared to radically change its focus to accommodate e-learning.

16. *How prepared is your organization to invest in and incubate e-learning for several years in order to get it firmly established?*
E-Learning initiatives must be shielded from the traditional practices and assumptions of the training organization that may tend to place it at a disadvantage.

The E-Learning Industry

17. *How prepared is your organization to deal with a large and increasingly complex e-learning marketplace?*
The e-learning industry is expanding rapidly. You must keep up so that you can be a smart consumer of external e-learning products and services.

18. *Does your organization have a good handle on what it is buying in the e-learning marketplace? Can it differentiate quality products and weed out redundancies?*
Buyer beware! Don't buy e-learning products without evaluating them. You must work across organizational boundaries to manage vendors and leverage your buying power.

19. *Is your organization prepared to outsource some of its functions and manage them externally so that it can concentrate its resources on more valuable areas?*
Outsourcing is here to stay and can be an invaluable management approach for e-learning. Training organizations will have to move away from a "we-can-do-it-all" attitude to one that embraces strategic partnerships.

Your Personal Commitment

20. *How committed are you, personally, to e-learning? Are you ready?*
E-Learning will evolve and expand, but it will not go away. As in any change, sound leadership will be needed at all levels in the organization.

APPENDIX

B

E-Learning Resources

Online Training and Performance Support

THE LATEST RESOURCES that bring instructional design and the Web together:

Valorie Beer, *The Web Learning Fieldbook: Using the World Wide Web to Build Workplace Learning*, San Francisco: Jossey-Bass, 2000. *An excellent overview of the critical issues related to Web-based learning. Outstanding links to other resources on the Web. Includes a Web site.*

Ruth Clark, *Developing Technical Training: A Structured Approach for Developing Classroom and Computer-Based Instructional Materials*, Washington, DC: International Society for Performance Improvement, 1999. *Dr. Clark brings learning research and theory plus a good dose of solid instructional design to technology-based training in a way that is easy to understand.*

Margaret Driscoll, *Web-Based Training: Using Technology to Design Adult Learning Experiences*, San Francisco: Jossey-Bass, 1998. *Provides extensive detail on the application of instructional design and technology for Web-based learning.*

Gloria Gery, *Electronic Performance Support Systems*, Gery Associates, 1991. *The classic book on performance support that defined the field.*

Brandon Hall, *Web-Based Training Cookbook*, New York: John Wiley, 1997. *A detailed resource on Web-based learning with extensive references to and reviews of vendors and vendor products. Includes a CD-ROM.*

Darian E. Hartley, *On-Demand Learning: Training in the New Millennium*, Amherst, MA: HRD Press, 2000. *A good focus on Web-based learning in the corporate environment, with many examples and links provided.*

William Horton, *Designing Web-Based Training*, New York: John Wiley, 2000. *A practical reference on online training, with lots of technical and instructional design information and examples.*

Kevin Kruse and Jason Keil, *Technology-Based Training: The Art and Science of Design, Development and Delivery*, San Francisco: Jossey-Bass, 1999. *Although not exclusively devoted to the Web, this book has lots of practical ideas and includes a related CD-ROM and Web site.*

Roger Schank, *Virtual Learning: A Revolutionary Approach to Building a Highly Skilled Workforce*, New York: McGraw-Hill, 1997. *Explores the world of multimedia design with extensive case studies and success stories.*

Wendy Webb, *A Trainer's Guide to the World Wide Web and Intranets*, Minneapolis: Lakewood Books, 1996. *A good introduction to the whole field.*

Knowledge Management

Some of the best thinking and best practices in this growing field:

Thomas H. Davenport and Laurence Prusak, *Working Knowledge: How Organizations Manage What They Know*, Boston: Harvard Business School Press, 1998. *An excellent business book that clearly articulates the power and potential of knowledge management.*

Nancy M. Dixon, *Common Knowledge: How Companies Thrive by Sharing What They Know*, Boston: Harvard Business School Press, 2000. *Looks at knowledge management from the perspective of contributors and users rather than the technology—the human dimension of KM.*

Harvard Business Review on Knowledge Management, Boston: Harvard Business School Press, 1998. *A collection of the classic HBR articles that defined the knowledge management field.*

Amy Jo Kim, *Community Building on the Web*, Berkeley, CA: Peachpit Press, 2000. *Rich with examples and techniques for building online communities.*

Carla O'Dell and C. Jackson Grayson, Jr., *If Only We Knew What We Know: The Transfer of Internal Knowledge and Best Practice,*

New York: The Free Press, 1998. *An excellent, in-depth look at knowledge management and approaches to establishing a KM system in an organization.*

Thomas A. Stewart, *Intellectual Capital: The New Wealth of Organizations*, New York: Bantam Doubleday Dell, 1977. *An excellent perspective on the value of knowledge in organizations—makes a strong case for knowledge management.*

Amrit Tiwana, *The Knowledge Management Toolkit: Practical Techniques for Building a Knowledge Management System*, Upper Saddle River, NJ: Prentice Hall, 2000. *"Toolkit" is an excellent description of this book—a complete guide to implementing knowledge management. Includes a CD-ROM.*

General Learning, Performance Improvement, and Technology Books of Interest

The foundation for e-learning lies in understanding learning and performance improvement; these are just some of the many resources in this area:

Robert O. Brinkerhoff and Stephen J. Gill, *The Learning Alliance: Systems Thinking in Human Business Goals*, New York: American Management Association, 1998. *An outstanding look at corporate training, with all its good and bad points. Takes aim at the bad practices and discusses how training must change for the future. Excellent insight into the field.*

Roger Craig (ed.), *Training and Development Handbook*, New York: McGraw-Hill and the American Society for Training and Development, 1996. *A robust and thorough collection of well-written chapters on all aspects of Training and Development, including elements of e-learning.*

Judith Hale, *Performance-Based Certification: How to Design a Valid, Defensible, and Cost Effective Program*, San Francisco: Jossey-Bass, 1999. *If you're planning a certification program connected with your e-learning initiatives, this book is a must.*

Randy J. Henrichs, *Intranets: What's the Bottom Line?* Upper Saddle River, NJ: Prentice Hall, 1997. *A practical, easy-to-understand treatment of intranets from both a technology and business perspective.*

Allison Rossett, *First Things Fast: A Handbook for Performance Analysis*, San Francisco: Jossey-Bass/Pfeiffer, 1999. *A practical approach to understanding organizational learning and performance needs, especially if time is of the essence.*

Clifford Stoll, *Silicon Snake Oil: Second Thoughts on the Information Superhighway*, New York: Anchor Books, 1995. *A funny and contrary view of the world of computers and learning—worth reading for its divergent perspective.*

Harold Stolovitch and Erica Keeps (eds.), *Handbook of Human Performance Technology*. San Francisco: Jossey-Bass and the International Society for Performance Improvement, 1999. *A complete and masterful collection of ideas, concepts, processes, and applications related to Human Performance Technology. More than 60 individual authors representing a "who's who" in the field.*

General Business and E-Business Books of Interest

There's a lot to learn about e-learning from the business press:

Joel Barker, *Future Edge: Discovering New Paradigms of Success*, New York: William Morrow, 1992. *The classic book on paradigms and paradigm shifting.*

Clayton M. Christensen, *The Innovator's Dilemma: When New Technologies Cause Great Firms to Fail*, Boston: Harvard Business School Publishing, 1997. *A business-focused book whose premise can help explain an organization's inability to grasp the nature of the fundamental change going on all around it.*

Stan Davis and Jim Botkin, *The Monster Under the Bed: How Business Is Mastering the Opportunity of Knowledge for Profit*, New York: Simon & Schuster, 1994. *One of the first books to recognize the value of knowledge and how knowledge can be a competitive asset.*

Larry Downes and Chunka Mui, *Unleashing the Killer App: Digital Strategies for Market Dominance*, Boston: Harvard Business School Publishing, 1998. *An excellent manifesto on how to build e-businesses that win in the marketplace.*

Michael Hammer and James Champy, *Reengineering the Corporation: A Manifesto for Business Revolution*, New York: Harper Business, 1994. *The business book that began the reengineering craze.*

Guy Kawasaki, *Rules for Revolutionaries: The Capitalist Manifesto for Creating and Marketing New Products and Services*, New York: Harper Business, 1998. *An entertaining book with keen insights on how to build a successful business on the Web.*

Peter Senge, *The Fifth Discipline: The Art and Practice of the Learning Organization*, New York: Currency, 1990. *An extensive look into learning organizations and how they form and work.*

Don Tapscott, *The Digital Economy: Promise and Peril in the Age of Networked Intelligence*, New York: McGraw-Hill, 1996. *An early and insightful work that laid some of the foundations for the Web society.*

Online Resources

Extensive resources and links covering a wide range of e-learning topics and issues:

AT&T Learning Network (www.att.com/learningnetwork). *A wide range of resources about online learning.*

Brandon Hall (www.brandon-hall.com). *An information-rich Web site with extensive information on the Web-based learning industry.*

Brint.com (www.brint.com/km). *An extensive portal on knowledge management issues.*

CIO's KM Research Center (www.cio.com/forums/knowledge). *From CIO magazine, a focus on knowledge management issues with extensive links to other related sites.*

Electronic Performance Support Systems (www.epss.com). *An extensive portal devoted to performance support and knowledge management resources.*

EPSS Infosite (www.epssinfosite.com). *One of the leading sites devoted to electronic performance support systems.*

Influent Resource Exchange (www.influent.com). *A community-driven resource for e-learning practitioners, including Web sites, surveys, white papers, and job postings.*

Institute for the Learning Sciences at Northwestern University (www.ils.nwu.edu). *A research and development lab dedicated to applying principles of cognitive science, computer science, artificial intelligence, and educational theory to improving the way people learn.*

Internet Time Group (www.internettime.com/itimegroup/elearning.htm). *A great deal of information, insight, and perspective on e-learning.*

Knowledge Management Consortium (www.km.org). *This "eKnowledge Center" is a portal to a host of information resources on knowledge management.*

Knowledge Management Resource Center (www.kmresource.com). *A portal to many other KM recourses on the Web.*

Lguide (www.lguide.com). *One of the first Web sites to provide independent ratings of e-learning products.*

Learnativity (www.learnativity.com). *An eclectic and independent site focusing on learning in general and e-learning in particular. Lots of valuable information and links not easily found anywhere else.*

The Masie Center (www.masie.com). *An e-learning think tank that sponsors online newletters, conferences, a resource-rich Web site, "links galore," and other services that monitor and help define the e-learning field.*

TRDEV-L (training.ed.psu.edu/trdev-l). *From Penn State University, a site for collaborating about e-learning.*

Web-Based Training Information Center (www.webbasedtraining.com). *An extensive portal devoted to online training resources.*

Professional Organizations

Provides resources and services for members and the industry at large:

American Society for Training and Development—ASTD (www.astd.org). *The largest professional training organization in the world—its site contains the "Learning Circuits" Webzine.*

International Society for Performance Improvement—ISPI (www.ispi.org). *Focused on the broad field of human performance technology, ISPI is the professional home of many of the leading thinkers in the area of performance improvement.*

Major Conferences

Opportunities to interact with leaders in the field and preview the latest products and services from the e-learning industry:

ASTD Annual Conference—ASTD (www.astd.org). *The largest training trade show and conference covering a broad range of learning and HRD topics, including e-learning, but is not an exclusive e-learning forum.*

KM World Expo (www.kmworld.com). *Covers the knowledge management industry.*

New Media Instructional Design—Influent Technology Group (www.influent.com). *Focus is on the use of instructional design to create/improve media-based learning programs.*

Online Learning/Performance Support Conference (www.trainingsupersite.com). *Focused exclusively on e-learning and performance support, with an extensive trade show.*

TechKnowledge Conference—ASTD (www.astd.org). *Focus is on building Web-based training and knowledge management.*

TechLearn—The Masie Center (www.masie.com). *Covers a broad range of e-learning development and e-learning industry issues.*

Training Conference (www.trainingsupersite.com). *Extensive trade show and program covering a wide range of corporate training topics, including e-learning, but is not an exclusive e-learning forum.*

Training Managers' Forum (www.trainingsupersite.com). *Designed for more senior training and learning managers. A broad coverage of the field with some emphasis on e-learning.*

WBT Producer and WBT Executive Summit—Influent Technology Group (www.influent.com). *Focus is on building Web-based training and knowledge management. The Summit is for more senior executives.*

Newsletters

The most current information on the e-learning industry:

Influential Trends—Influent Technology Group (www.influent.com). *Online, e-mail-delivered news covering the broad field of e-learning. Free.*

Learning Circuits (www.astd.org). *A Webzine on e-learning, found on the ASTD Web site.*

Learning Decisions (www.learningdecisions.com) *Published by the Masie Center and includes a monthly fieldwide survey on e-learning issues. Hardcopy, subscription.*

LINEZINE (www.linezine.com). *A Webzine exloring the issue of learning in the new economy.*

Online Learning News (www.emailpub.com/lakewood). *Online, e-mail-delivered news covering the broad field of e-learning. Free.*

Service Scan (www.servicescan.com). *Online, e-mail-delivered news covering the training world, including e-learning. Subscription.*

TechLearn Trends—The Masie Center (trends@masie.com). *Online, e-mail-delivered news covering the broad field of e-learning. Free.*

Velocity—Knowledge Capital Group (www.knowledgecap. com). *Online, e-mail-delivered news covering the broad field of knowledge management. Free.*

Professional Journals

Issues, new ideas, and thought pieces on the state of the e-learning industry and where it is going; many good e-learning articles in each journal each year:

e-learning—Advanstar Publications (www.elearningmag.com). *Covers the e-learning industry—issues, products, and professional development.*

Educational Technology—Educational Technology Publications (201-871-4007; edtecpubs@aol.com). *Articles on learning (including e-learning), instructional design, and performance improvement.*

Knowledge Management Magazine (www.kmmag.com) and KM World (www.kmworld.com). *Both magazines cover a broad range of knowledge management issues.*

Online Learning (www.onlinelearningmag.com). *Articles covering a wide range of e-learning issues and applications.*

Performance Improvement—ISPI (www.ispi.org). *Practical articles relating to improving human performance in organizations.*

Performance Improvement Quarterly—ISPI (www.ispi.org). *Research journal on human performance technology.*

Training and Development—ASTD (www.astd.org). *Articles covering a wide range of issues in the training (including e-learning) and broader HRD fields.*

Training Magazine (www.trainingmag.com). *Articles covering a wide range of training issues, including e-learning.*

Endnotes

Preface

1. Keynote speech to the Fall 1999 Comdex Trade Show, Las Vegas, November 16, 1999.
2. From the Foreword to *Unleashing the Killer App: Digital Strategies for Market Dominance*, Larry Downes and Chunka Mui, Boston: Harvard Business School Publishing, 1998, p. x.
3. "Industry Report: 1999," *Training Magazine*, October 1999, p. 40.
4. It is not possible to cite all vendors, products, URLs, etc., for a particular category or situation. I have made every attempt to select representative resources that either typify the point(s) being made or represent a best practice, but I make no representation about the quality or business practices of any Web site or company, unless specifically noted. You and the people you work with may have differing opinions about each of these sites, and you may have other sites you like better. I recognize that new companies and Web sites, with new products and services, emerge every day, and I'm sure that new and perhaps better examples will be identified that are not cited in this book. In addition, the Web links I've cited may change over time (in such cases, I suggest you visit the site's home page and conduct a site search). I encourage you to continue exploring the Web for new sites and practices that characterize this growing field.

Chapter 1

1. *Intellectual Capital: The New Wealth of Organizations.* New York: Doubleday, 1999, p. 165.
2. "Industry Report: 1999," *Training Magazine*, October 1999, p. 46.
3. 1998 ASTD State of the Industry Report.
4. Visit www.ispi.org for more information on Human Performance Technology.
5. *TechLearn Trends* #59, The Masie Center, Saratoga Springs, NY, 1998 <www.trends.@masie.com>.
6. *Knowledge in Organizations: Resources for the Knowledge-Based Economy*, Boston: Butterworth-Heinemann, 1997.
7. Peter M. Senge, *The Fifth Discipline: The Art and Practice of the Learning Organization*, New York: Doubleday, 1990, p. 14.

Chapter 2

1. "Managing Professional Intellect: Making the Most of the Best," *Harvard Business Review*, March 1, 1996.
2. December 4, 1995 (cover).
3. November 1999, p. 112.
4. November 1999.
5. See *"The Fall and Rise of PLATO"* in Chapter 6.
6. *Learning Decisions Newsletter*, Vol. 1, Issue 1, January 2000, The Masie Center, Saratoga Springs, NY.
7. *Business Week*, December 17, 1999. p. 40.
8. These sites and others referred to in this book are examples of the wide variety of e-learning Web sites on the Internet and are illustrative of the many approaches that are applied to the e-learning marketplace. They are not meant to serve as a comprehensive or a recommended list. Because of the rapidly changing nature of the Internet and the companies that do business on the Web, it is highly likely that some of these sites will disappear and new sites will emerge. The reader is encouraged to consistently scan the Web for new and perhaps more innovative examples.
9. These are examples only; I do not make any claim for the instructional quality or the depth/breadth of coverage of the programs on these sites.
10. Trace Urdan and Cornelia Weggen *Corporate E-Learning: Exploring a New Frontier*, Equity Research Report, © 2000, W.R. Hambrecht & Co., p. 21 <www.hambrecht.com>.

Chapter 3

1. "What's Your Web-Based Learning Strategy?" *Learning Circuits*, an ASTD Webzine about digital learning, February 2000 <www.learning circuits.org>.
2. Opinion and Arts Section, *Chronicle of Higher Education*, Vol. 48, August 1999, p. B8.

Chapter 4

1. *The New Pioneers: Men and Women Who Are Transforming the Workplace and the Marketplace*, New York: Simon & Schuster, 1999.
2. "The Attack on ISD," *Training Magazine*, April 2000, p. 48.
3. "Knowledge Management: Are We in the Knowledge Management Business?" <www.ariadane.ac.uk/issue18/knowledge-mgt/>.
4. Thanks to Carolyn Majkowski of DiamondCluster International, for contributing this metaphor.
5. http://www.epss.com/lb/concepts/con_frame.htm
6. These terms are often used interchangeably.
7. "Attributes and Behaviors of Performance-Centered Systems," *Performance Improvement Quarterly*, Vol. 8, No. 1, 1995.

8. For those not familiar with Microsoft Word or "Mr. Paper Clip," just think of a small, animated graphic of a paper clip with a smile on its "face," which pops up and presents dialogue boxes asking you what you want to do, or offering to show you what to do.
9. *Inside Technology Training*, January 2000, p. 17.
10. Presentation at TechLearn 99, Orlando, November 1999, sponsored by the Masie Center.
11. *CIO Magazine*, November 1, 1999.
12. Thanks to Allison Rossett for finding this example.
13. Valorie Beer, *Web-Based Learning Fieldbook*, San Francisco: Jossey-Bass Pfeiffer, 2000, p. 12.
14. This technology is licensed to other Web sites that want to assist users in finding specific information.
15. For detailed help on conducting needs assessments and performance analyses, see Allison Rosset, *First Things Fast: A Handbook for Performance Analysis*, San Francisco: Jossey-Bass Pfeiffer, 1999.

Chapter 5

1. "Emerging Trends in Instructional Interventions," *The Handbook of Human Performance Technology*, edited by Harold Stolovitch and Erica Keeps, San Francisco: Jossey-Bass, 1999, p. 891.
2. Companies like Centra (www.centra.com), HorizonLive (www.horizon live.com), Interwise (www.interwise.com), LearningSpace (www.lotus. com), LearnLinc (www.learnlinc.com), Microsoft's NetMeeting, Place-ware (www.placeware.com), and others offer Web-based synchronous systems.
3. What's Your Web-Based Learning Strategy?" *Learning Circuits*, an ASTD Webzine about Digital Learning, February 2000 (www.learning circuits.org.).
4. Hand in Hand, *Context Magazine*, April–May 2000, p. 31.

Chapter 6

1. *The Digital Economy: Promise and Peril in the Age of Networked Intelligence*, New York: McGraw-Hill, 1995, p. 255.
2. Some companies do not allow access to their intranet from home (or restrict access to selected employees). But if firms also want people to learn from home, there may be a conflict between corporate security policy and corporate learning policy that needs to be addressed early in the deployment of an e-learning strategy.
3. Although the Merrill Lynch Learning Network is a Web-based application, the TGA environment on which it is delivered has a more proprietary client-server technology that meets the specific requirements of the firm. Expanded Web-enabled capabilities are planned for the Learning Network and for TGA in the future.

4. Originally an acronym for Programmed Logic for Automated Teaching Operations.

5. Readers may remember that Wang Corporation's proprietary word processing technology died out around the same time, for the same reasons.

6. Now PLATO Learning, Inc. (www.PLATO.com)

7. Some companies are so decentralized, either by line of business, organizational structure, or geographical boundaries, that one corporate learning portal is not practical (or not desirable). In these cases, work to establish a single portal at the highest logical level of the unique organizational group.

8. Some of these systems include, but are not limited to, Docent (www. docent.com), Ingenium (www.asymetrix.com), Knowledge Planet (www. knowledgeplanet.com), LearningSpace (www.lotus.com), Pathlore—Phoenix and Registrar systems (www.pathlore.com), Pinnacle (www. pinnaclemultimedia.com), SABA (www.saba.com), Training Server (www. trainingserver.com), and Top Class (www.wbtsystems.com). Expect a continuous stream of mergers, acquisitions, and new entrants in this market.

9. Browsers were not originally designed for interactivity or multimedia; new versions will have more of these capabilities.

10. Some corporate IT departments restrict downloads through their firewalls.

11. Two examples of online testing Web sites are www.quizstudio.com and www.questionmark.com. Be sure these applications can integrate with your LMS.

12. Products like Autonomy (www.autonomy.com), Epicentric (www. epicentric.com), Intraspect (www.intraspect.com), Knowledge Track (www.knowledgetrack.com), OpenText (www.opentext.com), Plumtree (www.plumtree.com), SiteScape (www.sitescape.com), and Vignette (www.vignette.com) are representative of these applications. There are many others that cover the broad range of KM functionality, including portal-building, content management, archiving, searching, collaboration, community building, communication, and learning.

13. Information on standards is rapidly evolving. The best way to keep up is to consult these and related sites on a regular basis.

14. It's SCORM (Shareable Courseware Object Reference Model) specification is laying the groundwork for sharing learning materials across different learning management systems.

15. Many of the standard sites listed above have information on XML. For more specific technical information, go to www.w3.org.

16. *Working Knowledge: How Organizations Manage What They Know*, Boston: Harvard Business School Press, 1998, p. 18.

Chapter 7

1. Brinkerhoff and Gill, *The Learning Alliance: Systems Thinking in Human Resource Development*, San Francisco: Jossey-Bass, 1994, p. 57.

2. April 3, 2000, p. 154.

Chapter 8

1. *Virtual Learning: A Revolutionary Approach to Building a Highly Skilled Workforce*, New York: McGraw-Hill, 1997, p. 173.
2. Hammer, Michael and Champy, James, *Reengineering the Corporation*, New York: Harper Business, p. 32.
3. James W. Michaels and Dirk Smillie, "Putting More Now into Knowledge," *Forbes*, May 15, 2000, p. 88.
4. Research has consistently shown a reduction in learning time for most individuals. Citations: Brandon Hall, *Web-Based Training Cookbook*, New York: John Wiley, 1997; and Rob Foshay (editor) "Effectiveness of Computer Based Training" <www.plato.com>.
5. "Inside IBM: Internet Business Machines," December 13, 1999, p. EB34.
6. *Evaluating Training Programs: The Four Levels*, San Francisco: Berrett-Koehler, 1998.
7. *Intellectual Capital: The New Wealth of Organizations*, New York: Doubleday, 1999, pp. 230–233.

Chapter 9

1. *What's Your Web-Based Learning Strategy?" Learning Circuits:* an ASTD Webzine about Digital Learning, February 2000 <www.learningcircuits.org>.
2. *Inside Technology Training*, July/August 2000, p. 22.
3. Now DiamondCluster International.
4. *Business at the Speed of Thought*, New York: Warner Books, 1999, pp. 249–250.
5. There are some internal training organizations that provide services to external customers, not as part of the firm's business relationship (e.g., providing systems training to resellers and customers of a company's product), but as a separate line of business. If this is not fully sanctioned by the leadership of the company and held to the same productivity and profit standards as the rest of the business, the same collapse could be expected.
6. *The Innovator's Dilemma: When New Technologies Cause Great Firms to Fail*, Boston: Harvard Business School Publishing, 1997.
7. *Evaluating Training Programs: The Four Levels*, San Francisco: Berrett-Koehler, 1998.
8. *The Book of Knowledge: Investing in the Growing Education and Training Industry*, Merrill Lynch, Inc., April 1999, p. 137.
9. Boston: Harvard Business School Publishing, 1998.
10. "Hand in Hand," *Context Magazine*, April–May 2000, p. 31.

Chapter 10

1. Trace Urdun and Cornelia Weggen, *Corporate E-Learning: Exploring a New Frontier,* W.R. Hambrecht & Co., p. 1. Equity Research Report ©2000 from Web site: www.wrhambrecht.com.

2. VELOCITY Online, March 8, 2000, Release 2.5 <velocity @know ledgecap.com>.

Chapter 11

1. *The Monster Under the Bed: How Business is Mastering the Opportunity of Knowledge for Profit*, New York: Simon & Schuster, 1994, p. 42.

Chapter 12

1. Guiding principles are statements of how you will work/behave to achieve your goals. They reflect the beliefs and values of your organizaiton. Example: "We believe that e-learning has a critical role to play in how we grow the knowledge of our people and our business as a whole, and as such, we are willing to make the critical choices and investment decisions that will enable e-learning to become a reality."
2. Example: Chest pain can be a symptom of either indigestion or a heart attack; to know the root cause you must do further diagnosis.
3. Each of these examples is general in nature. Your e-learning strategy development efforts will have much more detail.

Chapter 13

1. 1999 Annual Report, p. 18.
2. *Unleashing the Killer App: Digital Strategies for Market Dominance*, Boston: Harvard Business School Press, 1998, p. 163.
3. April 24, 2000.

Index